THE BURDEN OF BAGGAGE

The Burden of Baggage: First Generation Issues in Coming to Christ
© 2019 by Roy Oksnevad

All rights reserved.

No part of this book may be reproduced, stored in a retrieval system, or transmitted in any form or by any means—electronic, mechanical, photocopy, recording, or otherwise—without prior written permission of the publisher, except brief quotations used in connection with reviews in magazines or newspapers. For permission, email permissions@wclbooks.com.

Scriptures are taken from the NEW INTERNATIONAL VERSION (NIV): Scripture taken from THE HOLY BIBLE, NEW INTERNATIONAL VERSION ®. Copyright© 1973, 1978, 1984, 2011 by Biblica, Inc.™. Used by permission of Zondervan.

Published by William Carey Publishing
10 W. Dry Creek Cir
Littleton, CO 80120 | www.missionbooks.org

William Carey Publishing is a ministry of Frontier Ventures
Pasadena, CA 91104 | www.frontierventures.org

Andrew Sloan, copyeditor
Mike Riester, cover and interior design

Printed for Worldwide Distribution

24 23 22 21 20   1 2 3 4 5   IN

IBSN's: 978-0-87808-082-3 (paperback)
978-0-87808-083-0 (mobi)
978-0-87808-084-7 (epub)

Library of Congress Cataloging-in-Publication Data

Names: Oksnevad, Roy, author.
Title: Cultural baggage: an Iranian example of coming to Christ out of oppressive societies / Roy Oksnevad.
Other titles: Risen from ashes to Christ
Description: Littleton: William Carey Publishing, 2018. |
   Originally published under title: Risen from ashes to Christ. |
   Includes bibliographical references.
Identifiers: LCCN 2018052455| ISBN 9780878080823 (pbk.) | ISBN 9780878080847 (epub)
Subjects: LCSH: Missions to Muslims | Christianity and other religions—Islam. | Islam—
   Relations—Christianity. | Church work—Iran.
Classification: LCC BV2625 .O37 2018 | DDC 266.0088/297—dc23
LC record available at https://lccn.loc.gov/2018052455

THE BURDEN OF BAGGAGE

First Generation Issues in Coming to Christ

ROY OKSNEVAD

The Burden of Baggage provides a realistic and detailed look into the inner joys and struggles of ex-Muslims now striving to live for Christ as a diaspora. Instead of glowing post-conversion stories, the book not only unveils their newfound happiness as believers and their fellowship with other Christians, but also the reality of pain and conflicts, community struggles over identity and belonging, and the pastoral and discipleship challenges of forming them into Christ followers. All who read this book will go away convinced of the priority of discipleship among Muslim converts to Christ—to pray, journey, and struggle with them more deeply and knowledgeably over the long haul.

John Cheong, PhD
missiologist and MBB discipleship researcher in Asia

Never has there been a greater need to understand Muslim people. Dr. Oksnevad, with over thirty years of experience and an impressive writing and research history, offers insights that will enlighten, instruct, and provide practical applications.

Duane Elmer, PhD
distinguished professor, international studies, emeritus
Trinity International University/Divinity School

I highly recommend Dr. Oksnevad's book. I am an Islamicist, and while we have many texts that generally cover missions to Muslims, there is very little good research on specific people groups; their challenges when they embrace Christianity; the problems when those challenges are responded to via acting out; and, more importantly, steps Christians can take to help a fledgling and sometimes flailing Iranian church. Dr. Oksnevad's work is a step in the right direction to address the realities experienced individually and collectively by Iranian Muslim-background believers in the West.

Steve A. Johnson, PhD
assistant professor of ministry care, Columbia International University

Dr. Roy Oksnevad is a great trusted friend, brother, and coworker in Christ with some of us at the Association of the Iranian Presbyterian Churches and Fellowships of North America, also known as Anjoman among Iranian Christians in diaspora. Roy has done an outstanding work based on his tedious study and research on the topic of success and failures/problems of the Iranian Christian churches in diaspora presented in this book. The Anjoman strongly recommends every Iranian church member in diaspora, pastor, leader, elder, and lay person to read and study this book and seek God to help them to first recognize/diagnose the problematic issues as well as to follow the biblical guidelines and counsels given in this book to rectify those issues. Let us remember that with God's help, everything is possible!

Tommy Mayvaian
moderator, on behalf of Anjoman

Thorough in the research presented and knowledgeable of the history and culture of the Iranian people, Oksnevad presents an insightful look inside the community of believers from Muslim backgrounds. It is noteworthy to see portrayed how Iranian culture carries over into the church, impacting both its strengths and vulnerabilities. Many insights into internal struggles in Middle Eastern churches in general are gained through this focused study on Iranian believers. This is the only book I know that portrays the MBB community from the inside out based on in-depth interviews.

Marvin J. Newell, DMiss
former senior vice president, Missio Nexus

The Islamic world is in turmoil. Millions of refugee families flee the Middle East to countries where they will not be persecuted for becoming followers of Jesus. Many are disenchanted with Islamic violence, rampant in their personal experience. Many are impressed with the love shown to them by Christians. We hear credible stories of hundreds of Muslim families turning to Christ every day. Yet the task of incorporating new followers of Jesus from Muslim backgrounds is filled with difficulties and challenges. Dr. Oksnevad provides the most valuable insights in *The Burden of Baggage*. The historical perspective reflects the complicated nature of understanding modern Islam today. His blend of insights from solid research and personal experience provides both theoretical and practical steps for helping Muslim converts grow in their newfound faith. This is a much-needed book for those helping new believers of Muslim background grow toward maturity in Christ. Such an important and timely book and resource is urgently needed. I highly recommend the book.

James E. Plueddemann, PhD
professor of intercultural studies, Trinity Evangelical Divinity School
former SIM missionary in northern Nigeria and former international director of SIM

The church among Iranians worldwide is growing fast in numbers, but is facing major challenges in growing in spirituality, health, and impact. Roy has spent countless hours researching the roots and causes of the cultural issues that threaten the budding church of Iran. This book is a "must read" for all Iranian Pastors or those who work among Iranian Christians.

Hormoz Shariat, PhD
president/founder, Iran Alive Ministries

Dr. Roy Oksnevad graphically exposes his diagnosis of distrust, insecurity, and disharmony in interpersonal relationships and leadership clashes in the post-conversion experience of MBBs in the adolescent Iranian church in the diaspora. The prescription he offers to nurture believers and congregations to maturity in Christ is also powerfully instructive for wholesome discipleship of MBBs from other ethnic backgrounds. Dr. Oksnevad's personal ministry journey with Muslims for over three decades and the research based on his personal in-depth interviews make this volume credible and compelling. Its content is groundbreaking and long overdue!

Dr. T. V. Thomas, DMin
chairman, Global Diaspora Network (GDN)

Contents

Preface	vii
Introduction	xi
A Brief History	1
Experiencing Church	19
The Luggage We Bring	35
Can We Just Play Nice?	57
All in the Family	85
Everyone Wants to Be a Leader	95
Conversion Is Like a Bomb Going Off	113
Where Do We Go from Here?	129
Conclusion	155
Appendix A—Research Methodology	159
Appendix B—Interviews	165
Appendix C—Research Questions	169
Appendix D—Distribution of Interviewees	175
Appendix E—Suggested Readings of Cultural Commentaries	177
Glossary	179
References	183

Preface

Much of the focus of missions today is driven by the task of world evangelization within this next generation. Books and strategies are touting new methods to accelerate church planting from addition to multiplication. It seems that the drive is for numbers—number of conversions, number of churches being planted, and number of movements to Christ. There is much written about conversions, testimonies, and church-planting strategies, yet relatively little has been written on what actually happens in these fellowships over the long haul. Do these fellowships grow and become mature bodies of Christ, or is the path more precarious? The reports are that there is an exponential growth of the church but little reporting on the health of these churches. When you talk with mission strategists, they see the hand of God and want everyone to jump on board. The idea is to get people into small groups through studying the Bible and then leave like the apostle Paul did so that the Holy Spirit can guide people into the true faith without the trappings of the church of the global North. It is assumed that prolonged outside influence will not allow the gospel to take on a truly contextual expression and thus be a detrimental influence to the expedient growth of fa movement. It is believed that without further outside influence, the group will auto-correct itself and a vibrant movement will spread like wildfire.

When you talk with academics they are seeing and dealing with churches that are struggling and in need of training. There is so little good training material translated or written for these new churches. The church is growing rapidly in the Southern hemisphere and Asia. The report coming out of the Center for the Study of Global Christianity reveals that the center of Christianity has shifted from the global North to the global South.[1]

> Between 1970 and 2020, each of the six major Christian traditions is expected to grow more rapidly than the general population in the global South. Simultaneously, Christianity is declining as a percentage of the population in the global North at a dramatic rate. Birth rates in many European countries in particular are below replacement level, and populations are aging. The significance of the global shift was recently demonstrated in the election of Cardinal Jorge Mario Bergoglio of Buenos Aires, Argentina, as Pope Francis, the first Latin American head of the Roman Catholic Church.[2]

---

1 The full report can be found online at www.globalchristianity.org/globalcontext.
2 "Christianity in its Global Context, 1970-2020: Society, Religion, and Mission" (June 2013, 7) https://www.gordonconwell.edu/ockenga/research/documents/ChristianityinitsGlobalContext.pdf.

Though the shift of Christians numerically has gone to the South, the theological shift has not taken place. So many teachers in the rest of the world have either received their training in Western institutions or their teachers are from the global North. Theological books are another influence which Kwok Pui-lan recognizes that,

> According to UNESCO, there were 292,000 new titles and editions of books published in the US in 2011, compared to 26,300 in Argentina in 2012, and 3,800 in Pakistan in 2012. The number of religious titles in the US far outnumbers that of other countries. Even though Christian demographics have shifted to the Global South, the production of academic theology is still concentrated in Europe and North America."[3]

William Dyrness notes that,

> Further, I am struck by the lopsided flow of information, which is almost entirely from North to South. For example, in 2006 (according to Bowker.com statistics) there were 292,000 books published in the U.S., of which 18,000 were religious titles. Compare this to 300 published in Kenya, of which 76 were religious and 1200 in Nigeria, of which 203 were religious (figures from 1994, 1995 the most recently available UNESCO statistics).[4]

Are these new churches auto-correcting and producing what the evangelical community would call an orthodox faith? The two driving theologies of burgeoning churches in the global South are New Apostolic Reformation (NAR) and Theology of Prosperity (TP). These movements have harnessed the digital world in a post-modern environment, making their message highly sought after. Societies that are hierarchical, with a strong mystical or folk element, will gravitate towards this expression. In the teaching of TP, "God appears as an extremely rich landowner, owner of all the gold of the universe. From this, they derive that Christians must be extremely rich and that they should wear gold."[5] The NAR fits the hierarchical paradigm as well.

The prosperity gospel would focus more on the individual's health and wealth. This group [NAR] is unique in that they really think God has put these apostles on earth to basically transform the world. It's a sort of trickle-down Christianity, where these apostles are at the top of the mountain, exercising this power from the top down. That's how the kingdom of God comes in.[6]

The NAR leadership has characteristics very similar to authoritarianism and messianism and is a form familiar to many who come from cultures where healthy boundaries have been violated on almost every level. Many are looking for a savior to bring about prosperity instead of shame.

---

3 Kwok Pui-lan, "Teaching Theology in a Global and Transnational World," American Academy of Religion (March 2014), https://www.aarweb.org/publications/spotlight-on-theological-education-march-2014-teaching-theology-in-a-global-and-transnational-world.
4 William Dyrness, "Where in the World Are We? Reflections on Fuller's Expanding Global Reach," Theology, News & Notes (Fall 2011), https://fullerstudio.fuller.edu/im-not-hearing-you-the-struggle-to-hear-from-a-global-church/.
5 Martin Ocaña, "The New Apostolic Reformation and the Theology of Prosperity: The 'Kingdom of God' as a Hermeneutical Key," Lausanne Movement, Oct 2, 2015, https://www.lausanne.org/content/88558.
6 Bob Smietana, "The 'Prophets' and 'Apostles' Leading the Quiet Revolution in American Religion," Christianity Today, August 3, 2017, https://www.christianitytoday.com/ct/2017/august-web-only/bethel-church-international-house-prayer-prophets-apostles.html.

Preface

I set out to take an in-depth look into one such people movement, Iranians in the diaspora, which is said to be one of the fastest growing movements in the world. This branch of the church is still in its infant stage of development. The growth has been so rapid that finding trained leaders and stable, mature members is a luxury. The Internet, satellite, and mobile technology have become teachers of many of these house churches.

People coming to faith in Christ do not do so in a vacuum; there is a context which greatly influences them. They bring their own cultural heritage, patterns of behavior, and values, which are uniquely shaped by their religion, culture, and family, into their new fellowships. The seductive message of NAR for self-proclaimed "Apostles" and the allure of prosperity in a culture that places high value on status and image are ripe for TP. Many countries in the world have similar cultural heritage, patterns of behavior, and values as found in the Iranian context. Trauma in its various forms from war, civil war, famine, and abuse, both sexual and emotional, are found throughout the world. Many societies like China or Uzbekistan are honor-based, meaning that they view the world through the eyes of the other. They seek to retain honor and avoid shame at all costs. Many cultures are hierarchical and not egalitarian such as Central African Republic or Venezuela, shaping both how the various institutions within society are formed—civil, religious, and personal. Totalitarian governments like North Korea gain legitimacy by creating a culture of distrust, one of the major obstacles to growth and maturity.

My personal experience is working among this burgeoning Iranian Christian community, and I spent a lot of time reacting to all the drama. Cultural dynamics were the default settings for behavior, for they were coming from a culture with little or no collective memory of Christianity. Within these contexts ministry seems to be one step forward and three steps backward. People are highly suspicious of each other and trying to get people together is a challenge. When someone stumbles in the Christian walk, he or she is quickly judged as not being Christian. People are highly sensitive, reflecting an entire culture of "doing a dance" so as not to offend the other person. Arguments break out easily, and so many involved in these conflicts have a zero-sum approach to life; it is all or nothing. In prayer, there are those who seem to hold God hostage to their demands; anything less is viewed as lack of faith. The idea of overlooking an offense is a foreign concept. Further, there seems to be an inability to distinguish between a minor offense to be overlooked and a major offense that needs to be dealt with. There is little collective memory of conflict resolution, so people resort to their default setting: deny the existence of conflict or simply leave the church when conflict arises. In a relatively short time, fellowships often experience a major split or fail to take root. Forgiveness, though talked about and often preached, just doesn't seem to make sense on an emotional level. Marital problems are frequent, and the divorce rate is exceptionally high. Women find a new lease on life in Christ and many want to be up front, and they dress in a way to get attention. Everyone wants to share their life's story and feels "called" to be a pastor. Very few want to listen to the pastor they have, for they feel that they could do better.

The Burden of Baggage

The church among Iranians worldwide is growing fast in numbers, but is facing major challenges in growing in spirituality, health, and impact. I tried to be as objective as possible as a researcher to ensure that my research would be an impartial study without foregone conclusions or preconceived ideas. I conducted fifty interviews, ranging from sixty to ninety minutes, with Iranian Christians in three countries. In order to balance the research, I interviewed pastors, church leaders, members, and attendees. I interviewed an equal number of men and women, and I purposely included first- and second-generation youth. I heard the honest concerns people expressed about negative situations in their churches. They wanted their voices to be heard, and they desired to live in harmony with their Christian brothers and sisters. They wondered if their experiences were unique or if other Iranian fellowships were experiencing the same things. The answer is no, their experience is not unique but is typical. Not only is this the experience of the Iranian church, but it is indicative of young churches throughout the world.

My goal is not to expose one movement, people, or church, but to look at the rapid growth of the church through the eyes of the Iranian experience and to start the discussion on the next dimension of rapid church multiplication—discipleship. Chapter one gives a brief history of the Iranian context. The incentive is to discover some of the cultural traits that have shaped the Iranian perspective and what ultimately influences the church. The second chapter relates the experience these former Muslims have of church, from when they first attended a church to their present understanding of church. It reveals both the strengths and weaknesses of the church in their own words. Chapters three through seven are the five main areas of research. Chapter three looks at the personal baggage people bring with them into faith that is informed from personal history, unique to the individual but also shared collectively in society. Chapter four takes a look at how people interact with each other, which is so central to how the Christian is to live out their spiritual life in community. Chapter five examines the influences of the family and family dynamics, which also play a large role in the life of the church. Chapter six seeks to understand the relationship between the leader and the congregation, between leaders, and how churches are structured, and how power is expressed. Chapter seven looks at religious elements and their influence. Is conversion a simple process or are there other contributing factors? The last chapter gives thirteen areas that are to be addressed for the new church to move from infancy to maturity. Even though the book takes the example of the Iranian experience, these dynamics are multiplied in many contexts around the world. As you read this book see if you can see vestiges of your own cultural baggage through the chapters describing the Iranian church. We all are culture bound more than we image, and it has a direct bearing on how the church is lived out in community.

Introduction

We are in a unique time in missions history. When I was in seminary in 1977, I was presented with the dispiritingly small number of missionaries deployed to the world's second largest religion—Islam. The missions community at that time was focused on reaching those who were open to the gospel (in sub-Saharan Africa, Latin America, and East Asia). It was considered a poor strategy to deploy missionary personnel to resistant religions. This was about to change in 1979, when a series of events took place. Iran's Western-friendly shah, who gained more power through the intervention of the United States and England,[1] left Iran amid pressure from the religious leaders and merchants; a relatively unknown exiled Islamic cleric returned to Iran, launching the first modern experiment of an Islamic republic; and the American hostage crisis in Tehran dragged on for a year under US President Jimmy Carter. Islam, a relatively unknown religion in the West, was now grabbing international headlines almost daily. The experiment in Iran has become a model that has inspired many other Islamic nations, such as Afghanistan, Somalia, and Yemen, as well as Islamic regions in Sudan and Nigeria, to seek to establish God's kingdom on earth.[2] We have seen an increase in terror groups such as ISIS, Boko Haram, al-Shabaab, Jamaat al-Islamiyya, al-Qaeda, Taliban, Lashkar-e-Tayyiba, Tehrik-e-Taliban Pakistan, and other jihadi groups.

What went unnoticed by the Western media was a silent revolution taking place. A prayer movement was started, calling on Christians to pray for Muslims throughout the world during the month of Ramadan.[3] This prayer movement has grown, and the church worldwide is participating in this mass prayer movement for the Muslim world. Many Iranians fleeing the Islamic regime looked for a God of love. We know that as radical Islam continues to morph, fellow Muslims who

---

1 Iran and other Islamic countries have a long history of Western intervention and exploitation, which has contributed to the overall negative impression of the West. For an overview of Western intervention in Iran, see the "Iran" page on the Intervention and Exploitation: US and UK Government International Actions Since 1945 website, http://www.us-uk-interventions.org/Iran.html.

2 According to some estimates, Boko Haram caused anywhere between one hundred thousand and one million deaths between 2010 and 2014. And in 2014 it was estimated that the northeast part of Nigeria had at least 3.3 million internally displaced peoples. Jideofar Abidbe, "Re-evaluating the Boko Haram Conflict," The Brookings Institution, February 29, 2016, https://www.brookings.edu/blog/africa-in-focus/2016/02/29/re-evaluating-the-boko-haram-conflict/.

3 The *30 Days of Prayer for the Muslim World* guide can be found at http://www.30daysprayer.com/. The editorial work for this prayer movement was initially coordinated in Australia, then in France, and is currently managed in Germany. The North American edition has been published continuously since 1993 by WorldChristian.com.

are caught in the wake of the venomous attacks are leaving Islam. Like the Iranians of the 1980s and 1990s, other Muslims are looking for something different than the toxic faith that seems bent on destroying everything they hold dear. Many are leaving Islam, disgusted with religion and claiming to be atheists. We are seeing Muslims worldwide turning to Christ in numbers not seen before.[4]

Church-planting strategies among Muslims were to integrate the new believers from a Muslim background into already existing language-specific churches, since it was presumed that they would know the language, religion, and culture already. Most Arabic-speaking fellowships I am familiar with are mostly Christian in background, like the fellowship in Belgium where I ministered—a small, isolated Christian-background fellowship primarily made up of Syrians. Muslim-background believers (MBBs) were unable to integrate successfully into the tightly knit fellowship, regardless of the intent of the Egyptian-born pastor. Not until the pastor started a unique MBB fellowship did the church begin to grow. This has been the pattern of ethnic Christian-background churches. Later I will address the reasons for this lack of integration into Christian-background believer churches and the role these churches can play, but suffice it to say that there are deep cultural, ethnic, and religious divides between Christians and Muslims from the same country, resulting in a lack of trust on both sides that hinders integration.

Iranians as a whole have been more successful than other groups in forming MBB churches, so my research centers on this group of former Muslims.[5] Because they have been more successful, their church dynamics can be more readily observed; and therefore the struggles these former Muslims have as they live out their Christian faith in community may well be a foretaste of what other new followers of Christ from a Muslim background will go through. The language-specific Christian fellowships of former Muslims play an important role in particular for the first generation with limited language skills and for those wanting to reconnect with their culture and heritage, much like the Farsi-speaking Iranian church. The Muslim-background church as a whole is in its infant stage, and this is a great learning time.

My wife and I have worked among Muslims for the past thirty years. Over the years of our ministry, we have seen MBB churches established that have been

---

4 David Garrison (2014) traces the history of movements to Christ from AD 632 to 2013. A major shift in Muslims coming to Christ happened from the 1980s onward, with exponential growth in what he identifies as the nine rooms of the Muslim world from 2000 to the present. Maps and other helpful information can be found at the *A Wind in the House of Islam* website, http://windinthehouse.org/.

5 Iranians in the diaspora have succeeded in planting uniquely MBB fellowships, while other groups from Muslim-majority countries tend to form Christian-background churches with a few MBBs in attendance. Even when the intent of the pastor is to start an MBB church, often the Christians from the same country soon become the majority group, changing the DNA of the new church. Many MBBs find it hard to be accepted when this dynamic occurs.

Introduction

chronicled by several authors,[6] but their experimentation in living out the Christian life together is fraught with turmoil. This book seeks to give an accurate picture of the MBB church as explained by MBBs; it is not a book on strategies by Western missiologists. The recommendations from research and corroborated by testimonies are to guide and lead the nascent church from birth toward maturity. The principles discovered in this process go beyond the initial study of the research and apply to a much larger audience establishing churches among peoples with little or no collective memory of church, and perhaps living under oppressive totalitarian regimes.

The strengths of the MBB church are many. For the purposes of this book, however, I will take an in-depth look at sources of tension to better understand what is happening and where our attention should be to move the young church forward. Remember, we are looking at a community that is still in its infant stage of development and naturally does not have the infrastructure found in older communities, such as trained leaders and stable, mature members. As the sources of disharmony are identified, the next stage is for the church to address the issues and concerns with some knowledge they may not have had before. It is not my intent to bring dishonor to the MBB church through this study. I have great love and respect for what God is doing among MBBs and in the nine rooms of the Muslim world.[7] It is my desire that this book will be a symbolic mirror to help the new MBB church analyze and prioritize the next steps to move the church from infancy to adolescence, and then on to adult maturity.

The broader reason I undertook studying the experience Iranians have in church was to better understand how new believers coming from a Muslim background are transitioning into their new faith in Christ. I want to better grasp their strengths and the areas in which they struggle. Could it be possible that the lessons Iranians are learning and the struggles they face may serve as a model for other Muslims coming to Christ—who have a similar cultural heritage, patterns of behavior, and values uniquely shaped by their religion, culture, and family?[8]

As is common with most first-generation churches, these MBB churches are very active in evangelism, and their worship experience is passionate and enthusiastic. The church exhibits deep cultural traits of loyalty, pride, and cohesiveness toward the family. They are altruistic, friendly, generous, caring, and kind to others—expressed in their commitment to hospitality (Dastmalchian, Javidan, and Alam 2001, 540–41). Their fellowship reflects the deep core value of family and friendship found

---

6 Most notable is Garrison (2014); Trousdale (2012) presents only glowing stories of churches and movements, with no feel of what it is like for the movements to actually live out their faith. There are other books that chronicle Muslims coming to Christ, such as Goode (2010) and Greenlee (2013). Books on discipleship give a better perspective of the struggles; see Little (2015) and Register (2009).
7 The term "nine rooms of the Muslim world" was coined by Garrison (2014).
8 It is beyond the scope of this book to take a deeper look at the psychological, individual, or cognitive dimensions of each of the fifty interviewees. That is for another study, requiring expertise in an area I have not studied.

within traditional society. MBBs often interact with each other more than once a week, as members are intensely involved in each other's lives throughout the week.

Yet the MBB church is in a constant state of flux, making it difficult to provide an exact number and exact locations of churches. For instance, the first Iranian church in California no longer exists. To my knowledge, four Iranian churches have been started in the Chicago area, and all four have failed. A church in Atlanta lasted only five years before it folded. A Somali MBB church in Minneapolis has struggled for its entire existence. The Arabic-speaking church I have worked with over the past eight years is still unable to establish a core group of believers, so necessary in forming a vibrant church. An Arabic-speaking MBB church in New Jersey started but eventually became a majority Christian-background believer church with only a few MBBs, who float in and out of the church. An MBB fellowship in the Chicago area went well until internal mistrust brought about the demise of this once-vibrant fellowship. The consensus is that MBB fellowships struggle most with interpersonal relationships and leadership.

Missiologists and church leaders understand that discipleship is a key ingredient in any new church. Discipleship is more than just gathering individuals together to study the Bible. God exhorts us in Romans 12:1,2 to no longer be conformed to the pattern of this world but to be transformed by the renewing of our minds. This renewal of the mind goes to the core values of new believers and their church community. Missionary anthropologist Paul Hiebert indicates that values are not immediately transformed upon conversion. Cultural beliefs shape the understanding of each individual's Christian faith.

> Leading individuals to faith in Jesus Christ is the evangelistic dimension of mission. People come as they are, with their histories and cultures. We cannot expect an instant transformation of their behavior, beliefs, and worldviews. It is important, therefore, to disciple them into Christian maturity. This includes a transformation not only in the way people think and behave but also in their worldviews. (Hiebert 2010, 12)

Missionary statesman and professor James Plueddemann writes, "From my experience, the greatest difficulties in multicultural leadership arise from tensions growing out of internal values" (2009, 71).[9] Traditional Western methods of discipleship do not address the core concerns that contribute to the conflicts found within these new MBB churches. Looking at the areas of conflict will give us a map of the areas to be addressed as we seek to move the church from infancy to maturity.

---

[9] I will not delve more into the interjection of values beyond this brief mention here, as it is beyond the scope of this writing.

Introduction

Where to Begin

Iranians are becoming Christians in large numbers and are being organized into Farsi-speaking fellowships or churches. I set out to interview fifty Iranians primarily from the second wave[10] in three areas: the United Kingdom, Canada, and the United States.[11] I used open-ended questions in guided conversations based on key areas to explore the relationships and experiences former Muslims have in churches consisting primarily of former Muslims.[12] The basis of the questions used in the interviews comes from several sources. Geert Hofstede's analysis of culture provided some of the categories that shape culture and values, as did Palestinian-born professor Mohammed Abu-Nimer's work on conflict resolution. In addition, over thirty years of experience working with believers from a Muslim background has given me firsthand knowledge of some of the issues faced in interpersonal relationships within the community.

The reason for using these sources is based on two factors. First, Middle Eastern countries are high on the collectivism end of the individualism-collectivism scale.[13] Second, there is little if any knowledge of fieldwork done on post-conversion life in the community (Miller 2012). Therefore, I allowed the MBBs to determine the fields and categories they understood as important in explaining the post-conversion experience of life in Christian community.

---

10 Research to date recognizes two waves of Iranians migrating to the West. The first phase was from 1950-77 and consisted mostly of students and visitors. The second phase was from 1978-95 and consisted mostly of refugees or exiles of the post-Iranian revolution. The major exodus from Iran took place after the Islamic fundamentalist government took over in 1979. In 1998 the new refugees were not numerous enough to constitute a third wave; however, there has been a steady stream of people leaving Iran that continues up to the present time.

11 See appendix A for the breakdown of those interviewed by sex, age, religion, current residence, the year they left Iran, number of years they have been a Christian, years they have been in their current church, if they were members of another congregation, and the place of their conversion.

12 See appendix B for the list of questions used in the interview. I did not ask every question, but used open-ended questions as a guide when the topics came up, so as not to prejudice the discussion. If a topic on the question sheet was not introduced by the interviewee, I would skip the question. For instance, I began with a general question, such as their church history and if they had left one church for another. The interview flowed naturally with questions concerning the length of stay in a church, the circumstances that may have precipitated their leaving the church, and the situation of the church that they left. Further questions to probe their church experience concerned the history of attendance at the church and the ebb and flow of the number of people in attendance. If there was a pattern of people leaving, it naturally led to questions concerning the historical circumstances around any exodus of members or themselves.

 I knew going into the interview process that some might use the interview to air grievances or injustices, and that there could be a tendency to exaggerate or to give me information they thought I was looking for. To ensure reliability and validity of the data collected, I sought clarity when generalizations were made. I asked for examples to illustrate the topic of discussion. At other times, I sought precision by asking the person to "unpack" an idea or concept. When certain characteristics of Iranian culture were mentioned, I asked if this pertained to the Christian community in the diaspora, MBBs, or ethnic Iranians such as Assyrians or Armenians. I sought further amplification to distinguish between cultural characteristics that might be found in the host culture in the West and the Iranian Christian community in the West. I would question the facts given from multiple angles to ensure that the information was accurate.

13 For a fuller discussion, see Hofstede (1991).

The Burden of Baggage

The first MBB church studied was organized in 1983. Many more have been started, and most are in an infant stage. When MBBs enter the Christian life, they bring their own cultural and religious values, which were referred to as "baggage" in the interviews. This study is particularly distinctive from studies of other ethnic immigrant groups because there is not a large pool of mature Christians or pastors in the country of origin from which to draw upon. For example, Vietnamese churches in the United States have ethnic Hmong to draw upon for church leaders, and Filipinos in the diaspora have a long tradition of Christianity back home.

The few Christian-background believers found in Muslim-majority countries have deep prejudices against their perceived religious oppressors, so much so that many MBBs do not feel welcome in the few Christian fellowships. Ethnic Christian-background leaders are reluctant to give leadership positions to someone from a Muslim background or allow their children to marry such a person. They fear that the MBB's conversion is not fully genuine and that at any time the MBB might go back to their Muslim community. Therefore, the new MBB churches are being formed with new converts who have little or no collective memory of the Christian church's rich heritage or of living examples of how the Christian life is lived out in the community, both of which contribute to the current disharmony.

The religious memory of Middle Easterners is Islam, along with its religious institutions and expressions. Even the Christian-background believers say that interaction with Islam paints much of their religious memory. Many Middle Easterners have lived under the watchful eye of secret and religious police who can indiscriminately sweep into private homes and detain individuals with impunity. This has created a climate of distrust and insecurity that has left an indelible psychological mark, affecting their perceived reality of the world. This climate of distrust and insecurity is not dissimilar to that created by oppressive and dictatorial regimes not associated with Islam. People living in such contexts will manifest many of the same patterns of behavior and values, which are uniquely shaped by this culture of fear and distrust.

Pastors in the newly formed churches have not received the conventional training that North American pastors have. There is very little time for the new converts to mature in their new life in Christ before they are placed into—or put themselves into—leadership. Many individuals interviewed expressed that the new converts resort to the cultural and religious patterns of leadership they grew up with to guide the new church. Finding this type of authoritarian leadership undesirable, those attending these fellowships seek a more egalitarian ecclesiastical expression. The church experiences interpersonal conflict, clashes over leadership and leadership styles, and hypersensitivity over perceived offenses—resulting in an inability to resolve conflicts, which is typical of a new church full of immature Christians trying to learn how to live out this new life in Christ in community.

Introduction

Churches tend to be small, between fifteen and thirty attendees. Most pastors are bi-vocational, meaning their time to prepare sermons and respond to the many personal and interpersonal crises of the community is limited. Newly arrived Middle Easterners look to the mosque or a Middle Eastern church as a safe place where their social and legal needs are met in their desire to become legal citizens. Many leave when their needs are met, causing a high turnover rate in these institutions.

Interpersonally, tensions quickly rise between attendees who come from vastly different educational and social classes, and the leadership's inability to respond to the brewing crises further contributes to the instability. There is little collective memory of conflict resolution, so many resort to the default setting of denying the existence of conflict or just leaving the church when conflict arises. In a relatively short time, fellowships experience a major split or fail to take root. Lay persons often split from the church because they feel that they are more capable than the current pastor to lead the church. Sadly, some disgruntled members take as many people with them as possible to start a new church or Bible study, with the intent of leading it themselves. The newly formed church is not exempt from conflicts, which often results in more splits since the new leader does not have the pastoral training or ministry skills necessary to form a healthy church.

If what I am describing sounds too negative, remember that Satan, our enemy, seeks to destroy all of God's creation. Christians in Muslim-majority countries blame Islam as the source of their problems, but Islam is not the enemy. The real enemy is Satan, who attacks families, societies, social networks, and cultures in order to destroy us. Without the presence of the church speaking and living God's truth into our culture, we will see a broken society. However, God's redemptive power can and will turn our families and society right-side up as the church lives as a redemptive community.

God uses the weak to shame the strong and the simple to shame the wise. God is using the MBB church in a mighty way. We live in the "already but not yet," meaning that we see God's firstfruits of changing us into his image-bearers; but we will not see the full culmination until we are with Jesus in heaven. This book is meant to give hope to the struggling church that God's divine power can transform his bride into a mighty people of God.

1
A Brief History

In an effort to understand the context from which the MBB community in the diaspora is formed, we will look at the history of some cultural characteristics and values found in Islamic societies. They make up part of the context into which the new faith is birthed. The Middle East is ancient and culturally rich. A prominent value in Islamic societies is hospitality, almost to a fault. It is not this aspect of Islamic culture that is associated with disharmony. The historical, political, and religious background is important to understand, for it identifies sources of disharmony in the past that shape some of the values expressed in MBB churches today. It is beyond the scope of this book to give a properly balanced and positive perspective of the two competing Islamic societies (the culturally rich and hospitable Muslims and the religious and political expressions) found in their countries.

Throughout the interviews conducted for this book, people mentioned the "baggage" they bring into their Christian experience. People are deeply shaped by their past. It is to this past that I now turn, which will better inform some factors associated with the struggle the MBB church is going through.

Pre-Islamic Times

The Arabian Peninsula, the birthplace of Islam, saw significant changes at the end of the sixth century. The two major empires were those of the Christian Byzantines to the north and west and the Sasanian Persians to the east, who battled each other for a trade route through the peninsula. The newly Christian Ethiopians aligned themselves with the Byzantines to establish a separate and open trade route to the east. They sought to control the Jews of Yemen and push north through the Arabian Peninsula, but instead they were evicted from Arabia and their regime weakened. They were to play a role later with the emergence of

Islam, accepting the few Muslim converts fleeing the persecution in Mecca as refugees before the *Hijra* in AD 622.

The Sasanian Persians experienced internal problems related to the Zoroastrian faith, leaving them weak and vulnerable. The Christian Byzantines had suffered conflict with the great disputes of the church (Lewis 1995, 45–46). The Arabian Peninsula had a number of foreigners, colonists, refugees, and other groups settling in the region, bringing new ways and ideas with them. Among them were Christians, Jews, and "other monotheistic communities of a 'Gnostic' type such as were then common in Syria" (Hodgson 1977, 159).

Scholars believe that these early monotheists were what the Qur'an calls *hanifs*. There were a few other men of the Quraysh tribe in Muhammad's time who were abandoning paganism and were attracted to this monotheism that valued life more highly than did tribal standards. They were not willing to accept any of the competing religions. These *hanifs* were the earliest converts to the new religion (Lewis 1995, 47). The idea that this monotheism goes back to Abraham is part of the Islamic self-understanding.

In the Islamic scheme of history, the time before Muhammad (AD 610–32) is called *Jahiliyyah* ("time of barbarism or darkness"). It is popularly believed that with the coming of Muhammad, light dawned in the world. The time of Muhammad is considered the height of spiritual enlightenment, and the rest of subsequent history is the loss of the perfect world's luster. The utopian understanding of the past creates a deep desire for a hero. The biographies of the life of Muhammad (*Sira*) bear this out. The evolving retelling of the life of Muhammad throughout the ages ends up with him becoming the ultimate model of human perfection.[14]

This utopian interpretation of history has led to an idealistic view of Islam and is a contributing factor in the disillusionment Muslims are experiencing in light of increased terrorism and destruction perpetrated in the name of Islam. Many secularized and conservative Muslims are disgusted with the carnage, and those living in areas of conflict have been driven from their homes, creating the greatest refugee crisis in modern history. As of the end of 2017, forty million people around the world had been forced to flee their homes due to conflict and violence in fifty seven countries and one territory. In 2017, a total of 30.6 million new displacements were recorded in 135 countries. Many of these areas are in Muslim majority regions or countries.[15]

---

14 Tarif Khalidi (2009) chronicles how the Muhammad of history has been sanitized of human faults and understood through a hagiographic interpretation to be the greatest of kings, the most rational of statesmen, the wisest of legislators, the most courageous of commanders, the most pious of believers, and the greatest reformer of ideas and manners.
15 The Internal Displacement Monitoring Centre (IDMC) provides high-quality data, analysis and expertise on internal displacement worldwide. http://www.internal-displacement.org/

A Brief History

Many Muslims who have heard all their lives that Islam is perfection are now skeptical of all religion. They have had their hopes brutally dashed at the hands of trusted Islamic and world leaders. This "Paradise Lost" is one of the contributing factors to Muslims considering the claims of Christ.

Shi'a History

Religion plays an important part in the identity of Iran. Iranians have a history of invasions; they were invaded by Greeks, Arabs, Mongols, and Turks. Nevertheless, during times of foreign rule the Persians retained their culture and succeeded in turning their conquerors into Persians. Prior to the Islamic invasion in the seventh century AD, Zoroastrianism was the religion of Persia, which has shaped part of the Iranian cultural identity. An oft-repeated theme of Iran's heroic tales is vengeance for the unjust death of an Iranian king or warrior. This Zoroastrian understanding of vengeance is one element that shapes the Iranian perception and reaction to injustice.

The long-standing quarrel between the two major sects of Islam, Sunni (meaning the usual practice of Muhammad and his followers) and Shi'a (meaning followers of Ali), stems from the very beginning of the religion. Muhammad's familial line felt that the pious and simple life embodied the teaching of Muhammad. They felt that Hussein, the second son of Ali and grandson of Muhammad, stood in opposition to the growing wealth and power of the Arab elites. Hussein called for social justice and standing against the darkness of evil, represented in the Umayyad dynasty (661–750). A split between the Sunni and Shi'a Muslims can be traced to 632, just after Muhammad died. The question of who should succeed Muhammad, whether the most qualified person or only someone from the family line, was bitter from the beginning.

The newly formed religion of Muhammad exploded into the Persian Empire under the expansionist "rightly guided" caliph, Umar. At first the Arabs did not press the Persians to become Muslims, but eventually Iranian Persians adopted Islam to escape the poll tax (*jizyah*)[16] levied on non-Muslims (Forbis 1981, 31), which was used to subjugate non-Muslims based upon qur'anic surah 9:29. The Arabs were unable to Arabize the Persian Empire, however. Persian culture and its centers of learning led the Islamic Empire into its golden age (750–1258) (Mackey 1996, 41).

---

[16] The purpose of the jizyah is clearly understood by Muslims. For instance, the hadith Sahih Bukhari (see http://sunnah.com/bukhari/58) *lays out the condition for jizyah. An Islamic discussion thread on a blog site gives the reason of humiliation and lowliness to slowly convert non-Muslims to Islam; see* https://www.quora.com/Why-does-Allah-stipulate-Jizya-tax-from-non-Muslims-living-under-Islamic-rulers. *Egyptian-born author Bat Ye'or has written two books on this topic (1985, 1996).*

Iranians eventually converted to Shi'ism as an integral part of Iranian identity; it not only spoke to Persian culture and the Iranian experience but warded off the threat of the Sunni Turks, who were expanding in the fifteenth century toward Iran. Shi'ism shares with Sunni Islam common beliefs in the oneness of God, the prophethood of Muhammad, and the resurrection. To these Shi'ite beliefs were added two others during the lifetime of Imam Jafar ibn Muhammad al-Sadiq (702–65):

1. *Adalah* (justice), meaning that men should strive to fulfill God's will in this world against Sunni injustice rather than wait for divine justice in the hereafter.

2. *Imamah* (imamate), meaning that the world needs the presence of an infallible guide who represents divine power and ought to be a descendant of Ali through his wife Fatimah (youngest daughter of Muhammad). (Taheri 2008, 24)

But it was not until 1490 that the thirteen-year-old Safavid Shah Ismail (1487–1524) converted everyone in Iran to Shi'a Islam "on pain of death" (Forbis 1981, 34). He "exploited the perception that Ali and Hussein were semi-detached from the Arab elite and effectively made them into virtual Iranians" (Bradley 2008, 7). Ismail did this by linking Hussein's marriage to Shahrbanou, the daughter of the last Iranian Sasanian king, Yazdegerd.

The life and death of Ali and the slaughter of Hussein on the day of Ashura are part of the metanarrative that has shaped the morality, values, and character of Shi'as, which also mirrors the national story of Iran (ibid., 8). The massacre at Karbala (a relatively minor civil war early on in Islamic history, in Iraq in 680AD) stands as a tragic moment when piety sacrificed itself for justice and is central to the Shi'as perception of Islamic history. Every year Shi'ites commemorate the slaughter of Hussein on Ashura, the tenth day of Muharram. Shi'ites re-enact the death by wounding themselves with knives, barbed chains, and swords while onlookers participate vicariously by pounding their chests rhythmically.

Sufism, or Mystical Islam

Orthodox Islam is not the only religious expression of spirituality in Iranian culture. The mystical expression of Sufism is entrenched in Islamic religious identity. There is a spectrum of folk Islamic practices, ranging from rejection of all forms of magic to overtly and consistently practicing magic.[17] Islam has in its various foundational documents the teaching of angels, demons, and jinn. Though many will deny using them when in fact they do, charms, amulets, fear of the evil eye, and using the Qur'an as an amulet to pass exams at school abound in daily life.

---

17 Love (2000) and Musk (1989) treat this subject in greater detail from a Christian perspective. Al-Ashqar (1998) gives a reasoned position from an Islamic perspective.

A distinction needs to be made between official and popular religion.[18] Musk points out that official religion tends to deal with universal issues underlying ideas of origin, destiny, and the ultimate meaning of life. It finds its social expression in complex institutions and organizations. Popular religion tends to deal with problems of immediate, everyday life affected by the unseen world and destiny (Musk 1989, 198–99). Though the modern urbanite Muslim may not practice folk religion in his or her daily ritual, nonetheless this spirit worldview "is discovered in the hadith literature, in the folklore of local communities, and in myths of origin. It is visibly worked out in rites of passage and at times of crisis" (ibid., 204).

For example, my former neighbor, a secular Indian Muslim who has lived in the United States for twenty-five years, has had little to do with Islam. He is here to make money. But at the anniversary of his father's death, I was invited to their little family worship time, and for the first time I saw him do prayers. He practiced a ritual of burning a paper with qur'anic passages, mixing the ashes in a glass of water, and drinking the water to honor the dead parent. On another occasion, when their teenage son became involved in gangs, the grandmother wrote passages of the Qur'an on scraps of paper, soaked them in water, and had the son drink the water to get the Qur'an into him to change his behavior. At special events and during life crises, these now-urban, Western Muslims turn to what they were taught to do, which involves the unseen world of spirits and powers.

The spirit world and dreams play a particularly important role in the spiritual life of the Muslim.[19] For example, Sahih Bukhari 87:112 states, "A good dream (that comes true) of a righteous man is one of forty-six parts of prophetism," giving credence to the belief in the meanings hidden in dreams. There is a body of literature dedicated to better understanding this phenomenon. Table 2.1 is one example of the type of systemizing used by Sufis in interpreting their dreams.

---

18 Some writers on Islam divide the religious system into orthodox and folk Islam. It is my contention that what is called "folk" is an integral part of Islam.

19 The topic of dreams and their interpretation is found in the various collections of hadiths, such as Sahih Bukhari 87, "Interpretation of Dreams," with sixty-one hadiths on the subject; or in Sahih Muslim, with forty references to dreams in book 29, "The Book of Vision." Muslims find qur'anic support for three vehicles of revelation: dreams, oracles, and words (i.e., speech). The prophet Ibrahim (Abraham) received guidance in a dream (37:102); God spoke to Moses from the fire (27:8), which is an oracle; and the angel Gabriel spoke to Muhammad through words (2:97), or speech.

Table 2.1. Monthly dream interpretation (Nizami and Chaudhry 1993, xvii)
Days of a Typical Month

False Dreams	Opposite Interpretation	True Dreams	Delayed Dreams	Worthless Dreams
1	2	5	6	7
4	3	11	15	8
13	23	12	16	9
20	24	14	17	10
21	–	18	22	–
29	–	19	25	–
–	–	27	26	–
–	–	28	30	–

The poetic writings of Sufi mystics Rumi (1207–73) and Hafiz (1315–90) are memorized by Muslims around the world. Hafiz's poetry is popular because "he somehow manages to sum up what it means to be a true Iranian" (Bradley 2008, 18). Even the Ayatollah Khomeini was a Sufi who wrote "fine mystical love poetry" (ibid.).

Many Muslims have multiple religious identities, depending on the situation. Though many fall into the two grand labels of Sunni and Shi'a, they may also carry Sufi (mystical) or folk (popular, using magic to ward off jinn) identities. The theme of many Sufi poems is the lover (Muslim) seeking his beloved—God. In Pakistan, there are contests in what can be termed a "sing-off" between Sufi masters who compete for the attention and money of their listeners.

Many Muslims who come to Christ bring with them two elements of the spiritual life: a devotional love and an understanding of the supernatural. Therefore, the Christian teaching about love resonates greatly with Muslims. Within the MBB churches in the diaspora, worship is often very emotional, and most churches tend toward a more charismatic expression, similar to some Christian mystic writings. Yet the expression of love for God can take on another dimension that borders on an obsession with love.[20] One MBB put it this way:

> "They (Iranain former Muslims or MBBS) are often very, very, very hungry for attention and for love. And that's how they view God. You can see in their prayers, it's all about love. For us (collective; referring to Iranians), it is not all about love, but it's a different kind of love. Usually, we have two words in Farsi: *asheghetam*, which means 'I love you,' and then we have

---

[20] A reason for this tendency is the popularity of great Sufi poets like Rumi, Yunus Emre, Hafiz Shirazi, and Rabiyyah al-Adawiyyah, to name a few.

doostet daram, which also means *I love you*. However, *asheghetam* has another dimension to it. It still means 'I love you,' but it's more romantic, or 'I'm enthralled with you.' It's now become the fashion among Iranian girls. They will say *Asheghetam Khoda* ['I love you, God'], which is just an example of how they view God. It's a very emotional relationship with God. It's all about God's love for me." (E5F)[21]

The second area of the mystical dimension of Islam that forms the worldview of MBBs is something that the Western church can learn from. MBBs have a worldview that is founded upon the supernatural instead of the amoral scientific worldview of the Western Christian. It is a shorter leap of faith for many MBBs to turn to God in every crisis. One MBB expressed it to me this way:

> "I think the strength of the church is that people come into it with a supernatural presupposition, meaning it's less of an intellectual leap for them to believe that God is who he says he is. He has the power to heal. He has the power to save. He has the power to provide. It's ingrained within Iranians for the most part. For the most part, the Eastern worldview is very much believing in a monotheistic God, and as a result of that, it's a highly spiritually charged environment that they come out of. They come into the Christian faith with just this wonderful openness to God, the Holy Spirit, and faith. Some of the most faith-filled people I know are Iranians. I love watching Iranians worship and I love hearing Iranians recite poetry that they have written for Jesus; it's so sweet and so endearing and it's such a childlike faith. Sometimes we miss out on it in the American church." (U4F)

The supernatural worldview held by many Muslims is an important dimension that affects the intense belief in a sovereign God found in many MBB fellowships.

Secularization and Westernization

Much of the Muslim world was impacted by colonialism. Muslims believed they were the best in the world until Egypt was humiliated in 1798 by Napoleon, who effortlessly took over the Levant with his superior weaponry and military tactics. Very possibly the eighteenth, nineteenth, and twentieth centuries have left an indelible mark on the conscience of Muslims. The invasion of Western powers and colonialism have left them with the sentiment that the rest of the world seems to have passed them by.

Further humiliation grew out of the destruction of the Ottoman Empire and dismantling of the caliphate in 1924. Mustafa Kemal Atatürk was responsible for the secularization of Turkey and the growing demise of the once proud Islamic

---

[21] I used a code to identify the individuals interviewed for this book. The letter E, U, or C stands for the location of the interview: Europe, the United States, or Canada. The number is used to indicate the person interviewed out of all the interviewees from that country, from 1-21. The last letter indicates gender: male or female.

civilization in Turkey. The Muslim world was not prepared for what they deem as the massive onslaught of Western imperialism beginning in the late 1800s. Western nations' military and political domination were obvious, but they were able to impose their influence more subtly economically.

Many Muslim-majority countries felt that the way forward was to imitate these Western countries by adopting modernism and secularism. The Pahlavi dynasty (1924–79) in Iran under Reza Shah sought to implement modernization along with secularization, which "required religion to be practiced at home" (Spellman 2004, 18). An adjustment to a double life of public secularism and private religiosity ensued. The modernization and secularization took much of the power and authority away from the *ulama (a body of religious scholars* who have been trained in the religious sciences of the Qur'an, Hadith, *fiqh*, etc.), thus severing the alliance between the *ulama* and the rich merchants and traders (*bâzâri*) in the market (*bazaar*) (ibid., 20).

Out of this humiliation grew the need for Islam to once again gain its rightful place of superiority, reflective of the Muslim's utopian worldview. The resulting Islamic ideology was characterized by four traits:

1. A nationalist tendency; that is, one that presents the recent past as an undeserved decadence and the future as a promise that sooner or later will be fulfilled.

2. An anticapitalism that is conceived chiefly as a token of separation from the West.

3. An egalitarian statism that consolidates communal unity (itself an indispensable condition of the promised renaissance).

4. An intrinsic and irreducible utopianism. (Laroui 1976, 96)

To revitalize the Muslim world, some Muslims have called for a complete separation expressed in the Islamization of knowledge. Muslims, from the intellectuals to the people on the street, recognize that the Islamic civilization lags far behind the rest of the world in almost every aspect of life. And because modernity and globalization are accompanied by a process of secularization, this perceived Western infiltration creates a crisis. The *ulama* point to a kind of Western neo-imperialism that is taking over, which they see as a cause of the decline in Islamic values and identity. Many Islamic scholars point to the state of education in the Islamic world as a foundational area of great concern. The results are (1) stagnation of Islamic learning, (2) lack of excellence in modern education, and (3) Muslim dependence on foreign ideas (Ba-Yunus 1988, 18).

In this way, Muslim intellectuals have determined that their present system of education is not only unproductive but also culturally alienating. At the same time, Muslim scholars accuse Western education of being amoral and a reason for the moral decline of Islamic values. Forty years ago, Al-Attas (1979, 10) warned,

> If Muslim scholars and intellectuals allow themselves, or are allowed to confuse the Muslim youth in knowledge, the deIslamization of the Muslim mind will continue to take effect with greater persistence and intensity, and will follow the same kind of secularizing course in future generations.

The desire is to create or recreate Islamic education with Islamic values. Even more broadly, Islamizing society has taken on a life of its own and is viewed by many as the way out of the backwaters of civilization, a catalyst to thrust Islam forward to its once dominant position. Islamization also came out of a deep desire for a new, distinctive Islamic identity in light of Western dominance. Luminaries such as Isma'il Raji al-Faruqi (d. 1986), Abu Sulayman (b. 1936), Seyyed Hossein Nasr (b. 1933), and Fazlur Rahman (d. 1988) were instrumental in starting the Islamization project in the United States in response to this secularization. Isma'il Raji al-Faruqi is known for his seminal work *Islamization of Knowledge: Central Principles and Work Plan* (1982).

Saudi Arabians have taken a different path. Rather than seeking to upgrade the educational culture in the country, they have sent their students to the world's best universities to pursue disciplines that lead to bachelor's, master's, and doctoral degrees and medical fellowships. American universities represent a top priority for the Saudi government, and according to Ibrahim Naffee of *Arab News*, in an article posted April 20, 2014, as of that date the number of Saudi students in the United States had reached 111,000.

Others have sought a more political expression in response to Western pressure, beginning with Islamic luminaries of the nineteenth and twentieth centuries, such as al-Afghani of Iran, who called for Pan-Islamic unity (1839–97); Sayyid Qutb of Egypt, author of *Milestones* (1906–66); Hassan al-Banna of Egypt, the founder of the Muslim Brotherhood (1906–49); *Ayatollah* Ruhollah *Khomeini of Iran* (1902–89); Osama bin Laden of Saudi Arabia, founder of al-Qaeda (1957–2011); and Abu Bakr al-Baghdadi of Iraq, the caliph of the Islamic State (IS) (1971–2017).

In particular, the more recent manifestations of radical Islam have been just as critical of Muslims who fail to comply with the Muslim leader as they have been of Western nations, creating inter-Islamic fighting on a global scale. Al-Qaeda is responsible for instigating sectarian violence among Muslims, only to be followed by Abu Bakr al-Baghdadi establishing IS, located in western Iraq, Libya, northeast Nigeria, and Syria. Its leaders regard liberal Muslims, Shi'as, Sufis, and other sects as heretics and have attacked their mosques and gatherings. Muslims have called other Muslims infidels and declared them apostates, thus justifying their attacks.

In response, King Abdullah II bin al-Hussein of Jordan set out a commission of Islamic scholars to address this sectarian violence in the name of Islam. They accomplished several things:

1. They came up with a precise definition of who is a Muslim.
2. Based upon this definition, they forbade *takfir* (declarations of apostasy) between Muslims.
3. Based upon the *mathahib* (schools of Islamic jurisprudence), they set forth the subjective and objective preconditions for the issuing of *fatwas*, thereby exposing ignorant and illegitimate edicts in the name of Islam.22

The Amman Message sought to protect the Muslim community from radical Muslims who issue declarations or religious verdicts (*fatwas*) calling for the killing of anyone, including Muslims who do not agree and support their cause, through pronouncing them apostate (*takfir*). It seems that now the Islamic scholarly community on the whole is distancing itself from radical Muslims, saying they do not represent Islam.23

However, there is still a range of responses from Muslim scholars regarding radical Islam. Some of the responses can be categorized as a perceived legacy of completion, polemics, mutual stereotyping, suspicion, and resentment.

Reaction 1: All Islamic History Is Sacred

The first tendency is to adopt defensive, apologetic, or vindictive approaches regarding Islam. In other words, some Muslim scholars feel compelled to defend and uphold Islamic history at all costs. Any self-criticism becomes a form of betrayal. John Azumah (2001, 176) cites A. Ahmed, who calls this Islamic scholarship an intellectual cul-de-sac, "in which important internal issues are either ignored or only superficially addressed."24

In these dialogues, the important internal issues are either ignored or only superficially addressed. History and faith have become fused in Islam to the extent that criticism of the Islamic past and its inherited traditions by non-Muslims is seen as an attack on Islam. Most Muslims find it difficult to distinguish criticism of the behavior of Muslims (past and present) from criticism of Islam as a faith. Muslim devotion puts up faith as an unintended object of attacks. The Islamic faith is used as a shield for the actions of past and present generations of Muslims.

---

22 The Amman Message states that it is not "permissible to declare as apostates any group of Muslims who believes in God, Glorified and Exalted be He, and His Messenger (may peace and blessings be upon him) and the pillars of faith, and acknowledges the five pillars of Islam, and does not deny any necessarily self-evident tenet of religion." See a summary of the text at http://www.ammanmessage.com/.
23 The typical response is to state that Islamic State has nothing to do with Islam. See http://www.beliefnet.com/columnists/commonwordcommonlord/think-muslims-havent-condemned-isis-think-again/; or Shaykh Hamza Yusuf on ISIS at https://www.youtube.com/watch?v=LGYYv6rjFQM and https://www.youtube.com/watch?v=hJo4B-yaxfk.
24 A. Ahmed is the author of *Postmodernism and Islam: Predicament and Promise* (1992). This remark is specifically referring to Said (1979).

A Brief History

Reaction 2: Rationalization: Cutting Off the Historical Legacy of Islam
Those who are representative of the second reaction may admit faults, but they seek to exempt Islam from these historical circumstances. The argument is that followers of Islam have deviated from the pure original teachings. Their understanding is that Islam is a set of teachings and beliefs confirmed by the deeds and practices of the Prophet Muhammad; the early true, pious Muslims; and the good, virtuous Muslims of all ages. It is believed that Islam was not really the motivating force behind atrocities. Therefore, the slave trade that came from the jihadi wars or the present atrocities committed in the name of Islam are tossed aside as deviations from "true" and "pure" Islam.

Reaction 3: Enlightened Conservatism
Those falling into the third type of reaction critically examine the whole of Islamic history and then discriminately employ what suits the contemporary context and is relevant for the erection of an Islamic future. These persons recognize that it is important not to judge past generations by current values, because values have changed and new approaches have to be adopted in some cases. When it comes to the growing radicalization of Muslims, the enlightened conservative's dismissive sweep of the hand in delegitimizing them is not recognizing that this too is a part of Islamic history that has deep roots in the past. Even though this situation does not suit contemporary contexts—nor is it seen by many as relevant for the future of Islam—it still is a part of the expression of Islam.

These factors give us the immediate background that shapes the cultural values of Muslims found in the diaspora. Both the secularization of Islamic society and the manipulation of religious symbols are keys that influence the worldview of the modern Muslim and may be one of the reasons Muslims are so open to hearing about Christ. The fixation on an "ideal" Islam may be one of the factors that creates a propensity for hero worship of leaders which follows converts into their new life in Christ. I will discussed this later. The new MBBs project a utopian understanding of Christianity in the church, which also creates disillusionment with the church and its leaders, something that needs to be addressed from the beginning.

History of the Islamic Diaspora in the West

Typically, early Islamic immigration to the West followed the lines of colonial occupation. Several countries broke this pattern, however. Germany, Belgium, and the United States received unskilled laborers to work in industry or building their infrastructure. Early on these Muslims were placed in select neighborhoods and often were understood to be guest workers—not expected to settle down and become citizens.

The Burden of Baggage

Early Muslim immigrants first came to the United States between 1875 and 1912. US immigration laws in the early 1920s imposed quota systems, significantly limiting the number of Muslims allowed to enter the country. Many assimilated into the general population. In 1965 President Lyndon Johnson signed an immigration act opening the way for a dramatic increase of non-Europeans to enter the country, most from the Middle East and Asia, with over half of them being Muslims (J. Smith 1999, 52).

Iranian migration before the Islamic Revolution of 1979 consisted mostly of professionals and businesspeople migrating to the West for higher education and remaining in these Western countries (Behjati-Sabet and Chambers 2005, 130). A significant shift after the revolution was that the arrivals were largely refugees or exiles (Bozorgmehr 1998, 6–8). Amir Taheri (2008, 298) notes that Khomeinism "has driven more than five million Iranians into exile and has turned a further four million into displaced persons inside the country. Khomeinism has provoked what the World Bank calls 'the biggest brain drain in history.'"

Behjati-Sabet and Chambers further explain that Iranians who migrated in the 1980s did so against their will—under unbearable living conditions, religious and political persecution, and tremendous pressure. These conditions typically make the process of adjustment and integration difficult. The majority of Iranians residing in Canada, however, came from large urban areas and belong to upper- and middle-class families who are relatively familiar with Western education and values (Behjati-Sabet and Chambers 2005, 128). Many Iranians in the United States came for social, political, or religious reasons; therefore, they are unlike many immigrants in search of economic opportunities. These Iranians have not isolated themselves and have excelled in business and education.

Contrary to the theory that identifies exiles as coming from lower educational and occupational backgrounds, "Iranian exiles are among the elites compared to other recent refugees" (Bozorgmehr 1998, 17). Iranians tend to be relatively economically well-adjusted and preoccupied with their homeland, as exemplified by the fact that they beam media production *into* Iran, in contrast to ethnic groups that import media programming *from* the country of origin. This same preoccupation is also found within the churches, which produce programming destined for Iran.

Bozorgmehr's research reveals that Iranians' business characteristics do not conform to the norm in immigration literature. In contrast to other new refugees or exiles, such as Koreans, who are mostly entrepreneurs in their own immigrant community, Iranians consist mostly of entrepreneurs and professionals catering to the general populace (1998, 19).[25] In other words, Iranian entrepreneurs are not dependent upon their ethnic community for success. This is significant in that

---

25 Though this research was conducted twenty years ago, I am confident that this is still the case.

Min and Bozorgmehr recognize that "Korean immigrants are more residentially segregated and more tightly involved in ethnic networks than Iranian immigrants as a whole" (2000, 726). In conclusion, Min and Bozorgmehr (732) state,

> Korean immigrants' concentration in several types of middleman businesses has contributed to a high level of ethnic solidarity because it often involves great business-related intergroup conflicts with both customers and suppliers. In contrast, Iranian entrepreneurs, who are concentrated in professional and white-collar businesses in white neighborhoods, have not encountered business-related hostility and conflicts.

Assimilation does not seem to be a major area of concern. Iranians are less segregated from native whites than Koreans are, though at the same time Iranians do not readily assimilate (Bozorgmehr 1998, 23). Organizationally, however, there is a significant difference. The Korean community has more than 150 active alumni associations in Los Angeles, whereas Iranians have few alumni associations, and those that exist are mostly dormant. A significant note for voluntary church organizations is that "Iranians had very little, if any, experience of participation in voluntary organizations in Iran, which could be carried over to the United States" (Min and Bozorgmehr 2000, 720).

The 1.5 generation[26] of Iranians has raised concern in the area of assimilation.

> The problem mostly concerned around these students' lack of respect for rules and regulations of the school. Iranians resisted the implicit educational mission of the school, i.e., to inculcate a commitment to American culture, and maintained steadfastly their affiliation with Iran. They devised various modes of resistance to overcome what they perceived as the school's preoccupation with rules and regulations. The teachers, in turn, perceived these actions as bypassing the rules. (Bozorgmehr 1998, 25)

More than 25 percent of Iranian-Americans hold a master's or doctoral degree, the highest rate among sixty-seven ethnic groups studied (McIntosh 2004). Iranians are a very class-conscious people, so socioeconomic class distinctions are important in their identity, both in Iran and in the diaspora.

Characteristics of Muslims in the Diaspora

There is a growing body of literature in the medical and mental health fields about characteristics of the Iranian diaspora, which is foundational to understanding sources of disharmony within the Iranian Christian community. "Regardless of the diversity of regional, ethnic, religious, and social class elements among Iranians, all have some cultural characteristics in common" (McIntosh 2004, 134).

---

26 The term 1.5 generation refers to immigrants who arrive as children and adolescents. They maintain characteristics from their home country to varying degrees. Most quickly assimilate and socialize with their new country, becoming bilingual and identify mostly with the host culture.

The same is true of Iranians in the diaspora. Pre-revolution Iranians were classified as immigrants since they left for economic or educational reasons. Post-revolution Iranians were considered exiles or political refugees since they left for fear of persecution, though "Iranians were not granted refugee status categorically" (Bozorgmehr 1998, 16). While they are less likely to be dissatisfied with their current jobs and incomes than immigrants, Iranian exiles or refugees suffer from drastic downward occupational mobility (ibid., 17). Besides the difficult social and economic adjustments, exiles face cultural and psychological problems. Good, Good, and Moradi (1985, 384), in their study of depression, made the following statement: "Dysphoria—sadness, grief, despair—is central to the Iranian ethos, an emotion charged with symbolic meaning." They saw this in poetry, preaching, and secular literature; both classical poetry and modern novels were filled with this melancholy and despair.

Nearly all Iranians continue to share in the emotions of despair brought about by tragedy, as represented in secular literature, poetry, and the arts. Iranian art forms and festivals that comprise the Iranian cultural identity do not look at the world through religious dogma, but through the human condition of suffering.

> These secular literary works treat cultural themes prominent in the discourse of Iranian patients–pathological grief, feelings of entrapment in repressive social relations, the desire to maintain self-integrity unsullied by demeaning social conditions, and despair at the awareness of the disjunction of the idealized inner self and outward social actions. These issues have special poignance for Iranian immigrants. (ibid., 390)

Good, Good, and Moradi used four symbolic domains for depressed Iranians, usually identified as *nârâhat*—"not comfortable," "upset," or "in distress" (ibid., 390–92).

1. *Gham o Ghosseh*—Sadness and Grief. This is explained as dysphoric mood and depressive illness.

2. *'Asabâni*—Anger. It refers to a state in which a person is irritable, agitated, easily angered, and nervous, and loses self-control in social interactions.

3. Insecurity and Mistrust. This mistrust is often exaggerated and focused on fears or delusions of infidelity, especially regarding kin and gender relations.

4. *Hassâsiyat*—Sensitivity. It is often links stressors in the environment with childhood experiences and personal character and is used to interpret dysphoria and depression etiologically.

Their study reveals that sadness, sensitivity, and mistrust are a distinctively Iranian depressive syndrome (ibid., 390).

People in the Middle East and North Africa suffer the world's highest depression rates. The economic growth rate in 2013 in the Middle East and North Africa proved too low to generate sufficient employment opportunities for a fast-growing population, and the rate of unemployment remains the highest in the world.[27] Another source of depression in these regions is the increase of conflict.[28]

People who have experienced traumatic events, such as those that are taking place in the Middle East, may well arrive in the West with post-traumatic stress disorder (PTSD). Anecdotal evidence, with all its recognized limitations, suggests that churches populated by MBBs may be experiencing the behavioral and social consequences of MBBs with PTSD and co-occurring disorders. If this is the case, then the church will need to develop resources to help individuals with mental and emotional challenges better navigate their lives so they have not only a more enriched spiritual life but healthier families and churches that glorify God.

Dr. Matthew Stone (2015), a clinical psychologist who has worked with Middle Easterners, describes PTSD in the following way:

> PTSD typically follows a traumatic event in which the person experiences intense fear, helplessness, or horror. Some of the more common such events include rape, assault, combat, kidnapping, being held hostage, or any experience in which the individual perceives the situation as likely to result in death or serious harm to the self. It can also be the result of an individual witnessing another individual experiencing such an event.

Stone suggests the following professional treatments: prolonged exposure therapy for PTSD, present-centered therapy for PTSD, seeking safety for PTSD with substance use disorder, and cognitive processing therapy for PTSD. These treatments can be subgrouped into exposure therapies and present-centered therapies.[29] Aside from referring people to professional counselors, much of what the church is doing through showing the joy of the Lord and preaching about the love of God can be healing. I have also laid out some approaches in chapter 8 for creating a twelve-step program like Alcoholics Anonymous to help with mental health issues.

This evidence supports the conclusion that mental health plays an important role in how Middle Easterners interact within the Christian community. The negative and depressed state will shape how a person interacts with others.

---

27 See "Global Employment Trends 2014," International Labour Organization, http://www.ilo.org/global/about-the-ilo/multimedia/maps-and-charts/WCMS_233936/lang--en/index.htm.
28 See Caitlin Dewey, "A Stunning Map of Depression Rates around the World," The Washington Post, November 7, 2013, https://www.washingtonpost.com/news/worldviews/wp/2013/11/07/a-stunning-map-of-depression-rates-around-the-world/?utm_term=.045a51e8465b.
29 Exposure therapy involves exposing the patient to the anxiety source or its context without the intention to cause any danger. Present-center therapy is to help the person become open to experience, learn to trust themselves, develop an internal evaluation of themselves and a willingness to continue to grow.

Understanding Post-conversion

Though the focus of this book is post-conversion experiences of MBBs, it is important to give some general insights on post-conversion experiences before we take an in-depth look at MBB churches specifically. Kathryn Kraft discovered in her research that the greatest struggles MBBs faced were the result of their conversion, not in the process of decision making (2007, 215). She views the MBB post-conversion life through the matrix of community expectations. Honor and shame are basic values.

> Especially in a communal culture, where family and society are considered more important than individual autonomy or self-expression, honour will likely be the guiding standard for its members. An honour/shame-based community is one in which decisions are made and behavior is pursued with an eye to how any given action will reflect on the individual, his/her kin, and his/her community. (ibid., 136)

Behavior is regulated by the community through the prism of honor and shame. Rich ethnographic research (Babbie 2007, 293) is needed to uncover the unspoken code of rules that only insiders know or are expected to know (K. Kraft 2007, 137). Kraft discusses the complication that shame-avoidance adds to the interviewing process when she references Alexander:

> Someone functioning in an honour/shame-based society will do anything to avoid shame by, for example, refusing to acknowledge that s/he has done wrong, or by deliberately shaming others. After all, it is exposing a wrong act that brings division and therefore makes it wrong. (Alexander 2000, 124; quoted in K. Kraft 2007, 140)

In his research on MBB discipleship, Little (2009) indicates that some MBBs become stagnant in their Christian walk before fading away or reverting back to their Islamic faith. This reversion goes beyond Hesselgrave's dissonance in the decision-making process (1980, 249); typically it is a result of persecution or familial pressure, idealized expectations of the Christian community, and interpersonal conflict.

Little's research focused on major obstacles to growth and maturity in MBBs' lives. Based on the answers of sixty respondents, he identified forty-one main obstacles, which were classified into five categories: (1) family and community, (2) Islamic ideology and theology, (3) social (other than family and community), (4) psychological, and (5) spiritual. Little (2009, 182) lists the top twelve obstacles as:

1. Pressures from Muslim family, family control, etc., especially while single
2. Local Muslim community's hostility, rejection, and/or expulsion
3. Vulnerability due to youthfulness, low social status, weak economic state
4. Fear of all kinds: of problems, suffering, persecution, and oppression
5. Lack of trust between and among MBBs and groups; lack of commitment to one group
6. Challenges for MBB families: child-rearing, education, marriage
7. The spiritual nature of the Christian faith—i.e., that it is about the Holy Spirit, prayer, and faith rather than performing religious acts
8. MBB lack of confidence, inherited complexes, emotional pain, victimization
9. Satanic hold of Islam, demonic and occult bondages, hate, anger, lust, etc.
10. Lack of acceptance of MBBs by local Christians and their churches and communities
11. The love of money is at the heart of most problems; MBBs need to learn to give
12. Living in a police state where change of religion is not officially/legally possible

Life in the diaspora can enhance the level of quality of life and achievement, but it can also add anxiety and distrust (Cohen 1996, 508). In addition, converts are thrust into a new set of values that are no longer the same as their community's, nor are they quite the Christian values they expect to find in the West. This ambiguity affects the MBB's relationship with the missionary. Kathryn Kraft notes that MBBs' expectations of foreign Christians are usually quite idealistic; and overall they set unreachable standards, which become a source of anomie (2007, 184). Struggles of immigrant congregations add another layer to the complexity that the MBB community in the diaspora faces.

In conclusion, an entire history makes up the complicated responses of MBBs. Some characteristics are cultural; others are deeply embedded in the psychological outlook they have of the world around them. Religion, social status, and the deep suffering that not only the individual but the whole society has gone through shape what they identify with, coloring their worldview. We will now try to describe the kind of church these MBBs are forming.

2
Experiencing Church

Much has been written about conversion, testimonies, and church-planting strategies among Muslims. The focus has been on how to communicate the gospel of Christ to Muslims and on gathering them into fellowships, but relatively little has been written on what actually happens in these fellowships. The assumption is that once a person is a new creation in Christ and believers are gathered in fellowships, house churches, or formal churches, these fellowships will grow and become mature bodies of Christ just like the church found in the rest of the world. The new believers are given all the tools they need in the Bible and through the guidance of the Holy Spirit. In addition, particular groups have produced Bibles and commentaries, Christian movies, and worship songs and have translated Christian books to help disciple the believers in their newfound faith.[30]

Providing tools, however, is only part of the equation. People coming to faith in Christ bring their own cultural heritage, patterns of behavior, and values—which are uniquely shaped by their religion, culture, and family—into their new fellowships. We will now examine how MBBs experience church.

In conducting interviews, I began by asking questions about the church that gave the person the parameters of the discussion before narrowing the questions to extract specific information about disharmony. These questions gave vital information about the MBB's first impression of the church, their current understanding of the church, and the general strengths and weaknesses of the church.

---

30 Organizations such as the Digital Bible Society (http://dbs.org/libraries/) provide material for new fellowships that are language specific, and satellite programs (https://www.sat7usa.org/) are beamed to where Muslims are located throughout the world.

The Burden of Baggage

First Impression of the Church

"What was your first impression of the church?" The responses revealed that the interpersonal love and compassion the MBBs found in the church made a lasting impression, drawing them back to the church from the very start. A typical response was, "Church was a place that I received love from people, even though I was not a Christian. The atmosphere was so good at church that I wanted to return again" (E19M).

The first impression of church gives an indication of what impacts MBBs. The love, care, and attention they received were by far the main elements that drew many MBBs to Christ, since they came from a culture in which hospitality and relationships were extremely important. Those who came from chaotic confusion, as asylum seekers or refugees, were impressed by the peace and serenity of a holy place. For those who were told in Islam that they were not to question religious convention but accept what they had been told, the church became a place where they could get answers to questions they had not been allowed to ask, making an important first impression. Some who knew nothing about church sought to use the church for their own advantage, but unexpectedly found Christ.

Even negative experiences could not dissuade new inquirers from returning to feel the touch of God they experienced in a relationship with Christ.

Current Understanding of the Church

In my questioning, I wanted to see if there was any difference between the first impression of the church and the current understanding of the church. So as a follow-up I asked, "What does the church mean to you today?" The most common expression of the church was in emotional and familial terms.

"Church has been like my family, the most trusted place." (E3M)

"Church is not a building; it is the body of Christ. I belong to them, and they belong to me. This family is much thicker than my blood." (E4F)

"The church is the body of Christ; we really are a family united in one body. This is the center in my belief in church." (E9M)

"Church means family." (E13M)

"Put simply, it's a family, the family of God." (U12M)

Others described the church as a place where truth seekers come to find the truth, find God, and look for something to fill the void in their lives. Church has a dual function: it is a place for those who know the Lord and a place for those looking for the truth (U9M).

Experiencing Church

Church was expressed as a refuge and a place of peace:

"I feel like it's not a place; God is there, and it's a place of peace. Church is us, people. Christ is the head, we are the body." (U17F)

"It's somewhere that I can release the stress and tension from the week, where I get spiritual peace and a learning experience. I still look forward to it every week." (C6F)

Church was also described in more dynamic or expressive terms:

"It's the body of Christ, it's an organism. It's not a building, it's the people." (U20M)

"Church is a place to come and see Jesus." (C9M)

"Church is the laboratory where we see the faith working out." (U22M)

"Church simply means the presence of Jesus on earth in a tangible way. You are his body, that's what it means… . I very strongly believe Jesus is in his church and the church is in Jesus. Jesus said, 'If you have seen me, you have seen my Father.' I think the church should say, 'The goal is that if you have seen me, you have seen Jesus.'" (U12M)

It is clear that the church plays an important role in the life of a believer from a Muslim background. The most common expression is speaking of the church in familial terms, expressing a deep emotional attachment and identity to the family of God. Worship, fellowship with people who are like-minded, and the teaching from the Word of God are primordial to the understanding of church. In addition, the Christian community and church are considered the refuge of peace in a hostile world. The understanding of church extends beyond the individual to the church's role in the greater immigrant community as a great conduit, a host, and a receiving station for refugees who have had to leave the family, culture, and country they love.

Church Growth History

Every church has its own history, so the next set of questions gives us a glimpse into how these new churches developed and the ensuing results found within them. I framed the question on church growth by asking, "How did your church grow? Was there a split? Did the attendance go up and down? Did people come and then leave? Did the church grow and then level off in attendance?" Most of the interviewees went into stories of the splits in the church rather than giving a history of the church's growth.[31] This section of the interview

---

31 I was not able to determine and group together the various stories about Iranian churches. Since interviews were conducted in areas where there is more than one Farsi-speaking church, and with the transient nature of Iranians moving from one church to another, it is possible that some of the stories of church growth cover the same church.

was useful in introducing many other subjects in regard to church growth, splits, or pastoral changes. These subjects will be dealt with later in the book. Though the general impression of those I interviewed was that their story of a struggling church was unique to them or their country, in actuality the stories were similar in each country.

The typical response indicated that there was growth until some crisis event resulted in a smaller group. One interviewee (U17F) said that they once had seventy to one hundred people, but now they don't have many. Another interviewee (C4M) shared that although on special occasions, such as a party for Nowruz, their church sometimes has over one hundred people, their normal attendance now is only between ten and twenty people.

One person told the history of their church:

> "We started with five couples and me.[32] We had a lot of ups and downs with attendance. A huge chunk of our church were refugees—maybe 90 percent recent refugees. Life was difficult for many in our congregation—a lot of broken marriages, single parents, issues with raising their children in the new culture, adjusting to life in America. It was a heavy burden to have so many refugees for our little congregation and to be involved in meeting needs in a crisis so often. The highest attendance was seventy and the lowest was twelve in our five years.[33] For the biggest part of those five years, our average was twenty-five to thirty adults."[34] (U22M)

The frustration expressed in growing a church came from the fact that all the effort put into helping people in crisis had so little return on the investment. One church in the UK has written more than eight hundred letters to the government for official papers. "But about seven hundred of them disappear when they get their papers" (E9M).

The vision to grow a church may be there, but the instability of the refugees' lives makes the plan uncertain. Typical is an MBB church in a British city with an attendance of ten to twenty people. They sought to cooperate with an English-speaking congregation with the idea of growing an MBB church out of the former. However, the core group was not stable. "A lot of them are young, barely any families. Most are young men" (E15F). Then, when these unattached young men get their paperwork from the government, they leave the church and the area. Now "only a few of those original people are still coming to church" (E15F).[35]

The instability of younger men is not the only obstacle that these churches must overcome in their attempts to grow a healthy church. One church under the

---

32 The core group of five couples that started the church was gone within the first year of the church's existence.
33 The reason for the high numbers was a major influx of Iranian refugees during that time.
34 This church lasted five years before it folded.
35 Attendance has been hampered by the government sending refugees to other cities.

leadership of a large American church had high hopes for growth. A small group from Iran came to this fellowship with a particular theological perspective and eventually broke away, starting a church in another state. Then a second group from Iran came, but "They couldn't get along, so they split" (U11M). The explanation given for the inability to get along was pastoral control: the leader excluded others. The result was two more splits; and then the pastor gave up on the church and went to another country to start anew. The current size of that church is 50 to 70 members, although it can be as high as 150 for a Christmas dinner.

Faced with the instability of immigrants and refugees, some church leaders have resolved that even if the growth pattern in their ministry is one of ups and downs, they will be the stabilizing force in the community. One puts it this way:

> "I think a living church has ups and downs. There are some people who attend faithfully—they come, they hear the sermon, they go home. That's it. There is not really a big difference in the five to six years that I've seen.[36] We have lost some people and we get new people (immigrants, refugees). As a servant of God, I try to help them. I believe that a living church is an up-and-down church." (C5M)

The new churches are not necessarily healthy, particularly when they are made up of disgruntled individuals. One man gave this historical perspective:

> "I think it goes to the late 1980s that one church was started here, and that one same church split to a second church, and split to a third church, and split to a fourth church. Then a couple of other churches popped up from other places, so that's six; and that one split—seven. This one lately split—eight. The half [church] is the guy with three to five people at his home. The churches in our area all started with one church. There is lots of hurt in these churches, and sadly nobody wanted to be accountable to each other. Our people come; they stay; but if they don't like it, they move on to the next church. Then, suddenly, as it has recently happened, five women from one church decided they are starting a church."[37] (C2M)

The average size of an Farsi-speaking MBB church in the diaspora is between fifteen and fifty attendees. Virtually every church experiences splits or major exoduses, typically when it is between one and five years old. The ebb and flow of attendees is partly due to the unstable situation of refugees, the attendance of non-Christians with no intention of seeking God, and the volatility of interpersonal problems. Some of these conflicts are between the leaders and the members, while others are between the members themsleves. Few churches are stable in their attendance, and even fewer have been able to sustain membership beyond one hundred. Disgruntled members feel like they can do a better job than what they experience in a church, so they branch off and start a home Bible study. But the

---
36 The church currently has about sixty to seventy people attending.
37 The last church meets in a home.

The Churches' Greatest Strengths

new churches are not exempt from the same problems found in the old churches, and soon they experience a split.

After hearing about these Iranian churches' struggles, I asked, "What are the MBB churches' greatest strengths?"[38] My purpose in asking this question was twofold: First, I wanted to give the MBBs an opportunity to expound on the strengths of their church. Second, this exercise would allow them to prioritize those strengths to help determine which aspects of the church in the diaspora are the most vital.

The strengths reflected the strengths found in Middle Eastern cultures—hospitality, generosity, and the emotional expression of one's feelings—coupled with the advantages of smaller churches.

"They love each other; they want to help other people." (U5M)

"One of the greatest strengths is small churches. People are close to each other, they pray for each other, they are like friends. They get close to each other. This is the benefit of the small church." (U18M)

"Hospitality and the ability to make strong, close friendships drew people back to the fellowship." (U9M)

"They are so hungry for God. It's hunger that I haven't seen anywhere else. They are so expressive of their love through their language and their body language. Iranians are very special people." (U5F)

Several mentioned that one of their church's greatest strengths was people's passion for their faith.

"The important thing is their zeal for God—they love the Lord." (U12M)

"One of the greatest strengths is the passion of the Iranian church: their zeal, their testimonies, the freshness of their experience with God. That's a tremendous strength." (U22M)

Here's how three others put it:

"Every first-generation Christian has one thing that the second generation doesn't—we have a zeal for the Lord because we know the Lord has done something in our lives, and we have experienced that. That's our strength. We are also strong in evangelism and sharing the experience with others." (U3M)

"Spiritually, I would say what makes the church strong is if the true love of Christ is there…. I think Iranian believers are capable, once these problems are under control, of creating a truly loving, attractive community where people feel very welcome—a place of healing, a place of acceptance. They are capable of doing that." (U21M)

---

[38] I did not ask this question of the interviewees in Europe, though several did offer strengths found in the Iranian church. Therefore, the lower number of responses does not reflect less interest in this subject.

> "MBB churches have a great potential of being a great strong church, should they be discipled, taught, and educated properly. Their strong points are their love, kindness, and hospitality, in my opinion—which you don't see in some of the Christian churches in North America. MBBs will go a thousand extra steps for you if need be. But they have to be taught to do this within the expression of church." (C2M)

The greatest strengths of the MBB churches center on their passion, hospitality, and fellowship. Spiritually, Iranians come with a worldview in which the supernatural is real, so expectations are that God will demonstrate his power when they call upon him. Hospitality, one of the greatest values of Middle Eastern culture, expresses itself in the church. Loyalty and fidelity to other MBBs are found in the church when individuals or church leaders go the extra mile to help someone, and often finances or time are not a consideration. Fellowship is a strong mark of the MBB community. Even though church services are long, people linger long after the service is over. Their desire to meet throughout the week and to visit each other in their homes makes the MBB church appealing and effective in its outreach to a hurting community.

The Churches' Greatest Weaknesses

I followed up with the opposite question: "What are the MBB churches' greatest weaknesses?"[39] Many stated that we had already covered most of the weaknesses in the interview process. The purpose of asking this question was twofold: First, although I initiated the research in order to uncover sources of disharmony in the MBB church in the diaspora, so many grievances were mentioned that it was difficult to determine the major offenses. This question afforded the MBBs an occasion to expound on the greatest weaknesses of their church. Second, this question provided the interviewees an opportunity to prioritize the major weaknesses to help determine which aspects of the church are the most significant.

The lack of good training and the lack of good leadership were identified as major concerns.

> "Like any other first generation, we don't have the wisdom and training. We're street smart, not people who have been to school. Our weakness is our lack of knowledge." (U3M)

---

39 As before, I did not ask this question of most of the interviewees in Europe, though the interview focused on the weaknesses in the Iranian church. Again, the lower number of responses does not reflect less interest in this subject.

"The weakness is that the leadership doesn't know how to engage the membership in ministry. They aren't giving them a chance to contribute, or they don't even know where they should contribute because they are not organized." (C6F)

Two others shared these primary concerns:

"The negative side is a lack of solid teaching. Most of the teaching and preaching are more emotional rather than solid systematic teaching. They struggle to take their members from point A to point B in discipleship and strategy for the church. I haven't seen any strategy or vision for the church. What are the steps or objectives to get there? None depends of the leaders depend on the Holy Spirit. Most of the churches I've seen are that way. We need more training and teaching." (U2M)

"The weakness is that everyone wants to be the leader, the boss, or to have the last word. That's the problem. Unfortunately, this is coming from experienced leaders and pastors of the church. It's sad. I see more weaknesses than strengths in the Iranian church. Normally I am an optimist, but not in this case." (U12M)

The lack of any collective memory of the Christian faith is viewed as a great weakness.

"[The Iranian] MBB church is not even in its youth or grown up. It has numerical growth, but the MBB church has not even come to its youth yet. There are many other mature ethnic churches with a better background. But not the MBB church." (U11M)

One person stated that Islam seems to dominate their behavior:

"There are more weaknesses because we are coming from a Muslim background. Even though we become a Christian, we still have that Muslim background in us. For example, sometimes we are still superstitious. Even though we are Christians we are plagued with doubts such as 'Where is God?' 'Where do all these problems come from?' 'Why did these problems happen to me?' When you are in the midst of a problem, you don't see many faith-strong Christians. Besides, we are not good encouragers. Another weakness is that we don't accept criticism, for we think we are always right. We are stuck in the past when it comes to church and our history." (U17F)

Interpersonal relationships between members was viewed as one of the greatest weaknesses of the MBB church.

"The greatest weakness is the inability to forgive each other for what they have done to each other." (C5M)

"The weakness is sensitivity, gossip, and distrust; they are major, major issues that we talked about." (U21M)

Two others gave their priority list:

Experiencing Church

"Our greatest weaknesses are relationship and community, by far. We do not do well as a group. It's not just a Christian problem, for I don't think our mosques or governments are any better. We don't work well as a group in our community. We don't understand community, such as compromise, or the give-and-take needed in interpersonal relationships. Those are my two top themes on weaknesses." (U22M)

"Middle Easterners are so concerned about what people think, what others are saying. Often church does become a bit like a social club, a bit cliquey, especially when we're talking about younger people. Dramas go on, judgments are passed, and gossip happens. These are weaknesses of the MBB church." (E5F)

The major weaknesses should not surprise us when we understand that the MBB church is relatively young and inexperienced. The lack of leadership, training, and maturity of the church, as well as problems of interpersonal relationships, are normative for a church comprised mostly of new Christians. Leadership is mentioned because leaders are seen as people who should be taking the church in a correct direction. Lack of training is connected to the leadership. The need for maturity is a consequence of little or no understanding of the church and the Christian life, which causes confusion. In addition, Muslims coming to Christ bring the cultural values often described as "baggage" from their earlier life without Christ, so interpersonal relationships are strained.

Reasons for Leaving the Church

A common experience everyone talked about was the high turnover rate of people leaving the church. Various reasons were given as to why the interviewees themselves or someone they knew left the church. I wanted to see if a pattern of behavior or circumstances emerged that precipitated this exodus. I categorized the various responses into the following categories:

For some the reason was geographical.

"It was always because of my moves." (U22M)

"I moved three hours away. It was useless to go all the time." (U11M)

"He and his wife were doctors, so for their jobs they moved." (C5M)

A common factor was the transient nature of Middle Eastern immigrants, who are not in a stable living situation. Some are told by a government agency where they are to live.

"I realized that all those people, after one or two years, they all got their visas, and they moved to different cities. It's the nature of their life in this country. They have no choice of where to live." (E16F)

The Burden of Baggage

Many Middle Easterners see the church as an ethnic community to help them transition to living in a new country, much like a cultural center. Once their needs are met, they leave.

> "After they got what they wanted, most of them disappeared after a couple of months or a year. Most will disappear.." (E11M)
>
> "After they got their green card, they stopped coming." (U17F)
>
> "Especially in the English church I saw a lot of people, MBBs, leave as soon as they got papers." (E3M)
>
> "Immigrants, refugees, and new arrivals come to church, have their needs met, then they leave the church. So I've become deeply suspicious of MBBs who come to church but really are just 'green card Christians' who want to take care of their problems, and then they leave." (U22M)

Some Iranians leave the Farsi-speaking church to integrate more fully into the new host culture.

> "They get tired of people [Iranians] always asking questions, so they leave. But few of them say, 'No, we don't want to stay in Iranian culture because we are in the West.'" (E11M)

The reason some MBBs left the church was the nature of the church they attended. Personal problems with the leadership or other members caused some to leave. In other cases, they left because of the dysfunction of the church itself, such as poor biblical teaching or personal offenses.

> "The main reason was from behavior and offending, as you said. They were coming to a point that maybe they think this is not true Bible, this is not Christian behavior, this is not true church." (E19M)
>
> "I know people who have left the [MBB] church and completely stopped attending any Farsi church. They have attended all of these [Persian] churches ... and eventually they attend an English-speaking church." (C2M)

I pressed to know if these people were now satisfied in the English-speaking church.

> "Yes!" (C2M)
>
> "I find it difficult to be in an established community of my peers. Those who are my age grew up; they all started dispersing and going to [national] churches. There was only me and another guy in our early twenties." (U4F)

Reasons for leaving the church also fell into the category of negative experiences.

> "The reason I left was because I got mistreated by my own people" (E10F). After trying different churches, this woman found a non-Iranian church that was "fantastic, so I stayed there" (E10F).

Experiencing Church

> "There are so many dramas, so many problems in their relationships with other girls and guys in that church. People often leave the church at that age." (E5F)

I pressed to see if those who left a church were mature believers or new believers in Christ.

> "A combination. Mature believers felt like they have been believers for a long time, but didn't have a place where they could use their gifts. The newer Christians felt like they weren't listened to. There was a combination who would leave, and a lot of real bitterness. Some went to other churches, some said they have had it, some went to American churches." (U6M)

Sometimes it is not possible to determine why people leave the church. Those who do so come from every segment: individuals who have not accepted Christ, new believers, and mature believers. Sadly, some who leave in bitterness try to cause damage to the church. The worst-case scenario is when all the members leave. A positive perspective of the high turnover rate, however, is that people have several occasions to hear the gospel.

Differences between the National and the MBB Church

The experience of many included attending a non-Iranian church. In an effort to distinguish the unique characteristics of the Iranian MBB church, I asked the interviewees to make a comparison between the national church (i.e., British, Canadian, or American) and the Persian church. This comparison helps us better understand the Iranian church's dynamics and sources of disharmony. I often pressed for further clarification on characteristics that are found in all cultures by asking what makes a certain characteristic unique in the Iranian experience.[40] The comparison was asked of those who expressed that they attended both communities, and therefore the number of respondents was lower.

The difference mentioned most often was the spiritual depth between the two communities.

> "For me, going to Iranian church means serving; I'm not looking to get fed since I'm fed in Canadian churches." (C7M)

> "I was fed more at the American church than at the Persian church, so I went to the Persian church more for the fellowship, but I continued going to the American church for the Word." (U13F)

> "Spiritually, the English church was very strong." (E3M)

> "I became a Christian in a Western country; the English words click deeper in my heart than Farsi words." (C7M)

---

40 The depth of knowledge of the host culture may be based more on impressions than actual fact. Perceptions are important to trace, however, as they can also lead to sources of disharmony.

"Many American pastors are more mature than Iranian pastors." (U21M)

"Number one, the English church is the spiritual food they are getting. Number two, the English church is a huge church…. You go, you get your spiritual food, and you leave. So there's no environment for conflict." (C2M)

One woman pointed to the maturity expressed in the two fellowships:

"My experience in the American church is that the people who storm out are a minority. It's like one or two or three crazy people. But in the Iranian church, the fact that the whole church just left because of this one event shows me that there is an underlying lack of maturity concerning Christian forgiveness and the process of Christian church discipline and how you go about that." (U4F)

Not everything is positive about the host culture, as this man stated:

"I still have not penetrated the American church behind the curtain, behind the scene. I've never been in leadership in an American church. I still don't know the nitty-gritty dynamics and struggles behind the scenes that American churches and organizations struggle with." (U22M)

"North American church has these walls. You never penetrate those walls. One thing about Iranians, it's easy to look over their wall. They allow you to get close to them. That's why they get hurt." (U9M)

At times, pastors, churches, and individuals in the host culture who have little or no cross-cultural experience seek to help an Iranian start a church. Westerners rarely have the experience or cross-cultural skills necessary to properly evaluate what is happening in the ethnic church.

"Most Western ministers in the English church cannot discern if an Iranian is telling the truth or not. Iranian unbelievers may cry in a church service, so now Westerners think they're believers." (E11M)

"I don't get excited when I hear an Iranian has accepted Jesus into his heart. That doesn't create an iota of happy emotions in me. I have become deeply suspicious of the motivations of an Iranian who comes to church. I get excited when I see growth in the process of Christian life; when lights come on; when there are a new maturity and commitments that are observable over a period of time. That's what gets me excited." (U22M)

There are significant differences between the Iranian church and the national church. Many Iranians perceive that the national church is more spiritually mature, particularly in the preaching and teaching of the Bible and pastoral leadership. The Iranian church has more young people, while the established English-speaking churches tend to be populated with older people. Cultural aspects of the national church are confusing, particularly when political and social life are mixed in with church life. The American church seems to have walls that do not allow outsiders in, while Iranians are very open

Experiencing Church

and hospitable. Though national churches and individuals have good intentions to help Iranians, most of them are naive about Iranian cultural signals.

The Second Generation's Church Experience

The second generation is the future of the Iranian church. Eight individuals, or 16 percent of the interviewees, commented on the second generation. Six were female, and all were from the second generation. The two males were older, but expressed concerns about the Persian-speaking church reaching the second generation. However, many members of the second generation are no longer in the Farsi-speaking first-generational church because of the disharmony they have experienced.

> "I felt more at home there in the British church. I could be myself, just not pretending anything. These people know us and where we are coming from, even though they didn't have a clue of our background. There was a sense of being comfortable and at peace. I love the worship and the music there, and I could connect to it more than when I went to the Iranian church." (E15F)

> "In general, I felt like the Iranian leaders were never anyone I could talk to. The community was kind of judgmental. If I ever had a problem, I would never ask them to discuss it or talk to them. I felt like I would not get good advice that I could use. They didn't take the young people seriously. None of them could relate to young people." (C6F)

Some of those in the second generation attend both a national church and the Persian church. Their spiritual needs are different than those of the first generation. In the following case, this young woman felt like she was part of a community in the national church, but in the Persian church she felt like she was an individual and not connected to a community.

> "The English church is where I'm fed. I am spiritually fed, mostly not by the speaker but by the people there and by the friendships that I have in the church there—whereas I probably just spend too much time criticizing what's going on in the Persian church. I'm not receiving anything from what's been said, from the style of worship, from this and that." (E5F)

When I pressed for clarification, she expanded the thought:

> "A speaker will emphasize certain points in his sermon. I fell under the 1 percent in the church to whom the point was not relevant. Just ways of thinking about things are completely different in the Iranian church. Their aims, their goals in life, and their way of looking at English people all differ." (E5F)

Sometimes the reason young people are not in the Persian church is pragmatic.

> "There were no others in my age group. I felt isolated. I don't know how others my age would have felt around a youth group." (C6F)

> "I do feel like I was unable to make intimate friendships with girls of a similar age. Their experiences are completely alien to me." (E5F)

> "Those who are my age all started dispersing and going to American churches. There was only one other person in my entire age group in the church." (U4F)

Language is also a problem for the second generation.

> "I've always had trouble expressing myself just because my Farsi vocabulary is so limited. Iranians love to joke about old TV programs, stories, stuff like that; and obviously I can't always understand them." (E5F)

Those in the second generation have not given up on the first-generation church. They have some great insights that can help the Iranian church be more effective in ministry.

> "In the Iranian church, they aren't grounded yet and don't have the Christian culture yet—they have the Iranian and Islamic culture. They just want to fit it into the Christian culture, and that doesn't work. That's why I like going to the British church—it's just better. But that doesn't mean I would give up on Iranians. These problems are with the first and second generations of Christians. Me, being the second generation, these problems are sorted out for me, being involved in the English church and culture. When I talk to other people, they say some of these things. Maybe when it's our time, these things will be sorted out. But we might not stay in the Iranian church. A lot of my friends don't stay in the Iranian church." (E15F)

> "It [The Iranian church] was a good place to begin their spiritual journey, but over time the second-generation MBBs] outgrew it and they were curious to try something different. Over time, they wanted to go into a more blended church where they could blend in… . They might go to the Persian Bible study on Thursday night for their connection and prayer group. But they wanted to be with the whole body of Christ for worship." (U1F)

I asked one young person if there was anything she wanted to share about her experience in the Iranian church.

> "I guess they get stuck in what they already know and they don't try to expand that. At a certain point, you already know what they know, and you can't learn anything new. It's good to expand your knowledge—research controversial topics to be able to talk to people about them and answer a lot of questions. Like, I see a lot of 'homophobia' in churches in general, but especially in the Iranian churches. It's an issue that needs to be solved. We're living in a world where those issues are practical and not just spiritual; the church needs to find a way to talk to kids and adults about it." (C6F)

Some older members of the Iranian church called for a strategy to reach out to the younger generation.

Experiencing Church

> "We should plan for the future. We have to be attractive to the second generation... . They have grown up here, and they are confused. They are not Iranian, and they are not British. They are in the middle. The second generation will disappear without good leadership." (E11M)

Not all of the second generation's views were negative.

> "[The Iranian church] is my connection to Iran as a second-generation [believer].... I love it, and I love the community." (E5F)

The perspective of the 1.5 or second generation is important in order to understand how the young people view church. The generation gap is exacerbated by the first and second generations living in two different worlds: the first generation lives with the history of Iran and the second generation looks to the future in the West. Spiritually, the Iranian church seems unable to meet the emerging needs of the second generation. Socially, there are few Iranian young people who desire to be with their Iranian peers. Language is also a concern, since the cognitive growth in the educational system is in English, not in Farsi.

Of all the issues, though, the second generation finds the disharmony of interpersonal relationships—exhibited by the lack of forgiveness and repentance, being stuck in the past, and unable to move forward—the most frustrating.

Suggestions from the second generation are not meant to be critical but instructive in helping the Persian church become relevant to the next generation, who are being raised in the West.

Summary of Church Background Experience

Iranians' first impression of the church, whether national or Farsi-speaking, is very positive overall. The church is a place of peace and very attractive to new attendees. The church becomes a surrogate family, as most described the church in familial terms—expressing deep emotional attachment to the church and its members. The history of the church, however, is sordid. Most Persian-speaking churches remain small, around twenty-five or thirty attendees, and have experienced at least one and often multiple splits—making the churches fragile at best. The Iranian church's greatest strengths center on its members' passionate worship, generous hospitality, and rich fellowship, which are experienced multiple times throughout the week.

The Iranian church's greatest weaknesses reflect its relatively new genesis. Immature leaders and members, the lack of training, and struggles in interpersonal relationships remain its weak points. The unstable and transient nature of recent arrivals is reflected in the high turnover rate in the churches. The spiritual depth and maturity of national churches are attractive to Iranians who have grown beyond the Persian leadership, but cultural differences are confusing. Many in the second generation experience a cultural gap because they live more in the host's world, while those in the older generation still remember their home country. The second generation greatly desires the Farsi-speaking church to move beyond its weekly personal dramas and mature to become a forward-looking church with broader experience than the small ethnic church it is today.

3
The Luggage We Bring

There are various layers in all of our lives and in the institutions to which we belong. In the rest of the book I will break down these layers into five core areas. First—and the focus of this chapter—is the dimension that is unique to the individual. We will call this the emotional/behavioral/cognitive dimension and individual features that make up part of the individual's normative responses. Second is the interpersonal dimension, which explains how people interact with each other. Third is the familial dimension, which considers how marriage, nuclear family relationships, and extended family relationships influence the individual and the church experience. Power is the fourth area under consideration, for it is so integral to our churches and our lives. Lastly we will examine religion, which is not just the doctrine or beliefs of an individual or church, but profoundly shapes the values, traditions, and culture of a people.

The personal dimension is not a psychological analysis of MBBs. What I am after is to initially investigate, describe, and explore the nature of conflicts and to examine the factors that lead to tensions within the nascent Iranian Christian church. In my research, therefore, I wanted to know to what extent the reactions in the context of the church came from the person's own filters/reactions/perceptions as expressed through envy, honesty, shame and honor, trust and fear, fate, and boundary issues.

Rules/Boundaries/Freedom

The first set of questions was to determine if the newfound freedom in the West may be a problem in the Iranian church. Many discussed rules, boundaries, and freedom and the confusion some Iranians struggle with in understanding and living the new Christian life. This section revealed a broader problem of rules or boundaries as an area of concern within the Iranian church experience.[41]

---

41 Both K. Kraft (2007) and Mernissi (1992) refer to the role of rules and boundaries as integral to the Muslim experience. Kraft, in particular, explores what happens at conversion when the oppressive boundaries

Boundaries are an important element in Middle Eastern societies. There are two aspects of boundaries to consider to better understand the responses of Iranians and other Middle Eastern people in churches. First, when anyone ventures outside the prescribed boundaries, they are viewed as bringing chaos not only on themselves but on the community, the nation, and even the religion.

Fatema Mernissi (1940-2015), a Moroccan sociologist, described the foundation of Islamic societies from the eighth century onward through boundaries, or *hudud* (limit or restrictions). She argued that in the Muslim collective mind, community is built around boundaries, walls, and separations. Boundaries exist for defensive purposes, to separate and control differences within society, as well as to maintain a well-organized Muslim community (Mernissi 1992, 7). Oftentimes this same worldview is brought into the MBB church, expressing itself through limits and restrictions.

Second, Sandra Wilson describes how people who grew up in unhealthy families are taught to be numb to violations of personal boundaries. The tendency is "to think and live in extremes… we express our overdependency with either nonexistent or fortresslike boundaries" (Wilson 2002, 129). Those coming from life under a highly oppressive regime are taught very similar messages about boundaries and thus react similarly. Conversion into the freedom of Christianity, where the oppressive boundaries are removed, causes confusion. Kathryn Kraft states, "This loss of structure leads to a degree of anomie" (2007, 189).

The difference between rules and control within the Iranian community does not seem evident to new Iranian arrivals. "In Iran, boundaries were forced on you. You were a good person because the pressure was always there" (U2M). Now Iranian Christians are free from the control, and some forget about Jesus because of the freedom they now experience. One woman expressed frustration: "Freedom is freedom, not to do whatever you want to do" (E4F). She went on to say that some people coming to their church want freedom, "but they don't understand what it is."

The confusion over the rules and standards Christians are to live by leads to live-in situations, loose sexual mores, alcohol and drug abuse, viewing pornography, indiscriminate consumption of music, and inappropriate dress (U22M, E4F, U2M, U17F, C5M, E10F). Without clear rules about respect, how to dress, and dating in a Western setting, MBB Christians are left on their own to navigate their emotions and hormones. Reconstructing how boundaries should be set in the church causes tension and disharmony. Some pastors are too strict and act like moral police.[42]

---

are removed.
42 I will give more detail of this consequence and its repercussions in chapter dealing with leadership.

One of the reasons people leave churches is because they feel that pastoral leadership is inappropriately strict when they set boundaries. "Most of the time it was the overbearing rules of the pastor. Everybody talked to the pastors, had secret talks with him, and then the pastor independently decides what to do. That's why most of the time when the church gets up to fifty to eighty, they split. There are no rules; just whatever the pastor decides" (C9M).

This confusion over boundaries can be found in the way MBBs interact with each other. There is a sort of naiveté in just how open people should be in communicating in church. Some people, when they come to Christ, believe that they need to be completely open about all their past sins. There is no experience in how to share discreetly with a few trusted individuals or where proper boundaries are to be drawn.

Several people indicated that confidential information was shared in prayer or that problems were shared as a prayer request or in sermons (C9M, U4F, U9M), resulting in fuel for gossip. This goes back to learning how to set up healthy, appropriate boundaries instead of sharing without any sense of propriety. "Iranians don't have any boundaries... . We are quick to express our feelings to each other, even if we've only met twice. Some don't know their limits" (E19M).

Part of the confusion over boundaries can be the visceral overreaction to *any* boundaries that remind the person of the past oppressive control from of a totalitarian regime from which they have escaped (E10F, U1F, U6M, U17F, C5M). "It's more how they react when they see legalism—which was definitely practiced in the prior church—being very, very legalistic. There was this legalism that shackled people, and they really felt burdened by that" (U6M).[43]

The lack of boundaries is also a concern when the pastor is not strict enough. The result of a lack of boundaries is that a few members take on the role of trying to bring order to what was perceived as chaos. Predictably, the pastor is considered the "nice guy," while those trying to bring some semblance of order to the worship service are viewed as the "bad guys."

One member expressed their frustration that led to their leaving the church, "I felt like the police who was beaten over and over. So, because of that, I was like the bad guy in that church, with a couple other people [who sought to bring order to the church meeting]. So the members took it out on us; I felt beaten. I was there five to six years" (U13F). However, when this believer attended another church where boundaries were set, she said, "I could sit there and enjoy the service and serve, and not worry if people were doing the right things or how to stop the conflict. I didn't have to worry about that. I could just be a member, serve, and get fed" (U13F).

---

43 There was no indication in the interview that this lay person has a problem with authority.

Conversely, some felt that other churches were too strict, for they would not allow them to behave in the way that they had become accustomed to in their home church.

Boundaries are a particularly difficult area for MBBs who have come from controlling situations to navigate, and they are a component leading to disharmony within the MBB church. Inappropriate and strict boundaries create an oppressive legalism that imitates the oppressive experience of the past. The emotional hurt suffered by MBBs in the past creates an overreaction to any boundaries, whether overly strict or lacking. Confusion over setting appropriate boundaries in church can lead to unchecked conflict and misrepresentation of true spirituality, and it sets up an unfortunate tension between a passive leader and one who polices members.

Henry Cloud and John Townsend's book *Boundaries* (1992) is an excellent resource in describing boundaries, offering resolutions to boundary problems, and developing healthy boundaries.[44] To use their nomenclature, "Boundaries help us keep the good in and the bad out" (ibid., 33). Boundaries are like fences, not walls; they are not used to control people. These fences need a gate to let the bad out of us and allow the good to come in. The gate closes to keep the bad out.

People coming from abusive cultures often experience confusion over boundaries, particularly when healthy boundaries have been violated from the governmental level down to the personal level. One aspect of growing in the Christian life is learning that we don't have boundaries where we need them (such as saying no to control, pressure, demands, or sometimes the needs of others that are imposed on us) and that we have constructed boundaries where they shouldn't be (like saying no by default, or avoiding good).

When coming from a culture where it is shameful to say no, establishing boundaries is particularly difficult to navigate. We live in a world where there are both aggressive controllers (who don't listen to others' boundaries) and manipulative controllers (who try to persuade people out of their boundaries). These pressures are found in the church and in the culture. I will cover how to establish healthy boundaries in greater detail in chapter 8, "Where Do We Go from Here?"

Honesty/Lying/Falsehood

Among MBBs, a culture of fear and distrust is endemic. Javad Larijani, a conservative member of the Iranian parliament, once said, "Being able to keep a secret even if you have to mislead is considered a sign of maturity. It's Persian wisdom. We don't have to be ideal people. Everybody lies. Let's be good liars" (Sciolino 2000, 35).

---

44 I have found this book most helpful in dealing with controllers and manipulators. The book helps define boundaries, describes what is going on, and gives helpful solutions. This helps detangle the emotional element in codependent relationships and gives a path toward healthier relationships.

Lying in a guilt-innocence worldview is always considered wrong. But in a shame-based society, lying to protect the honor of the tribe or nation is acceptable. Only selfish lies are considered shameful. An Arab proverb says, "A concealed shame is two-thirds forgiven" (Muller 2000, 81).

Lying within Iranian society is considered so commonplace that it causes perennial public concern (Forbis 1981, 93). Many point to the practice of *taqiyeh* (dissimulation)—arising from Shi'a's minority position within Islam, particularly during the Abbasid caliphate—as endemic to society.[45] A Persian proverb encapsulates this idea: "Conceal thy gold, thy destination, and thy creed" (ibid., 92). William Forbis suggests that a great body of literature on Iranians portrays the values of "dishonesty and its variants—deception, cheating, hypocrisy, guile, duplicity, pretense, knavery, fraud, mendacity, and corruption," in works such as *The Adventures of Hajji Baba of Ispahan* (ibid., 93).

A culture of fear and distrust goes beyond lying and can leave an indelible mark on society. Daniel Bar-Tal, an Israeli professor of research in child development and education, identifies two types of fear reaction: the first type results from cues that directly imply threat and danger, while the second results from conditional stimuli that are nonthreatening in their nature (2001, 603). Bar-Tal reveals that fear is stored in memory and dominates and controls thinking. Prolonged experience of fear causes overestimation of dangers and threats. His research reveals fear's tendency "to cause adherence to known situations and avoidance of risk, uncertainty, and novel situations; it tends to cause cognitive freezing, which prevents openness to new ideas" (ibid., 604).

Bar-Tal also states that societies may develop collective emotional orientations. Intractable conflict tends to dominate the collective fear orientation and thus becomes embedded into the collective memory over time. Fear often becomes contagious.

> Oversensitized by fear, a society tends to misinterpret cues and information as signs of threat and danger, searching for the smallest indication in this direction, even in situations that signal good intentions. The fear also leads to great mistrust and delegitimization of the adversary because of its harmful acts and threats. (ibid., 609)

This culture of fear and distrust appears to be an underlying reason for the disharmony and conflict so prevalent in Iranian fellowships. Jewish cultural anthropologist Raphael Patai states that discord in the Arab world has always been present, even since pre-Islamic days. At the slightest provocation, violent verbal abuse and threats erupt, easily degenerating into physical violence.

---

45 For a fuller discussion on *taqiyeh* and its influence on Iranian society, see Forbis (1981); Sciolino (2000); Mackey (1996); and Taheri (2008).

The situation is complicated by the fact that "unity" is merely a very abstract and remote ideal, while strife has its historical antecedent and underpinning in the age-old Arab virtues of manliness, aggressiveness, bravery, heroism, courage, and vengefulness, which have been extolled by poets for more than thirteen centuries and survive in the Arab's consciousness, predisposing him to conflict even though he believes in Arab unity and brotherhood. (Patai 2007, 239)

Herbert Kelman explains one of the dimensions of protracted ethnic conflicts:

> Threats to identity create a zero-sum view of the conflict, where one's very existence seems inextricably linked to the negation of the other. An acknowledgment of the identity of the other is perceived as an act of self-destruction, as recognizing the experiences of the other fundamentally brings into question one's own interpretation of history, the conflict, and of the responsibility one holds for the past, present, and future shared realities. (Kelman 1997, quoted in Hicks 2001, 129).

The topic of honesty, lying, and falsehood has as its backdrop avoidance of risk, uncertainty, and novel situations. In addition, Donna Hicks has noted that intolerance of uncertainty and ambivalence is a way of measuring egocentrism. "The more one steadfastly holds onto beliefs, especially when there may be disconfirming evidence, the more egocentric (embedded in one's own perspective) is one's understanding of the world" (2001, 135).

Global Leadership and Organizational Behavior Effectiveness (GLOBE) is a long-term program designed to conceptualize, operationalize, test, and validate a cross-level integrated theory of the relationship between culture and societal, organizational, and leadership effectiveness in sixty-two societies. Iran ranks on the lower range in the GLOBE sample for assertiveness. "Iranians are less confrontational and aggressive in social relationships" (Dastmalchian, Javidan, and Alam 2001, 540).

When someone suffers from a history of traumatic threats, an overload of the senses takes place. Hicks believes that the assimilation/accommodation process shuts down in an effort to stabilize core beliefs. The process causes beliefs to become "rigid and extremely resistant to change, complexity is lost, certainty of our assessment of what is 'right' rises, and the feeling of ambivalence about what we 'know' is lost" (2001, 137). She describes the defense mechanism of self-preserving/other-annihilating which leads to revenge and threats of violence. When people find themselves under perceived threats of trauma and humiliation, their survival mechanism includes the following: (1) closing down the learning process; (2) certainty about beliefs solidifying and becoming rigid; (3) feeling the need to place blame or deflect responsibility; (4) breakdown in social interaction through retreat; (5) breakdown in trust; and (6) revenge (ibid., 137–41).

The Luggage We Bring

Anthropologist Lila Abu-Lughod recognizes a pattern in Bedouin society whereby individuals—in cases of loss—react with anger, blame, or denial of concern. The response of blaming others, learned early in life, provides a focus for anger (1985, 251). Abu-Lughod believes that

> by responding to loss with anger and blame or denial of concern, individuals both live in terms of the honor code and dramatize their claims to the respect accruing to the honorable. Through their responses people disavow experiences of helplessness, vulnerability, passivity, or weakness which would compromise their images as strong and independent. (ibid., 252)

Furthermore, Hicks believes that

> the threats experienced by parties in conflict are experienced not only as threats to one's identity, or our collection of beliefs about who we are, but more broadly [as] a threat to the way we maintain our inner sense of coherence and stability. In so doing, the threat not only challenges the beliefs we hold about ourselves (our identity), but how we arrive at those beliefs, and how we ultimately use those beliefs as stabilizing mechanisms that allow us to function in the world. (2001, 141)

International correspondent Elaine Sciolino further explains that, in Iranian society, "The lying, the compulsion to beat the system in the name of freedom, the insecurity that comes from not knowing when the state might intrude into a private space all create anger. The feeling is just under the surface, but it can explode unexpectedly" (2000, 107). It is this collective consciousness that Iranian exiles and refugees come from.

When I explored the topic of interpersonal relations in the church with the MBBs, lying came up spontaneously when discussing honesty and trust. Twenty-two people, or 44 percent of the respondents, expounded on some aspect of this topic. Honesty and lying are considered sources of disharmony in the Iranian church. One person said it this way: "We don't trust each other. I'm 100 percent sure on that" (C4M).

Many pointed out that Iranians have been lied to in every domain in life. The government was singled out as a lying institution, with the result that Iranians in general don't trust anyone. The basic sentiment was that lying is found within the very fabric of Iranians (U1F). Islam was blamed for the culture of falsehoods or lying, as this man explained: "There is baggage that comes with Muslim background, especially in the area of dishonesty. It's not a big thing to be dishonest; if you're dishonest toward a non-Muslim, it's a good thing. That baggage that comes along with an MBB has to be dealt with care" (U6M). Another expressed it this way: "Gossiping and lying are worse with Muslims" (E18M).

Many pointed to lying as a part of their background and culture. "It's not something crazy among the Persians, lying. No, we have a problem for almost fifteen centuries. Every single day Islam was in the midst of our life. That's why we are like this. I think it takes time to get better—better than this" (U12M).

Many reasons for falsehoods were expressed: Lying is for survival. Lying, cheating, and taking advantage of others and their ideas reveal a person's "smartness" (U7M). This type of behavior was condemned for its lack of integrity.

Developing trust can be difficult, especially when trust has been broken on multiple levels. "We had issues with … mistrust of each other. In terms of character, integrity, motivation, [our doubts] were huge" (U22M). It doesn't help that the Iranian government has created a culture of distrust through spies who have followed emigrants into the diaspora.

The Iranian concept of *ta'arof* was mentioned several times as an example of how persistent falsehood is within the Iranian community. In my interviews, I gave a positive spin to *ta'arof* as a cultural attribute of politeness. There was some recognition of the positive aspects of *ta'arof*. For example, "Some *ta'arof* is great. Some *ta'arof* is just being polite. And that's really the intention behind it, which is great… . But it's very easy to cross over the line when it comes to *ta'arof*" (E5F). Despite the positive comments, many Iranians I have talked with over the years see *ta'arof* in a negative light—as deception, lying, and dishonesty.

Some Iranian believers hope that when their non-Christian compatriots become Christians they will grow out of lying as the Holy Spirit convicts them that this behavior is wrong. Others have a less optimistic view, recognizing that lying is a part of their old life that is not easily transformed (U1F). Nonetheless, there is hope that over time the prevalence of lying will diminish.

One man who was concerned for the second generation stated that "the second generation … is longing for transparency and honesty" (U3M). He raised this cautionary note: if the church isn't transparent and honest, "we're going to lose them; we'll lose the battle and lose them."

Iranians appreciate the value of truthfulness in Western culture and lament the fact that Iranians in general lack that type of honesty (U14M). One woman expressed her frustration with a cultural characteristic that inhibits honest relationships in which people can help each other going through trials. She believes there is more acceptance of expressing your weakness in Western churches. "For instance, saying that you are going through depression is a taboo and an embarrassing thing. Don't tell anyone that you are depressed because people will start judging you. If you are a Christian, you need to be a happy person" (E5F).

Nevertheless, there are MBBs who, through great effort, vulnerability, and transparency, have achieved some level of trust. Trust is achieved in these churches, and they begin to grow numerically. "Iranians like people who are open and honest" (U21M).

A pastor opened up to the people in his church, sharing his experience. At first the people didn't have much respect for him, but the level of love was high because he was trying to be open and transparent. He felt that over time people grew to trust him, being persuaded that what they saw was what they got. His willingness to take a long-term perspective in building trust helped people become committed to him (U21M).

In summary, lying, falsehood, and lack of trust are major areas that cause disharmony in the Iranian church in the diaspora. Falsehood is said to be embedded in the fabric of Iranian society with the Islamic influence of *taqiyeh* and the Persian concept of *ta'arof*. Lying is also part of the survival mentality. Lying, cheating, and taking advantage of others is even considered intelligent. The result is that trust within the society is broken, so Iranians tend to trust non-Persians more than they do their own people.

The positive side is that Iranians do desire honesty, and a few people have achieved honest and transparent relationships within the church. It will take time for the transformative work of the Holy Spirit, coupled with Christian leaders modeling open and honest relationships, to create trusting relationships in the body of Christ.

Negative Attitude

During the interview process I pressed for reasons and motives for the sources of disharmony. Though I did not specifically ask a question about a negative attitude, the issue was raised by four interviewees, or 8 percent of the group, who indicated that Iranians view life through a negative lens, which is also a characteristic of Iranians in the diaspora.

One person put blame on the Iranian Revolution of 1979 and its ongoing repercussions. He remembered that Iranians, before the revolution, were very generous and hospitable. This common courtesy slowly diminished as people were forced to stand in line for hours to buy the basic necessities of life—such as milk, meat, and bread—and they soon began to fight over these necessities. "People have gone through several decades of that; I would say their basic posture is one of negativity, fear, suspicion, competition, fighting for scarce resources" (U22M).

This negative attitude has infiltrated the church as people search for motivations behind just about everything.

> "I think Iranians are fundamentally suspicious of the outside world, because of suspicions about scarce resources, competition, betrayal, gossip, etc. It is hard to develop trust." (U22M)

> "They are so negative. [They think] you knew it and you intentionally have a problem with them or intentionally wanted to dishonor them." (U21M)

This suspicion, fear, and survival mentality seems to close down communication, and a survival-of-the-fittest perspective drives behavior. Information needs to be concealed because, as one Iranian expressed it, "This is a very hostile world; everyone out there will take advantage of you if you open up to them" (U22M). Honesty and vulnerability are not seen as an option.

Some pointed to how years of oppression since the 1979 Islamic Revolution in Iran have created a negative perspective of life. Negativity, fear, and suspicion affect communication, so Iranians are afraid to share information and resources. The interviews revealed that Iranians' first response in the church is typically to be suspicious, looking for ulterior motives. The deteriorating situation in Iran further engrains this negative viewpoint, creating a greater chasm between new arrivals and those who have been in the West longer.

Shame/Honor/Pride

Understanding the cultural value of shame, which shapes many Islamic and Eastern societies deeply, may give insight into common reactions expressed in interviews concerning personal interaction in the MBB church. Stephen Pattison, a professor at the University of Birmingham, observes that "there are two broadly different kinds of cultures throughout the world, shame cultures and guilt cultures" (2000, 54). Roland Muller (2013) adds a third culture characteristic of fear and power which is predominant in animistic civilizations.[46] Every society has all three of these cultural elements, but the emphasis may lie more with one or two.

Shame cultures are understood to be structured around shame, honor, and pride, or esteem. They promote social conformity by external sanctions for good behavior. "The emphasis is upon appearance and conformity in response to an external social view" (ibid., 54). Offenses are perceived as actions that go against social mores, punishable through public shame, ostracism, and rejection by the social reference group.

Pattison contrasts shame cultures with guilt cultures, where the individual has an internalized sense of wrongdoing and a sense of conscience. Punishment is forensic and not dependent upon the loss of honor or of global stigmatization of the person.

It is important to have a working definition of guilt, which is "essentially a legal concept; when you transgress a law you are guilty" (Noble 1975, 22). On the other hand, "Shame is essentially a personal concept" (ibid.). As Patai notes, "Shame has been defined as a matter between a person and his society, while guilt is primarily a matter between a person and his conscience" (2007, 113).

---

46 Muller (2013) identifies these three cultural responses to sin as found in Genesis 3.

Achieving one unified understanding of shame is not possible. "Many disciplines bear on the understanding of shame—from literature to biology, psychology, philosophy, and sociology. There is no one way of understanding shame and it can mean many things to different disciplines and people" (ibid., 13). One broad way of understanding shame, however, is that it is the internal pressure to behave in an honorable manner, the psychological drive to escape or prevent negative judgment by others (ibid., 113).

Pattison makes a distinction between "acute, reactive shame"—which is temporary and limited in its effects and is by no means all negative—and "chronic shame"—which is extended in time and influence and "can cast a permanent shadow over a person's life, character, and personality" (2000, 83). His conclusion, however, is that

> any experiences that induce a sense of persistent inferiority, worthlessness, abandonment, weakness, abjection, unwantedness, violation, defilement, stigmatization, unlovability and social exclusion are likely to be generative of chronic shame… . Perhaps the lowest common denominator in all the factors outlined here is the experience of human individuals being dishonoured, disrespected or objectified. (ibid., 108)

Honor, within the Middle Eastern perspective, is to be upheld at all costs, so shame is avoided. "Honor is greater than life itself" (Noble 1975, 66). "Honour is the value of a person in his own eyes, but also in the eyes of his society. It is his estimation of his own worth, his *claim* to pride, but it is also the acknowledgement of that claim, his excellence recognized by society, his *right* to pride" (Pitt-Rivers 1966, 21).

In the Middle Eastern context, life revolves around honor and shame. Honor, saving face, and shame have a profound impact on behavior. Competition, envy, and rivalry are on the dark side of the honor-and-shame value system (Mischke 2010, 8). "One is considered justified, for instance, in resorting to prevarication in order to save one's face. If it comes to saving somebody else's 'face,' lying becomes a duty" (Patai 2007, 111).

The worst thing is for a man to expose his inner self with all its errors and weaknesses.

> But over and above his own behavior, his self-respect depends on whether or not others respect him, that is to say, whether they show a respectful attitude toward him, whether they treat him with the respect he feels is due to him. Therefore, the code of behavior followed by the individual is primarily calculated to impress others with those qualities of his personality that will induce them to respect him. (ibid., 107)

Chronic shame, which has long-term negative consequences, can be described in the following four reactions.

1. *Withdrawal.* Pattison (2000, 11) suggests that withdrawal can be literal and physical and/or psychological and internal. The defense mechanism is a withdrawal to safety. The withdrawal response is often accompanied by distress and fear, which are interpreted as depression rather than suffering from chronic shame. My interviews revealed this propensity for withdrawal in conflict or perceived conflict.

2. *Attacking self.* Pattison notes that a chronic "attack self" response to shame can be related to fundamental masochism. "The person constantly seeks to be in the position of suffering victim; you are never powerless, alone and abandoned so long as you are a victim, the unconscious script runs" (2000, 112). He suggests that the means used to attack oneself include self-ridicule, putting oneself down all the time, and being perpetually angry with oneself. Should this reaction be found within the church, the person needs to give up the inner hostility or shame-related feelings of abandonment, powerlessness, and unlovability, or emptiness may result.

3. *Avoidance.* People view themselves as defective. Strategies of avoidance can include self-aggrandizement and seeking perfection, which deflect attention from a defective self. This reaction involves performance and denial, which are costly. This may be reflected in part by the Iranian community's high achievement both in business and education, particularly in North America.

A related strategy is *self-deception*. Pattison quotes Nathanson on this point; self-deception may reach such a critical stage that those who engage in it become "people whose very identity is a lie, who live with a sense of self so false that they may be seen as imposters" (Nathanson 1992, 350; quoted in Pattison 2000, 113). In the church, for instance, the tension between the pastor's outward identity and his personal life—the fact that his projected image does not match reality—may be a factor in disharmony within the church.

Other strategies of avoidance are *flight*, often into addictive substances, and *caring for others*, from which people who experience chronic shame might get their self-worth.

4. *Attacking others.* People using this behavioral reaction to chronic shame externalize their discomfort. Rage, whether through active or passive aggression, poisons relationships. The strategy is to direct rage toward a scapegoat and project self-contempt onto others. Blaming others is also a way to avoid owning shame in the unsatisfactory self. "Contempt, blame, and envy can coalesce in externalizing scripts for shamed people. They may then, for example, have very strong negative feelings towards authority figures" (Pattison 2000, 116).

Pattison concludes by saying,

> This selective account of some of the ways in which people react to shame shows just how pervasive and varied are the implications of this condition.

> From laughter to despair, from hiding to grandiosity, shame has enormous implications for the way in which people think about themselves and others. It also affects their behavior. One must beware of associating all the woes and defensive reactions of humans everywhere with chronic shame. (ibid., 119)

Shame is often associated with morality. Chronic shame may create a strong reaction to other people's opinions and cause the individual to be hypersensitive about the effect other people's attitudes and actions have on them (ibid., 124). Pattison indicates that a general problem for shame-prone people is that they may radically overestimate or underestimate their place in relationships and events. "A person may be as mortified over a small or trivial offence as they are over a major offence" (ibid., 128). In the moral dimension, Pattison believes shame is a more primitive social condition than guilt. He even states that "chronically shamed people are pre-social and pre-moral" (ibid., 124).

The majority of Iranians I interviewed remarked that "Iranians are sensitive." This sensitivity expressed itself in "dramas" over seemingly anything—for instance, getting offended if they believed that someone didn't greet them in the proper way. A glance, a raised eyebrow, or the intonation of the voice all become major signals of communication that can be easily misread. Chronic shame theory seems to give meaning to the hypersensitivity over perceived offenses that are often overlooked in Western churches.

I did not specifically ask about shame, honor, and pride in the interview process. But these topics were raised in multiple places in the interviews, such as in questions dealing with sin, forgiveness, and conflict. Nineteen respondents, or 38 percent of the group, used expressions of shame, honor, and pride; and all seemed to use the terms interchangeably. This emotional element is thus a major operational force in the MBB community and a source of disharmony within the Iranian church in the diaspora.

This cultural characteristic of honor and shame was often expressed in terms like the following: "Iranians are constantly aware of respect and not shaming each other. It's very complex" (U1F). Shame was defined as "not [being] able to live up to the standard that someone set for you" (U3M).

> "The Middle East and Asia are shame-based cultures. Then comes the Western [world], which is right or wrong cultures. We don't really care about right or wrong. If you are right about me or wrong about me, that's not the thing. It's about honor and shame. You just don't say certain things. If you said it, you brought shame; and when you bring shame to me and to my family and to my name, you're not easily forgiven. That's how I look at it. It's cultural and historical because we are a shame-based culture. We do a lot of things for honor. People kill their daughters because they had a boyfriend, so they brought shame." (U19M)

Pride is used to express a strong-willed attitude.

> "Again a split? Again I think of pride; I think in every conflict the root is pride somewhere. Pride and gossip and, again, not being able to negotiate. Americans are sometimes more open to negotiation, but Iranians are never ready to give in. If they give in, they feel [they have] lost. They have been taken advantage of." (U21M)

Iranian culture was blamed for creating a survival mentality resulting in a pride that does not take others into account. Sometimes people accuse others of pride when they do not agree with what they are saying or doing. One pastor shared that people complained that he was focusing too much time on the needs of the new refugees and not enough time on the needs of the people in the church. Pride also shows itself in doing jobs in the church. "Everyone wants to draw attention to himself in the church. Individualism is a problem in the church" (U18M). Pride is seen as the way people defend their honor.

Protecting one's honor or name was recognized as an important quality. "Protect their name. Protect the honor. Even protect the name of the church…. They don't want to be criticized for their teaching or the style of their ministry and their leadership" (U19M). This person went on to say that this protectionism is "strong in our culture, so they hide information."

In the discussion about pride/honor and shame, I asked if vulnerability was hard. "Yes, that's right," one interviewee answered. "You may lose your honor. There is the honor-and-shame part of it and there is the fear that it will be used against you" (U21M).

> "If you use that information against me, talk behind my back, what are others going to think about me if they find out negative things about me or my family? What are they going to think? How will it make me look as a person and as a believer? Part of the culture is we don't talk about our problems because it will make us look bad. We magnify other things to make us look good, because if I look good, I'll be respected, I'll have things. If not, they'll look down on me, not respect me; I'm a nobody." (U13F)

I wanted to know what it is like to minister in a church and culture in which the reaction to honor and shame is so prevalent. A pastor confided,

> "They feel dishonored again; it goes back to honor and shame. If somebody does something to you, dishonors you, you really get hurt. You come to a wedding or a party and they sit you somewhere improper; you get hurt. 'You didn't give me the honor and you devalued me; you put me down in front of others.' Honor and shame are a high value. If you offend people many times as a pastor, people get offended; because on Sunday I'm talking to somebody, and somebody [else] comes and says 'Hi,' and I'm focused [on the person here] and I don't hear or answer [the other person]—and the other person gets hurt." (U21M)

One of the most powerful combinations of emotions expressed within the Iranian church is honor, shame, and pride. Protecting one's honor or name is a value that seems to trump all other values. The lens of honor defines relationships, the way people do ministry, and how Iranians interact with each other. Iranians hide information from each other to protect their honor.

Churches split as a matter of pride and honor. The pride-and-honor perspective influences the way conflict is addressed. Listening to other people and to their opinions in conflict is seen as a loss of face and honor. This concept of honor is so pervasive that even the perception that the person is dishonored results in conflict. Moreover, shame reaches into the family, where it is used as a tool in disciplining children. Humility is a quality that seems to elude most Iranians, even in the church in the diaspora.

Individualism

One of the topics that came up as a problem in the church was the inability to work together. Forbis has proposed that the major conflict in Iran is between individuals rather than between classes, religions, tribes, or races. He believes Iranian history teaches "the importance of a man's survival, of looking out for himself" (1981, 90). His conclusion is that

> this excessive individualism works out as unwillingness to collaborate. Team sports are weak in Iran, which goes in for weight lifting, wrestling, horsemanship, tennis, and skiing—in fact, the Persian language used to have no word for "team," and had to borrow it from English. In its more harmful form, excessive individualism brings envy and malice, exploitation and manipulation, rascality and guile. (ibid., 91)

Forbis describes the priorities in most Iranians' minds as self first, family second, and the nation third (ibid., 92). Zohreh Khazai Ghahremani, in her article "Yeki Bood Yeki Nabood" (literally "One Was and One Wasn't," the Persian equivalent of "Once upon a time … ,"), notes that "such a phrase being hammered into us from childhood may well be the reason why we choose to be alone, always 'yeki' and never a team… . We Iranians are a nation that adores number one" (2011).[47]

Well-organized and collective societies count heavily on interpersonal trust in order to function. Some writers describe Iranian society as a nation of self-interested individualists with a tinge of mistrust.

Mohsen Mobasher argues that "the Iranian community in exile suffers from a major identity crisis and lacks a unified sense of national identity that binds Iranians together" (2006, 100). Drawing his insights from the cultural trauma theory of the

---

[47] *Ghahremani is a dentist and a featured writer for the website Iranian.com, an online English community site for the Iranian diaspora.* Launched in 1995, Iranian.com is a vibrant forum for Iranians worldwide who care deeply about all things Iranian—identity, culture, music, history, politics, literature, and one another.

2004 book *Cultural Trauma and Collective Identity*, he proposes that "the trauma of the hostage crisis and Iranian Revolution was the impetus for the birth and popularity of a set of new ethnic labels including Persian, Persian American, and Iranian American among Iranians in the United States" (ibid., 107).

Iranian nationalists are proud to be affiliated with the Persian culture and heritage, but are ashamed and embarrassed to be identified with the Iranian national government. Many have lost their sense of pride in, or commitment to, their religious tradition and identity (ibid., 101). Iranian community organizers tend to promote the public celebration of Persian cultural festivals and criticize or condemn participation in Islamic rituals. Iranian media in the West reflects this anti-regime and anti-religious bias.

> Iranian television and radio programs produced in Los Angeles have been the chief purveyors of the non-Islamic Iranian national identity.... Therefore, discussions about the social and political conditions of Iran, treatment of political dissidents, and loss of national dignity and international respect under the Islamic government have been a central feature of the Iranian media in exile. (ibid., 111)

The cultural trauma and nonreligious practice of Iranians may be a factor in "a rise in the number of Iranian-born Muslims who have converted to Christianity or openly condemn Islamic faith as a fanatic religion that is inconsistent with modernity and progress" (ibid., 104).

My research questions did not specifically ask about an independent or self-centered perspective. However, four interviewees, or 8 percent of the respondents, mentioned that self-centeredness was characteristic of Iranians and a reason for conflict within the church. Shame theory identifies this self-centered perspective as a normative response, so I include their remarks. During the discussion about conflict in the church, some interviewees described the inability of Iranians to work together; I followed up by asking if it is hard for Iranians to work together.

> "We are coming with the same backpack, with the same disease.... It's all about me, who I am." (U7M)

> "I think a lot of it goes back to the culture—Iranians are very good at individual sports, like wrestling and weight lifting, but team sports where they have to work together—soccer, volleyball—they suck, they don't work together.... But when they have to work together, it's not part of the culture. It's always *me*. What can I do for me so I can be successful? That culture has come to the church. There isn't a lot of unity. They don't say, 'I humble myself for the sake of the church or the team.'" (U13F)

The individual or independent perspective in the diaspora church is considered a carryover from Iran—part of the cultural baggage. The propensity to be self-centered, and the lack of a cultural collective memory of cooperation, is one of the ingredients in the proclivity toward church splits. The church becomes a place where members draw attention to themselves.

Sensitivity

The topic of sensitivity—that is, how easily Iranians get offended—was raised throughout the interviews, although the questions did not deal explicitly with that topic. But sensitivity surfaced in questions dealing with communication, getting along with one another, criticism, forgiveness, gossip, and conflict. Seventeen people, or 34 percent of the respondents, talked extensively about the hypersensitivity of Iranians, which appears to be a normative response in an honor-and-shame society. This is a particular area of concern, for when individuals are easily offended, the result is people leaving the church.

When asked if Iranians are easily offended, the responses varied. "You can talk to them and you can preach, but they will say, 'You know something about my life and you're preaching that to me.' You say something in regard to something, anything, and they feel offended" (U10F).

Sensitivity within the Iranian community is complex and has many contributing factors.

> "We, as ex-Muslims, have all this baggage of insecurity, and come to Christ. So we wouldn't lose this baggage of insecurity overnight. It's like an iceberg. It takes time, it takes prayer, it takes God's grace, it takes good teaching.... The more insecure they are about the basics and their tomorrows, the more insecure they will be about their faith as well. I think it impacts them very, very, very greatly." (E2M)

I wanted to know how the dynamic of sensitivity, or getting offended, is different in the Iranian culture than in any other. A typical response I received was, "If you talk with Persians, you'll find that there is enormous social pressure to fit in. The way you serve tea, how you greet people, the way you say goodbye. There's always the fear that you won't measure up" (U1F). Some even pointed out that Farsi has expressions and ways of speaking to deal with this sensitivity.

> "Even the language–Farsi is not a direct language. It has many connotations and implications–they are hidden." (U2M)

> "If we're in the car, and you're in the backseat–they have a saying–'Excuse me that my back is to you.'" (U1F)

I asked who was more sensitive—men or women. Both men and women responded by saying that women are very sensitive. In a church in which women would come to services dressed inappropriately, a sermon was preached on modesty based on the passage in Romans 13 and 14 about the weaker brother and not being a stumbling block. "A bunch of those people were offended, and some of those ladies left the church and never came back" (U22M).

I asked if older women can also be very sensitive. "Yes, especially the older generation. But some of the younger ones, especially if they've been trained that way—to be very formal—could be offended" (U1F).

I asked how this sensitivity expressed itself.

> "Disagreeing with someone in an Iranian context is like you are personally attacking them. People get offended when you say you disagree…. It's very hard for them to disagree and still be friends." (U22M)

> "If the pastor tries to tell them that what they are doing is wrong, they get offended and leave the church." (U2M)

I asked if their church preached or taught on the topic of being overly sensitive.

> "It's one of the topics many times of the year; either in sermons or indirectly we talk about how to get rid of that sensitivity. The reason our church is relatively healthy is because we address those things all the time and we ask people to pay attention, to get over it and to grow." (U21M)

Navigating the emotional sensitivities is difficult since there are multiple levels of sensitivity. Some believe the baggage of past hurts and insecurity is the driving force behind the sensitivity. Perceived disrespect or being overlooked causes hurt feelings. Even the Farsi language reflects this hypersensitivity and a tendency toward exaggeration. The Iranian inclination toward indirect communication means that feelings are not expressed, so people must speculate and make accommodations for unexpressed sensitivities. Women who are not recognized for their contribution are often offended and leave the church. Disagreements are considered personal attacks. Pastors who are aware of these sensitivities and give considerable time to addressing them are seeing people grow in this area. It will take time, though, for the first generation to experience grace and healing to grow past their hypersensitivities.

Shifting Blame

As I asked questions dealing with conflict, I expected to hear more stories about shifting blame. Only seventeen people, or 34 percent of the respondents, talked specifically about blaming others. Throughout the various questions in almost every category, much of the blame for behavior was placed on Islam or how the interviewees were raised in an Islamic system. It was difficult in this research to explore the area of shifting blame in depth, so I only mention it briefly here. The most common claim was along the lines of "To be honest, I blame Islam" (U12M) for what Iranians are suffering now (U14M, C5M, E6M, E15F, U6M, U21M, U2M, E18M, U19M, E14F, C3M, C2M, C6F, E1M, U22M, E1M).

Intolerance

One characteristic that surfaced in the interviews is a very strong will and seeming inability to flex with other ideas, which I call here intolerance. Though only five respondents, or 10 percent of the total, mentioned this category, this behavioral trait is inferred in the answers in the section "Maturity of the Believer and the Church" below. In the section "Reasons for Leaving the Church" in the previous chapter, intolerance is one of the many explanations given for the hypersensitivity and inability to overlook an offense. The characteristics of toxic faith described in chapter 4 specify intolerance, rigidity, a position of superiority, and judging others. "The pastor had a very strong personality … very active and passionate about ministry. But he was very strong-willed. He was very abrasive with the way he dealt with people" (U22M).

Problems often become so big that there is no avenue to deal with them. One person expressed that it is hard to work with people, especially if there isn't 100 percent agreement. He felt that there is no tolerance or maturity among the members, so if the leader is not paid, they leave (U2M). One respondent characterized the Iranian way as "our bluntness, our rudeness, thinking that our way is better than everyone else's. You put two Iranians together and you have three opinions. We are just better than everyone else. But every culture is like that—we're just better at it" (U3M).

I asked how this intolerance affected the church. One woman explained why her church has decreased in number: "We don't have unity. Everybody has their own mind and doesn't want to listen to others. We need to accept our downfalls" (U17F).

The respondents agreed that intolerance and strong will are characteristic of Iranians. Within the Iranian church in the diaspora, intolerance is viewed negatively—seen as not being open to new ideas, and as a problem with pride. This rigidity provides one explanation for why Iranians leave the church. This intense independence can be channeled into a positive asset, however, if there is a willingness to work with others. As the church matures, there should be a decrease in intolerance and an increase in the ability to work together.

Immaturity

My questions did not seek to uncover the problem of immaturity, but the topic arose from the discussion in multiple areas. In an attempt to better understand motives, I asked about the reasons behind the stories that were shared. Twelve respondents, or 24 percent of those interviewed, thought that a lack of maturity was behind much of the negative behavior exhibited in the churches.

They expressed the view that believers coming from a Muslim background have little or no collective memory of what church is or how to behave as a Christian. This research category grew out of responses that brought up the issue of immaturity in some form in the explanations about conduct.

Some interviewees called Iranians' conduct in church childish.

> "Sensitivity is weakness and childish. If you are strong in your identity and strong in your faith, people could speak negatively about someone like they did with Jesus and you would not be offended. That is a measure of your growth." (U21M)

> "One of the major parts of a pastoral ministry in the Persian community is to just bring people closer to each other. It's like you're dealing with your children, just playing nice with each other. 'Be nice to each other. Don't say bad words to each other.' I preached a series of sermons about this. Seriously! This is my observation about the Persian church. This is not pastoral principles, this is fathering principles. These forty- or fifty-year-old men, I have to sit with them and say, 'Play nicely with each other and don't say bad words. Why did you just do that? Why did you push him?'" (U19M)

The immaturity of the leadership, particularly of pastors, was also a concern. Even if a person is a pastor or desires to be a pastor, that does not necessarily mean that he reacts with maturity and wisdom. "Iranian leaders—yesterday they became Christians, and today they want to be leaders; they need to be fed by the Scriptures" (C7M).

The immaturity of new believers is something every growing church will have to deal with, although the particular way immaturity manifests itself will vary depending on the church's cultural background. "If the pastor says something, they don't want to obey" (U17F).

There was a joke in one church that the welcome packet should include a microphone. "That desire to be behind a microphone, to give a testimony, to sing a song, to give a message, and to lead worship—that created a lot of conflicts. The hunger is for being seen, [being] up front, calling the shots, being a leader" (U22M). This thirst for attention results in Iranians recording their testimony and sharing it wherever they can get a hearing, with little or no forethought.

The Iranian church in the diaspora is made up of individuals who have little or no experience in any church. Many are new believers. Relationships between members, as well as relationships between clergy and members, was expressed as childish at times, particularly when it comes to hypersensitivity. The path to becoming a leader or pastor is often short, not allowing time for wisdom and maturity. People react impetuously in their life together, getting offended and leaving the church and trying to take others with them, or speaking without thinking. In their unbridled enthusiasm and passion for their new faith, believers make some rash decisions and express a desire to share what they have experienced with whoever will listen, often without consideration of where they fit within the life of the church.

Summary of the Emotional Component

In this chapter, we have looked at the emotional/behavioral/cognitive and individual variables. Appropriate and balanced boundaries is something the Iranian church in the diaspora struggles to establish. Church members grapple with oppressive legalism on one side and unrestricted boundaries on the other, reflecting confusion over the freedom they have found in Christ. The Islamic teaching of falsehood (*taqiyeh*) and the Iranian culture of politeness (*ta'arof*) result in a lack of trust within the Iranian Christian community. Achieving open and transparent relationships built on trust is an important ingredient for growth in the Iranian church. The negative suspicion coupled with a shame/honor cultural lens and hypersensitivity undermines many authentic attempts at ministry.

These emotional behaviors indicate an immature Christian community in which many members and leaders are relatively new in the faith. The expansive growth of the Iranian church requires pastoral leadership but does not allow for the maturation process to take place. Believers' enthusiastic and passionate response to their new faith in Christ results in an infant church whose members are unaware both of the complex baggage they have brought with them into Christianity and of how to minister to the needs of a growing community.

4
Can We Just Play Nice?

The way people interact with each other is an important dimension to consider when looking at the church. MBBs, like all of us, bring their own cultural ways of socializing and relating into the church. Some of these strong cultural traits are very beneficial. When individuals who come from the same cultural experience meet together, there is a familiarity that makes them feel at home, something that is not found in Western churches. They might experience familiar cultural elements in the way hospitality is expressed, the customary heartfelt greetings, the way people communicate, their passionate worship, or the way they enjoy one another without an agenda.

On the other hand, every culture has some blind spots that perpetuate some of the negative responses, which they might find frustrating. When someone comes to Christ, these ingrained ways of relating to one another do not automatically become redeemed or reflect the new patterns of behavior taught within the Bible. It takes time and maturity to unlearn certain behaviors. Some will not disappear in the first generation but will fade in subsequent generations.

So much of the Christian life is lived out in community, yet it is in this area that we fallen human beings seem to have the greatest difficulty. It is a multifaceted dimension of our faith requiring a greater explanation of the dynamics that vary from culture to culture. This includes variables in communication, victimization, criticism, revenge and forgiveness, "saving face," and conflict resolution, or conflict management. The respondents in my research considered the interpersonal element a major area of weakness within the church.

> "Getting offended, interpersonal relationships—that's number one, that's off the charts." (U22M)

> "I would say 100 percent of the problems are related to the relationships." (C2M)

Middle Eastern cultures are context-dependent cultures, meaning that relationships are important factors in any institution (Weir 2001, 14). Business models found in the Middle East are based on relationships. "All is directed towards the long-term accumulation of position, prestige, standing, relationship and respect" (ibid., 16). The family and its role in wider social networks are important factors in business, and these family networks may also be assumed to exist within the nascent church.

Both Kathryn Kraft (2007) and Don Little (2009) mention the importance of relationships and the breakdown in relationships as the new disciple works through living the Christian life. When cultural patterns of kinship are confused within the MBB community scattered throughout the world, the natural, culturally acceptable patterns for relationships enter into disarray.

Communication

Communication is important in any culture and is indispensable in how people relate and interact, and in context-dependent cultures it comes with high expectations. Anthropologist Edward Hall explains how messages are perceived and understood in context-dependent cultures.

> A high-context (HC) communication or message is one in which most of the information is either in the physical context or internalized in the person, while very little is in the coded, explicit, transmitted part of the message. A low-context (LC) communication is just the opposite; i.e., the mass of the information is vested in the explicit code. (1976, 91)

On a day-to-day basis, the individual in a high-context culture needs to supply the missing information. Hall breaks down this process into two entirely different but interrelated processes: inside the organism or person and outside the organism or person. The thought process internally reads past experiences, and the external-looking thought process is reading the situation or setting in which an event occurs (ibid., 95).

> High-context cultures make greater distinctions between insiders and outsiders than low-context cultures do. People raised in high-context systems expect more of others than do the participants in low-context systems. When talking about something that they have on their minds, a high-context individual will expect his interlocutor to know what's bothering him, so that he doesn't have to be specific. The result is that he will talk around and around the point, in effect putting all the pieces in place except the crucial one. Placing it properly—this keystone—is the role of his interlocutor. To do this for him is an insult and a violation of his individuality. (ibid., 113)

Iran is a high-context culture in which language has become an art form. As we discussed earlier, the unique Persian word *ta'arof* has both a positive and a negative aspect. On the positive side, *ta'arof* is a system of politeness that includes both verbal and nonverbal communication. It has deep roots in the Iranian tradition of treating your guests better than your own family and being a great host. The art of *ta'arof* becomes a ritual, a game that both participants are aware of playing.

> Ta'arof is the active, ritualized realization of differential perceptions of superiority and inferiority in interaction. It underscores and preserves the integrity of culturally defined roles as it is carried out in the life of every Iranian, every day, in thousands of different ways. (Beeman 1986, 57; quoted in Sahragard 2003, 399)

Ta'arof can be described as a verbal dance between an offeror and an acceptor until one of them agrees. One never knows the true intention of either party and may not be sure if they really want to offer/take something or not.

> In the Iranian context, ta'arof refers to a way of managing social relations with decorous manners. It may be charming and a basis for mutual goodwill, or it may be malicious, a social or political weapon that confuses the recipient and puts him at a disadvantage. Ta'arof is the opposite of calling a spade a spade; life is so much nicer without bad news. (De Bellaigue 2012)

Ta'arof complicates communication with its aversion to blatantly telling the truth, particularly when it is shameful.

Communication in Middle Eastern society is high-context and complex. Iranians raised in this high-context culture look beyond the words to fill in the missing information, which is extrapolated from their past experiences and their reading of the context in which the conversation takes place. *Ta'arof,* which includes both verbal and nonverbal communication, must always be considered, but even then the parties are not always sure of what is being said. Lying and cover-up have become normative, creating dual behavior.

This background information gives the context for how the MBBs in my study expressed their understanding of communication. Sixteen people, or 32 percent of the interviewees, made references to communication style as a source of disharmony in their churches. This is a multifaceted element that intersects with many aspects of how Iranians interact.

I began with the following statement: "Every culture has ways of communicating and most have trouble in this area." I followed this by asking how Iranians rate in their communication skills. The responses were strikingly similar.

> "Top issue, in my opinion: we don't know how to communicate." (C2M)

> "Communication is very important, and it is very delicate. You have to be very careful." (U18M)

> "We Iranians don't know how to communicate. We've been yelled at, so we want to yell at people. 'If you disagree with me, I will disagree with you.' 'We

are enemies, so we can't work together.' So basically there are no problem-solving skills. It's only I, me, myself; the trinity: within myself, in me, within me. And what I say, you don't do; so we fight." (C2M)

"We are easily offended; but we don't learn to listen, so we constantly offend others." (U3M)

"I feel mostly that Persians don't communicate. They hold everything inside, and then they blow up at each other. I see at work, with Americans—when they don't like something about you, they say it in your face. But Iranians hold it inside, and then they blow up at you." (U17F)

"The issue is that people misread each other all the time. A lot of times that is because of our own issues. We have envy,[48] and we have so many character flaws that really inform our worldview [the lens in which we see the world]. It's not just our culture. It's our own sin, our own circumstances, our own experiences throughout life, and our own fears and anxieties. I think this person was interpreting out of her own brokenness. I have no problem with that. The problem is, how then do we apply the Scripture to our relationships and to our communication?" (U4F)

I wanted to know how communication is on a communal level, between churches members, and if this is also an area that causes disharmony.

"Really there is no communication. In all the churches I've been to—and I've worked with many leaders—there isn't a lot of communication. One of the main complaints they have against the pastors and leaders is they don't communicate. Even among the leaders there's not a lot of communication. In every church I've been in, or the churches my friends are in, a decision is made, then the members find out. It could be a very important decision, but they are told after the fact, or by accident. So there is no communication; it's all across the board. All churches are like that." (U13F)

I was told that when communicating within the Iranian context, it is important to protect the relationship and not offend others. "If you're friends just coming together, just two to three people, they never say they do not agree with you" (C3M).

To clarify, I asked if they still agree even when one person is not right. "Yes, even when they are not right" (C3M).

Our conversations led to a discussion of the way people communicate, which they described as indirect communication, and the concept of *ta'arof* was mentioned. When a person is offended, it plays out like this:

"I think communication is multifaceted, and there is verbal and nonverbal communication. What people say to you in person can be very gracious and welcoming, or hospitable; but behind your back, they're not. So obviously

---

48 There is often confusion between the words *jealousy* and *envy*. Envy involves a two-person situation, whereas jealousy involves a three-person situation. Envy is a reaction to lacking something, whereas jealousy is a reaction to the threat of losing something. In the interviews, people used the word *jealousy* when the correct word was *envy*. To convey the correct meaning, I changed the word *jealousy* here to *envy*.

there's a communication issue there, where there is not authenticity in communication. You are not communicating what you are thinking, because it actually would be ruder to actually say what you are really thinking than to be insincere and inauthentic." (U4F)

"People have had to learn how to look past politeness and interpret nonverbal clues. I think people take little things that someone says or did. There is a Persian saying, *'Chap chap 'beh' man neghah kard,'* meaning 'This person looked at me from the corner of the eye'—in a kind of glaring way. I think, because of that, they've had to acclimate and evolve into trying to analyze every little thing that someone says or does to try to understand how the person really feels about them. I think there is this overanalysis versus just taking somebody at face value; you can't take someone at face value." (U4F)

For clarification, I asked, "If people fail to communicate with people, are they left trying to guess what people are thinking?" The answer was, "Yes, we do that all the time. 'Why was that person feeling that way?' 'Why was that person treating me this way?' 'What is wrong with that?' You always think, 'What is wrong? What did I do wrong?' So you do speculate about things" (U10F).

But there is hope for the new generation of Iranians. "This new generation that has been growing up over here, we are more open. If something bothers us, we don't hold it for that long. We say it" (U17F).

It requires much wisdom to navigate all the subtleties found within the Iranian manner of communicating. The matrix through which communication is interpreted is informed by past experiences brought into the relationship. Because so many nonverbal signals are given when communication is superficial or when Iranian politeness is expressed, the other party is likely to overanalyze any form of nonverbal communication. The results are miscommunication and hurt feelings.

Failure to communicate honestly, particularly from the leaders of the church, offends the membership. The sharing of confidential information within the Christian environment varies from sharing indiscriminately (where personal details then become fodder for gossip) to not sharing at all.

Relationships

To get a better handle on interpersonal relationships, I explored the types of relationships found within the church. Thirty-two respondents, or 64 percent of the group, indicated that tensions arise from miscommunication or a lack of communication. Three main categories emerged: relationships between members, relationships between members and clergy, and relationships between clergy.

Relationships in General
Rejection is a part of interpersonal relationships. "Yes, if you've spent any time in Iran, you're constantly knocked down. You want to feel respected and that you are equal to others" (U1F).

People experience rejection when expressing opinions or ideas. C2M shared that whereas in the West people can disagree about ideas without rejecting the person, "We [Iranians] interpret it to the rejection of the person. The minute you criticize somebody's idea, thought, writing, you refuse me. It becomes personal" (C2M).

Interpersonal relationships are the major area of struggle in any community of faith.

Between Members
Eleven people, or 22 percent of those interviewed, spoke of relational problems between members of the church. "One other main problem that Iranians have—we don't sit down and talk and work things out" (E16F).

> "The biggest challenge was interpersonal relationships between the people. I don't remember a time when people were upset because of a theological issue or argument or doctrinal difference. It was always about interpersonal relationships—the way people reacted to each other, came across to each other. The problems were not with me as pastor but with each other. Very few left because of me; it was because they didn't get along with each other." (U22M)

> "People come because they think it [church] is a safe place; they think that's the only place to have relationships with God and each other. The problem is we don't understand each other; if we don't understand, then we don't accept each other, then we don't love each other. If we love each other, then this comes to make us separate. I think that comes from our culture." (C4M)

Interpersonal conflict seems to be normative in relationships. Some believe that what causes tensions is the fact that the community is so close-knit. The precarious nature of relationships influences Iranians to choose to hide information out of self-preservation, and getting along with each other can change drastically when some are hurt. Forgiveness and reconciliation are important areas to consider in light of these tensions.

Between Members and Clergy
Thirteen respondents, or 26 percent, shared that the dynamics between the pastor and members mirror the problems among members. "A lot of the splits are over the role of the pastor and how the pastor was treating the congregation" (U9M).

> "Iranians can be very offended because of that ta'arof thing. Some leave because [the pastors] are controlling. They want to do what they like, the way they want. They say, 'God told us to do this; we are led to do this.' The pastor says they have to serve in a certain way, and then they get offended

and leave. They don't want to cooperate or compromise. They don't want to work in teams or be one-minded." (U15F)

The expectations placed on the clergy are high.

"They look at the leadership like they are their parents. So when they don't meet their needs, it's like the dad letting them down." (U1F)

"The Iranian church goes down and up. The problem is because we don't have good relationships with each other—the pastors, the leaders, and the believers." (C4M)

"At the end of the day, I think the issue was that people had elevated [the pastor] too highly.... I think he was placed on an unfair pedestal.... I think they just questioned that they trusted this person, and they had looked to him for guidance and wisdom, and they just never expected him to make a decision like that. I think they questioned him and what they believed about him." (U4F)

The relationship between the members and the pastor becomes particularly strained when the pastor is seen as controlling. C9M related a situation that resulted in forty to forty-five people leaving the church. It occurred during a Bible study, when a member asked the pastor about something he didn't understand.

"A member asked the pastor to answer a certain question, but he didn't. The member insisted, and so he asked him again in front of people to answer. The pastor either couldn't answer or didn't, so he called the member to the office and told him not to come anymore." (C9M)

Pastors have a very difficult time leading a church that views decisions as black and white.

"The issue is, you're either on my side or you're against me. As a pastor, I was always a loser, because no matter which side I took, I lost. Some people got up and left." (U3M)

"The pastor didn't allow me [to teach]; he wanted to control me." (U18M)

Relationships between members and the clergy, according to the interviews, are strained. I will expound upon this later in the chapter on pastoral leadership. The high expectations placed on the leadership of the church create a disharmonious relationship. The tension centers on the pastor's unwillingness to compromise and work with the members, or on the members wanting to impose their will upon the leadership of the church. The lack of trust between leaders and members is a major source of disharmony.

Between Clergy

Nine people, or 18 percent of those interviewed, spoke of envy or broken trust between pastors. The problem between clergy was mentioned as a source of isolation and an area of great concern within the larger body of Christ. In all three locations where this research was conducted, key leaders have initiated conferences to bring about unity and training for the greater Iranian Christian community. But envy and insecurities between the pastors prevent broad participation. One pastor confessed that, as pastors, they don't trust each other.

> "Why do we talk behind each other's back? I think the problem is that we don't have a good relationship between us pastors, not between the people." (C4M)

> "One negative thing is many of them don't like to get together and learn from each other. They are individualistic; they don't trust each other. But there is a great wisdom in sharing their problems." (U16F)

In frustration, one woman said,

> "Persian churches—no communication, a little competition with other churches. They all say we need to be like this and that, point finger at other leaders. They are not running the church like Christ. We are all part of the same family. But if you go visit other churches, they don't like that... . They don't want you to go to other churches. It's controlling." (U13F)

As a solution, one Canadian offered this suggestion:

> "I think it would be good to have a meeting with a few brothers ... [and] invite all the Iranians. We don't want to judge each other; we just want to talk about the future. Not the past—the past is past. That's the thing I wish and dream, to have all the Iranian churches ... to agree together to trust each other, and have a good relationship—so more people trust us. The trust in the church is broken, and the trust outside the church is broken too." (C4M)

The lack of trust between clergy creates seclusion. In diaspora churches with multiple pastors (all bi-vocational), envy and insecurities around loss of power cause splits within the church. The members of the congregation are forced to choose sides, creating further confusion. Territorialism is not beneficial for the congregation or the clergy. Pastors need each other to share the struggles of ministry, so ministerial meetings and pastoral conferences should be welcomed instead of avoided.

Sources of Conflict

Conflict is central to understanding tensions in Iranian Christian fellowships. A working definition of conflict is "A process that begins when an individual or group perceives differences and opposition between oneself and another individual or group about interests and resources, beliefs, values or practices that matter to them" (De Dreu et al. 2007, 7).

Mohammed Abu-Nimer, an expert on conflict resolution, recognizes the importance of preserving and protecting the honor of all parties in conflict management (1996b, 44). Though the field of conflict resolution discusses conflict/anger inoculation in theory, Abu-Nimer relates that escalation can quickly engulf the entire community when disputes are over sacred resources (e.g., money, debts, or land), and values such as honor, shame, dignity, social status, and religious beliefs are at stake (ibid., 46).

George Foster described sacred resources as "wealth, land, happiness, honor, and the like" (Foster 1965, 296; quoted in Neyrey 1998, 17). This perception views the things of this world in terms of a zero-sum game. "Any advantage achieved by one individual or family is seen as a loss to others, and the person who makes what the Western world lauds as 'progress' is viewed as a threat to the stability of the entire community" (ibid., 18).

A major complication is avoidance of underlying issues, which reflects the core values/motivations of harmony, avoidance of conflict, and maintenance of order (Abu-Nimer 1996b, 46). It is important to identify the underlying assumptions and procedures of dispute resolution and discover any patterns of effective biblical resolution that are culturally appropriate.

Conflict avoidance is an especially prominent dimension in high-context cultures. Friedman, Chi, and Liu suggest that we must look at people's motivations in conflict avoidance (2006, 87). Expectancy theory highlights three places where the motivation to avoid conflict may be a factor. First, direct confrontation will hurt relationships; this is dubbed the *expectancy effect*. Second, maintaining good relations may pay off later, which is called the *instrumentality effect*. Third, maintaining good relations is inherently valued, referred to as the *valence effect* (ibid., 77–78).

In a behavioral science study, De Dreu et al. (2007) recognize the complexity of conflict, which can be caused by a mixture of resources, information, and values. Often the content of the conflict changes and transforms. But the most significant aspect of conflict is what parties do with it—in other words, how they react and manage their conflict. These researchers identify strategies for dealing with conflict as cooperative, competitive, or withdrawal from the situation (ibid., 11).

According to De Dreu et al., conflict has three cognitive functions. First, it can be a key driver of change, for without conflict there is no change. Second, conflict can help to define boundaries and clarify who and what belongs where. Third, conflict brings creative potential that allows people to redefine themselves, to change and to adapt, and to innovate and create (ibid., 10).

Middle Easterners view conflict as negative and dangerous, something that should be avoided because it brings destruction and disorder (Abu-Nimer 1996a,

29–30). Lack of trust among compatriots, indicative of high-control societies, complicates conflict resolution.

> Iranians hold to an abiding fear that an individual can trust no one but his kin. And only within the family do Iranians escape the rivalry, conflict, manipulation, and oppression inherent in a political system that has never escaped absolutism in one form or another. Thus, in pursuit of group survival in an environment characterized by insecurity, the patriarch has always directed the family's defense, provided its material needs, defined its interests, managed its affairs, and demanded its obedience. (Mackey 1996, 94)

I believe that the negative view of conflict and conflict avoidance are major contributors to the breakdown of relations within the nascent MBB church.

Conflict is part of the human experience; the church is not exempt. I sought to understand the nature of conflicts, consequences, and attempts to bring resolution. Twenty-seven people, or 54 percent of those interviewed, expounded on some aspect of conflict. Twelve people, or 24 percent, indicated that conflict is a problem in the Iranian church. I asked how Iranians deal with conflict within the church.

> "The way to keep people attending church is to hide the problems under the carpet. Sweep them there; just keep the people intact. So the numbers were saying, 'Yes, the church is growing,' while inside was turmoil." (C2M)

> "One person goes to another and says he did this or that. They become angry and gang up. The communication breaks down. They ask someone to mediate. We have done this, but nothing happens." (U16F)

> "The issue here is that they decide 'You are either with me or against me.' Even when three of us sit down and talk about it, if you take the other person's side, then I'm that guy who is not willing to accept that maybe the other person is right. It's not like when someone says 'He's right,' and he repents. To repent is to commit another shameful sin, because you're agreeing that you were wrong to begin with." (U3M)

Pastors have their own conflicts and have trouble handling them. One person expressed his frustration by saying, "Pastors don't deal with the problems; they don't want to hear about the problems because they think they know everything" (C9M).

Sometimes pastors don't have anyone to go to in a crisis. The conflict can range from his marriage problems to the church splitting.

> "They don't have anyone to be accountable to. There's no denomination, no accountability. If the pastor and elders get along together, then there is hope. But if there's a struggle between them, they don't know where to go." (U2M)

> "I think they couldn't even handle conflict within their small leadership group. So how could they handle it in the church between the members? It was [because of] conflict within the leadership group that a lot of the

members left. So if you can't do that, you can't expect them to go any further than that either." (C6F)

When conflict does arise, some Iranians have little or no collective memory to know how to handle conflict.

> "What makes it Iranian and worse is that Iranians gossip more; they don't resolve conflicts. They don't communicate to understand each other. That's Middle Eastern black and white: either you're my friend or you're my enemy. There is no negotiation to better understand each other and talk about each other and come to a common ground. That's not a part of the culture. Compromise is not a part of Iranian or Middle Eastern culture. Either you win or you lose. Either you're right or you're totally wrong. That makes it worse. All cultures have it, but what makes conflict in Iranian churches worse ... [is that] something comes up and you have no way of resolving it. It stays there and the problem grows." (U21M)

To better understand why there seems to be so much conflict within the Persian church, I asked for a comparison between the English-speaking church and the Persian church.

> "If they [disaffected churchgoers] move to another Farsi church, you take your baggage there. The other people are there with their baggage, and then you fight over where to put your baggage. But here [in Canada], in this big megachurch, your baggage goes with you, but nobody would take your baggage and look at it. You just go there, do your worship ... leave, and go home. It's like a good restaurant—you have good food and you leave. There are no relationships." (C2M)

In summary, conflict is an all-too-familiar part of the Iranian church's experience. The cultural way of dealing with conflict is to hide the conflict or lash out against the offender, a typical response in an honor-and-shame culture. According to the interviews, it seems that pastors are no better at handling conflict than their congregations, possibly due in part to a lack of education or an unwillingness or inability to deal with the conflict. Finding common ground is nearly impossible in handling conflict when conflicts are seen through an all-or-nothing mentality.

Conflict Resolution

Understanding conflict is only part of the equation. It is important to see what others have written on conflict resolution to get a better grasp of what is happening. Conflict resolution is multilayered and requires a sincere, profound exploration of the underlying emotional legacies of fear, hatred, sorrow, and mistrust resulting from decades of warfare and unending cycles of victimization and vengeance (Irani 1999, 4–5).

Conflict comes from different beliefs regarding data, issues, values, interests, and relationships. Some of the issues that need to be discussed are the importance of patrilineal families, the questions of ethnicity, the relevance of identity, the nature of tribal and clan solidarity, the key role of patron-client relationships, religious beliefs and traditions, and honor and shame. Methods often used in conflict are shunning, disinheriting, and even killing to restore the family honor within the community.

Fundamental to conflict resolution is, first, the recognition of the legitimacy of the "other."

Second, there must be a recognition of a plurality of views and seeking to live with divergent views. There must be a move beyond victimization by pushing through mistrust, hopelessness, and despair (Mercadante 2000, 301). This is far easier said than done. I spend a lot of time just trying to get people to stop reacting to one another and really listen to what is being said or not said. Political science expert George Irani adds another step to healing: overcoming feelings of victimization, which he considers the most important (Irani 1999, 5).

Third, conflict resolution theories mention three dimensions to peace building. They are the "head, heart, and hand ... , which correspond to cognition, emotion, and behavior" (Abu-Nimer 2001, 689). Abu-Nimer adds a fourth dimension called the spiritual gate, which includes prayers and rituals (ibid.). His comparison between the assumptions of Middle Eastern and Western approaches to conflict resolution is most helpful.

Table 5.1. Approaches to conflict resolution (Abu-Nimer 1996a, 29–31)

Western Assumptions	Middle Eastern Assumptions
Conflict is positive.	Conflict is negative and dangerous.
Conflict is normal.	Conflict should be avoided.
Conflict can bring growth and creativity.	Conflict brings destruction and disorder.
Collaborative and cooperative frameworks are the essential components of conflict resolution.	Group affiliation (family, clan, religion, sect, or other collective identity) is the most central and important identity that should be protected and sustained through conflict management processes.
Facing a conflict is a necessary and recommended strategy.	Spontaneous and emotional acts characterize Middle Eastern processes of conflict management, particularly in regard to the parties' interaction. Such behavior is not only an integral part of the mediation and negotiation strategies, but it also reflects a strong characteristic of Arab society in general.

Since everything is based on rational reasoning, any conflict can be settled and managed through rational planning. Every Western conflict resolution model has four to twelve stages of intervention.	Social norms and values rather than legal forms are the main rules of commitment. Therefore, written agreements (or signing) are not part of the process. Instead, parties and third parties rely on established social and cultural values and norms in reaching and implementing the agreement.
The individual's interest, position, needs, and desires are the essence of the conflict resolution processes.	Codes of honor, shame, and dignity are the main components which are used by parties, mediators, and conflict resolvers to describe or establish any process.
The outcome reflected in a written agreement is a central component of the conflict resolution process.	Unity is the ultimate and common goal for groups. Unity means agreeing on the same ideas, principles, and actions.
Legal formality and procedures are essential parts of the conflict resolution processes.	Conflict resolution and mediation are based on hierarchical, authoritarian procedures and structure (older people, males, and powerful officials).
Material resources are often the codes which Western parties and mediators use to describe or establish a process of conflict resolution.	Processes and outcomes are more relationship-oriented than task-oriented. A strong emphasis is placed upon the relationship of the parties to each other and to the remaining members of the community. The parties' major concern is with their image in relation to each other.
The actions of the parties and intervenors in the resolution processes are task-oriented. Achieving a task and focusing on the negotiable issues (materialistic aspects of the dispute) is an important element in the steps toward an agreement.	The intervention mostly depends on and involves the use of arbitration and mediation as the essential components of the Middle Eastern approach to conflict.

Irani (1999, 4) gives some helpful insights about conflict resolution:
1. Western conflict resolution deals with definite, programmed, institutionalized relationships. Middle Eastern conflict is often unprogrammed, informal, and with random relationships. Organization helps in conflict resolution.
2. Conversational culture is expressed through people usually talking all together at the same time. Help people move toward a solution rather than just expressing themselves.
3. In intense argumentation, remaining silent is sometimes interpreted as meek acquiescence or agreement. Draw people out, particularly Western workers who remain silent.

4. Mediators or third parties play a key role in disputes. They are perceived as having all the answers and solutions. If they do not provide these answers or solutions, they are not really respected or considered legitimate.

In Middle Eastern Iranian culture, problem solving and conflict resolution usually occur in stages and according to a certain pattern. Every effort is made to keep the problem private. Should the parties involved (e.g., marriage partners, in-laws, business partners) fail to resolve the conflict, perhaps because of the extreme emotionalism of those involved, a third party is asked to impartially intervene. This person is trusted and respected by both sides, usually an elderly man who is well-known and respected in the community. If reconciliation occurs, it is on the basis of "forgive and forget," and the problem is never mentioned again, whether resolved or not (Behjati-Sabet and Chambers 2005, 144).

Conflict resolution is the goal of Western intervention, while conflict control or reduction is the goal of Middle Eastern intervention. Several obstacles hinder conflict resolution. First, strong beliefs are normative; and when one party believes the other to be misled and in need of correction, there is little that can be done. Second, mistrust and suspicion of outsiders, in particular of Western methods, is also normative. Third, recognition of the legitimacy of differences in beliefs and interests is a basic assumption of conflict resolution; but in Middle Eastern cultures it is considered a weakness.

Multiple issues complicate the process of conflict resolution. First, there is a conceptual category that the individual does not have the same validity and importance as in Western cultures. "The individual is enmeshed within his or her own group, sect, tribe, or millet" (Irani 1999, 14). Second, family loyalties, the use of control and power to protect the family name, hinder the honest seeking of conflict resolution. Third, widespread corruption, the maintenance of honor at all cost, and hierarchical and patriarchal structure that have a higher sense of duty than justice all create a limited sense of justice. Said and Funk recognize that if the ideals of community in the Muslim world are to be reached, these ideals must underscore the dignity of the individual rather than guarding the reputation of the family or group, maintaining a public image, and avoiding dishonor at all costs (Said and Funk 2001, p 9).

Thomas and Sandra Wisley (2006, 102) note that forgiveness and reconciliation are conditioned through cultural filters. The background filters should be taken into consideration in the process of forgiveness. They are:
1. Experiences, past and present
2. Beliefs about what is possible and not possible
3. Environmental conditioning

4. Parental and family upbringing
5. Cultural cosmology (belief systems)

Conflict and its repercussions is a major area of concern within the Middle Eastern community in the diaspora. These societies are built upon shame, honor, dignity, social status, and religious beliefs, all of which directly contribute to conflict avoidance. The lack of trust within these communities undermines efforts to resolve conflict. All too often the strategy of withdrawal is used.

Conflict between Believers of Different Ethnic Groups
Knowing that tension does exist between the Armenians, Assyrians, Jews, and Persians, when appropriate I asked if the conflict expressed could be traced, to some degree, to a breakdown of relationships between various ethnic groups. Thirteen interviewees, or 26 percent, confirmed that ethnic tension between the believers from a Muslim background and those from another religious background played a major role in the conflict.

> "We come from very different cultural backgrounds, socioeconomic, educational, and religious backgrounds. We all come under one roof because we don't have a lot of options—we don't have ten churches in each city to choose from. So that creates a lot of tensions and clashes." (U22M)

Often the various ethnic groups will separate into MBBs and Christian-background believers (CBBs).

> "There was a lot of contempt and arrogance toward ex-Muslims from the Armenians and Assyrians. Some of them even called our church 'the church of the Muslims.' We were kind of Negroes." (E2M)

> "Assyrians think of Persians as second-rate Christians, because we weren't born in a Christian family." (U18M)

Tensions exist on all sides. Jewish Iranians are successful in business, so "that didn't go well with the Muslim-background believers" (U3M). The Armenian Iranian church is larger than the Muslim-background churches (U12M).

> "In the back of the mind of Assyrians they think that since Muslim-background individuals are not born in Christian families, they are not qualified. Some Armenians have that thought too. That was one thing they had conflict about—superiority." (U18M)

> "After so many splits, the Assyrians started saying, 'These conflicts happen because these people are not Christians, or are baby Christians, and that's why they are not transformed.' The Persians started saying, 'The Assyrians are arrogant or think they are better than we are.'" (U13F)

The ethnic tensions between the interethnic groupings found within Iran carry over into the Iranian church in the diaspora. When the church was small, the ethnic groups went to the same church, but tensions were found under the surface. Ethnic tension was a factor in several churches splitting. The pervasive feeling among Christian-background believers is that ex-Muslims are second-rate Christians and cannot be trusted. When I probed into various leadership tensions, it was determined that ethnic strains were part of the problem that added to the disharmony. There is enough blame on all sides of the tension. Each ethnic group brings its own baggage to the church.

Confrontation and Results
To further clarify how conflict is dealt with, I asked how Iranians confront others during a conflict. Ten individuals, or 20 percent of those interviewed, shared attempts at confronting conflict. However, Iranians have little or no collective memory of how to confront others. Since this is uncharted territory, confrontation becomes a source of disharmony within the Iranian church.

The cultural background from which Iranians come is shame and honor, so this shapes the response to conflict.

> "Even when you see what they are doing, you have to be careful how you confront them. They have the shame of why my thing has been exposed; they don't want things to be exposed. So we have to expose the Word of God to them." (U18M)

> "Pretending is a huge theme of our church culture; repressing feelings is a huge part that we've had to deal with in our culture. You don't feel free to express what is inside of you. Disagreement is a personal attack on character and integrity and identity on the other person. So when you put all of that together, of course, there is no freedom to confront. If you disagree with him, that's war. You've set up your position against someone else." (U22M)

> "I actually tried everything by the book about the cycle of conflict, but it never worked for some reason. I think a major part of managing any conflict is communication, honesty, and forgiveness. When you have issues—I mean serious issues now—none of the techniques are working. They don't want to sit and talk." (U19M)

The process of conflict and finding possible resolutions takes several paths.

> "At first, they get angry. There are two options: they go to talk with the person, or they leave the church. I was in the church many years; maybe one hundred people have gone, and they never come back here." (E18M)

> "In this sense, your internal experience is experiencing aggression toward a person and toward a set of circumstances. But your mode of coping with that is, instead of confronting what the issue is, you will retreat from it or you will act out your aggression in a passive way. In a passive way would

be gossiping. Or 'I'm going to continue going to this church, but in the meantime I'm going to talk to other parishioners and try to get a support system going so that we can all eventually break off and start our own fellowship,' and not lead on as to what I am thinking." (U4F)

Some pastors have a difficult time confronting problems. One pastor confessed that for a long time he wasn't able to confront others at all.

"I try to do it in a more tactful way, but I wouldn't say that I was ever confrontational in a strong way until our last two or three years. I was more direct because I changed myself. But most of my pastoral ministry I wasn't confrontive. I allowed some things to grow in the church and not confront it. It split our church at one time." (U21M)

On a positive note, one church has found a way to express discontent.

"We have this box where they can put their opinions about the church. The leadership looks at those notes. The members have a right to share what they think. I think in our church the leadership is not too bad at listening to the people and the criticism of the members. I said they're not too bad in comparison to maybe churches in Iran." (E17F)

Confronting the problems in the Iranian church is difficult, resulting in people leaving the church. Culturally, Iranians find it difficult to confront one another. The first response to confrontation is to run and hide. The ensuing result of confrontation is hypersensitivity to honor and shame and the visceral negative reaction it elicits. Disagreement is offensive, and confrontation means fighting. Rather than using direct confrontation, people gossip; so others leave the church.

Pastors find these issues particularly hard to confront due to the sensitive nature of the people and the desire to be polite. Some pastors feel that confrontation will result in an exodus from the church, so they often chose to overlook the problems. Culturally acceptable mediators have not been able to bring conflicting groups together. With little or no memory of how confrontation is done in a positive way on the one hand, and fear of the unknown consequences on the other, conflict is avoided and people end up leaving the church.

Experiments in Conflict Resolution

Finding ways of resolving conflict is an important dimension for any church to be healthy. Conflict can be handled in several ways—it can be handled in a constructive way, it can be delayed to another time, or it can be avoided and allow to be destructive. The purpose of the questions on the topic of conflict was to discover these churches dealt with conflict. Thirteen individuals, or 26 percent of those interviewed, gave opinions on the topic of conflict resolution.

"If you're not going to solve the conflict, you would have to avoid it. That avoidance eventually gets to the point where you just have to leave the church, because you either have to face it or leave it. Most people end up leaving the church." (U9M)

"Conflicts are avoided, not resolved; you don't see them [the conflicting parties] anymore. I don't think that a win-win situation exists a lot." (U13F)

Leaving the church instead of resolving conflict is "the easiest option. Being there and going through all the suffering and just communicating and trying to resolve issues takes a lot of energy and time. And they just cut it short" (U19M).

"They run from it, always." (C9M)

"Not necessarily a place to run to, but just to run." (U9M)

"I think it's cultural that Iranians do not resolve conflicts. They have no idea what conflict resolution is. They are either your friend or your enemy. There is no agree-to-disagree kind of option here. There is no in-between. There is no period of time where you say, 'Let's take a break, let's come out of this, let's look from outside in, let's give each other time and space. Let me hear your side and allow me to express my side. Think about it. Pray about it.' None of that. 'You don't want to serve me anymore; you don't want to preach to me anymore; I'll be somewhere else.' It doesn't matter that there is a service there at church, meeting twice a week. 'But if you don't want to do that, I'm out of here.'" (U9M)

Conflict resolution requires sensitivity, understanding, and wisdom. But the process can result in greater problems. Even the most sensitive and nonjudgmental approach can yield the same results of people getting offended.

"I confront them very carefully. I don't make assumptions or accusations. I try to talk with them and uncover the facts, as much as possible without offending. I've figured out what the problem is, I go and talk to them firmly; then they get offended, and that creates an even greater mess. It needs to be dealt with, but with respect and not believing the first person or the person you might feel closest to, but really be[ing] fair. And some of the Iranian pastors that I've seen don't always do that. They use their authority to clear that up. A lot of people get offended." (U6M)

Many aspiring pastors see only the public, up-front side of pastoral ministry: activities such as preaching and teaching. But there is an unseen side to pastoral ministry that is relational. Not everyone seeking to be a pastor understands this dimension of pastoral work.

"[In] those years, relationships were a problem. My first gift is not pastoral. Teacher, evangelist, maybe, and more apostolic—trying to make something happen at gatherings. So pastoral was not my gift. So when the relational problems developed, I didn't know what to do. And it always happens. You gather people who don't know each other. And you can't call it a church; it's a gathering. From a gathering to a church, these are the things that need to happen; and part of it is conflict and conflict resolution. So when the conflicts came or when people lost interest in that gathering for different reasons, I couldn't solve that problem." (U21M)

One individual I interviewed was part of a church that seemed to have been able to find a way of building a culture of learning to deal with conflict. It started with the leadership team and then filtered down to the congregation.

> "You learn how to sit down, build a relationship with the church member, and sit down [and] softly but clearly talk about what needs to stop. 'I'm with you and will fast with you, and let's pray. I'm with you and I'm not against you.' Never as 'I'm the pastor, and you do it or else.' But it's a softer approach. But when you get to the leadership level, you agree to be more straightforward. That makes it easier. Again, we don't take advantage even as leaders. I'll talk to you and try hard not to break the relationship. But you are more straightforward." (U21M)

To reiterate, conflict resolution is an area in which pastors and members struggle. There is little collective memory of resolving conflicts. The normative response is avoidance or running away. Attempts at conflict resolution consume much time and energy, often creating more problems, and often resulting in the typical avoidance by running away. Conflict is viewed as "zero-sum," where one's very existence seems inextricably linked to the negation of the other, and mutually beneficial results are unheard of. Strong-armed approaches by the pastor are offensive. Teaching on the subject yields little behavioral change. However, some pastors and teachers preach and teach conflict resolution methods. One person suggested that conflict resolution must be modeled by the leadership so members can witness that example.

Forgiveness. Forgiveness is central to the Christian faith. I introduced the topic of forgiveness as a response to the topic of disharmony, and thirty-one individuals, or 62 percent of those interviewed, made significant remarks about forgiveness within the Iranian church. The interviews explored various aspects of forgiveness, including how Iranians forgive, whether it is difficult for Iranians to forgive, and stories about forgiveness.

Though forgiveness is central to the message of Christ, the Iranian cultural context makes it difficult to forgive. There were a variety of explanations like the following: "Our culture is shame based. We go by the shame; even though we are changed, we can't forgive easily. We don't forget things" (U20M). Three people considered forgiveness harder for those who come from an Islamic background than for Westerners (U12M, C3M, C2M).

After the interviewees talked about a lack of forgiveness within the church, I followed up by asking why forgiveness is so difficult for Iranians.

> "Maybe it's harder for Iranians because we prefer not to talk about forgiveness." (E17F)
>
> "There are lots of emotions—they forgive each other, but I don't know how deep it is, or if they really understand Christian forgiveness." (U2M)

There is a conscious effort to be a forgiving community. This can be particularly difficult when Iranian believers have experienced so many difficulties in their family and country (C8F). So often they find themselves talking about the past instead of moving on after they have forgiven someone (E17F).

> "Yes, forgiveness is very weak in Iran. They put up with people. There is a saying which talks about your rights: 'It's not what you give, it's what you get.' It's a very, very famous statement. Yes, I have seldom witnessed a genuine story of forgiveness. They bear the grudge. People just vanish. It's like they don't exist any longer. They don't talk to one another.
>
> "Yes, I've been told by Muslims, 'When Jesus forgave somebody, he had no other choice. He was quite weak. That's why Jesus did it.' For Muslims to become a Christian, it is like World War II. It's like someplace has been bombarded. It takes ages to rebuild the place. It was that way for me, and I am witnessing exactly the same thing.
>
> "Now if people say, 'Now I've been changed, just like that,' they are lying or they do not know what they're saying. It's a lifelong process of [rebuilding] a demolished city. The message of the gospel is like bombarding a city in which the people are finding themselves among the ruins. Everywhere has been marred or destroyed. The technical term is called an 'epistemological transformation.' That is what is happening." (E1M)
>
> "The basic misconception is that if I forgive him, it means he was right. Again, right and wrong. Two things: They feel they are approving what they did was right. Number two, they feel like they were taken advantage of. The person who forgives is just simple, naïve. 'They took advantage of me, and I'm so weak that I accepted, and I forgive them.' They see that as weakness." (U21M)

I followed up with questions asking how the church teaches the topic of forgiveness. The regular communion service and a conference were mentioned.

Again, disharmony is a major part of the Iranian diaspora church's experience. Forgiveness is the Christian way of dealing with hurts, offenses, and strained relationships, but it is a foreign concept for the Iranian MBB. Iranians tend to be past-oriented people who find it hard to forgive grievances and move on in the relationship. Forgiveness is viewed at times through the lens of weakness, and forgiving someone is considered an affirmation that the other person is right.

There is a fear that forgiveness will lead to being taken advantage of. The maturity of the believer and having time to heal wounds are key elements in achieving true forgiveness. The depth of the wounds in the past makes it hard to practice forgiveness. Yet the Iranian church in the diaspora teaches often on forgiveness; the church calendar offers regular occasions to speak on this topic, which is so central to the Christian message.

Revenge. If forgiveness was not achieved, was revenge a problem? Though I purposely didn't want to introduce the topic of revenge in my questions, I asked questions about criticism, forgiveness, gossip, and conflict to see how people respond to relational problems. Middle Eastern literature identifies revenge as a normative response to hurt. However, only five individuals, or 10 percent of those interviewed, made mention of revenge in particular, though several talked about disgruntled people leaving the church and taking as many people with them as possible. Revenge can take many forms in the church.

> "I come from a shame-based culture. One of the most important attitudes is revenge. So forgiveness takes a long time to find its way through layers of culture that are based on revenge." (U3M)

> "It's all about revenge, revenge, revenge. Everything is about you; you're the center—someone hurts you, you hurt them back. Everyone is trying to get something before the other people do. Everything is yours; you're the center." (E15F)

> "Under the culture is the religion—it is revenge and not to forgive. If I don't forgive you, it means that I am stronger than you. In Christianity, it is the opposite. In the church, if I do something to another Christian by doing bad things or being rude, I then go to that person and say, 'I'm sorry I did that.' They answer, 'Don't do it again, OK?' They don't say, 'I forgive you.' I have to work really hard to show them attention and respect, and give and give until this person can forgive me. Our memory is badly scarred and hurt, and it takes time to be healed." (E14F)

I asked how revenge is expressed in the church.

> "Gossip, leaving the church, trying to do whatever you can to bring the other person down." (U3M)

> "At the beginning of this interview, I told you that Iranians carry baggage from the background of Islam. It gives you the freedom of revenge and the sinful lifestyle. When the person comes to Christ with this baggage, it's going to take time to leave all the nonsense behind and become a good person. That baggage we all have—pastors, leaders, members." (U12M)

Envy. Only four people, or 8 percent of those interviewed, mentioned envy as a problem. Envy was mostly brought up when I asked questions about relationships between clergy. Nine people, or 18 percent, spoke of envy or broken trust between pastors.

Envy is one dimension of disharmony between pastors. In one church, one recognized leader did the preaching and another did the evangelizing. The latter shared his experience. "As the church was growing, the preaching pastor became more insecure, feeling that I may be a threat to him. So he started talking and poisoning the church against me, even though I had no intention of getting into ministry. That brought a lot of conflict" (U21M). The end result was that "the church split, and it really hurt the church" (U21M).

This category of envy must be understood in light of the category of status, of which Iranians are very conscious. Envy is the normative response to other people's status. People get envious over cars, houses, family, position, and other status symbols. Envy is found among clergy who are envious of the gifts other members or clergy have. It is yet another source of disharmony within the Iranian church in the diaspora.

Judgmentalism. The interviews revealed that a judgmental attitude is another area Iranians in the diaspora churches struggle to bring under control. Many of the sensitivities mentioned in the responses in the chapter "The Luggage We Bring" involve some aspect of judgmentalism. Fourteen people, or 28 percent of those interviewed, mentioned a judgmental attitude as a serious problem.

> "That mentality is already here; it is judgmental—constantly judging one another is part of the culture. Even though we see right now, behind everybody's mind, they start evaluating, reading their mind, start talking about people. This is what's going on in the mind of everybody. We are judging, evaluating; and in our mind, there is a lot of conversation." (U7M)

I asked what criteria someone would be judged on in the Iranian church. One woman gave the following answer:

> "Everything—your weight, your makeup, how you cook, the behavior of your children, how successful your husband is, the size of your home, the cars you drive. Persians are very materialistic. They are materialistic. Why do they drive Mercedes or BMWs? Why put their children in private school? Because they want the administration to respect them, so they are going to pay them for that service to teach their kids. Why are they all doctors and engineers? [Because] you must have the title to get the respect." (U1F)

A judgmental attitude can restrict how openly people share their testimony or hide information to protect themselves.

> "Here the people try to hide everything. I have never given my testimony, because they will judge me. They won't look at my new life; they'll just look at my background. If they know I smoked or had a boyfriend before, or [had] been on drugs, they won't talk to me anymore. Their reaction will go to my son, and he doesn't know anything about my background. I'm frightened here." (E12F)

Two women put it this way:

> "There is always the risk of someone being offended or judging you, or they could be overly sensitive. So you're always walking on eggshells." (U1F)

> "Misunderstanding–somebody does something and they judge them quickly: they are hard-hearted. It becomes a stumbling block." (U16F)

Judging others can extend indiscriminately to anyone attending church, even to those who are not yet Christians. There is a particular danger in smaller Iranian groups that an immature believer with good language skills might become a translator and use that position to control others and gain status. As Iranians mature in their faith, however, the judgmental attitude begins to subside.

Gossip. Gossip is a particular problem the MBB church struggles with. Sixteen respondents, or 32 percent, expressed that gossip is a major area of concern that leads to disharmony and people leaving the Iranian church. When gossip was mentioned, I followed up by asking for examples and how it is different from gossip in any other culture.

> "I think those two things–pride and gossip–really were some of the main issues in terms of people leaving the Persian church." (U4F)
>
> "The greatest sin that destroys Iranian churches is gossip and envy and things like that. That destroys the relationships and disintegrates them." (U21M)
>
> "Gossip, lying–this is common." (E18M)
>
> "The older attendees are not there anymore. They have gone to other churches and British church, or they have stopped going to church [altogether]. I got really upset. It's because of all the gossip." (E15F)

I asked how Iranians' gossip differs from gossip in the English-speaking church. The interviewees revealed that Iranian gossip is more intense and pervasive than what they found in non-Iranian churches (U22M, U3M, U21M, E10, E18M).

> "Gossip is in every culture. It reflects that you don't measure up with what they think you should be doing in your life. I don't think it's any worse in Persian church. Persian Christians are hurt, because it represents the old system. They have the naïve view that when they enter the church that everything is going to be OK. They get hurt really easily because they are sensitive. An Iranian guy said, 'We don't think with our heads; we think with our hearts.'" (E18M)

Gossip has a direct effect on the people in the congregation. Iranians keep "things hidden so people won't know a lot of things about you and try to control what other people know about you and your life" (U22M).

> "Openness and transparency are very rare in our culture, and even in church unless you work on it. If you are transparent and somebody knows something about you, he may gossip; or at least he will keep it. And later, if you become his enemy, he will gossip so he will have something against you. If he is a friend now, he may not be your friend next year.
>
> "That is why marriage counseling is rare even in church. A husband and wife may have major problems, and they don't even go to their pastors because,

first, they feel ashamed that we Christians are fighting inside. Second, they are afraid that what they share will somehow get out there.

"The pastor can be my friend, but next year he may not be my friend and he might use my personal information against me or gossip and destroy my reputation. That's what causes unhealthy churches. These are elements that make Iranian churches unhealthy which need to be addressed." (U21M)

Rumors and false stories are a source of disharmony in the Iranian church in the diaspora.

"Some people sit together; they build up stories against someone." (C5M)

"The end result in the church is that 'the accuser and the accused both disappeared since that.'" (E1M)

An aspect of gossip that comes up often is speculation about male/female relationships.

"The English church I go to is a young church with lots of young people. People date for a couple of months, then break up; and people don't really talk about it. But at Iranian church, you can't go back to that church. There would be a lot of gossips, and what they say about you makes you feel uncomfortable." (E15F)

I asked if there is a lot of teaching on the subject of gossip in the Persian church. "A lot. We've got good resources" (E15F). An answer suggested for the problem of gossip is creating a vulnerable and trusting environment at church, which begins with the pastor. "It helps eliminate the gossip" (U21M).

Gossip is considered a major concern within the Iranian church in the diaspora and the greatest sin that destroys Iranian churches. Many of the older Christians leave the Iranian church over the unbridled gossip. One particular subject is the male/female relationships within the church. The young people recognize that talking to the opposite sex does not elicit gossip within the English-speaking church as it does in the Iranian church. Some speculate that Iranians focus more on others than looking at themselves as the problem, so gossip is pervasive. The Persian church frequently addresses the topic of gossip, yet it remains a persistent problem.

Status. Status is an important part of an honor-and-shame culture. The topic of status was mentioned by eight people, or 16 percent of those interviewed. Iranians seem to be very conscious of looking good in the eyes of others. Sizing up or judging others based on what they project is a characteristic of Iranian culture, which is expressed within the Persian church.

"You Americans thrive on the fact that everyone is on the same level. We don't live that way. For instance, where you live, what you drive, what education you have, how pretty you are, is how we measure each other." (U3M)

> "We in our culture like to please people and always be somebody that looks good; and if, God forbid, you're not that type of person or don't meet that standard, people will think less of you. So I always have to put up a front and can't make mistakes. I have to be good. Mistakes are not accepted. For instance, you're supposed to know everything because you're a leader or teacher. You can't act human and say 'I don't know,' or that you've made a mistake. You're expected to know, put on a face that you have more than what they have. So we put on our best dress, wear our gold, even if you have to borrow it. We have to show status, for appearance means a lot. You have to please people. This is the culture, but sadly this mentality has come into the church. We live for people. If people think you are happy, then you are successful. You could be successful and not be happy, but then people wouldn't think you're successful. What matters with Iranians is that others see you as successful." (U13F)

A person's social standing and education are important to other Iranians and have implications for ministry. The educated upper classes are easier to minister to, but with the poor it "is difficult, and we should spend time with them to help them to grow in Christ" (E11M).

Some prefer not to get involved in the games people play. "Frankly, my eyes are closed and my ears are plugged. I do not get involved or try to evaluate. I stay away from this type of comparison" (U8M).

Cultural class and status are significant values Iranians bring with them from a hierarchical society into the diaspora. The church is not exempt from the cultural value of status, which is a source of disharmony. The appearance of success is important to maintain, as it also reflects the values of an honor-and-shame society. Churches are evaluated by the social status of their members, and symbols from language to dress are scrutinized. At times, people are pushed to live beyond their means to maintain status and respectability.

Criticism. I asked a question that introduced the topic of criticism, but it did not generate a lot of dialogue about the topic. Six people, or 12 percent of respondents, talked about criticism directly. The cultural characteristic of judgmentalism could also be included in this section, but I have separated the two.

I asked if Iranians are easily offended.

> "Very easily. And they don't take criticism well—even myself. But I have changed; I am changing." (C2M)

> "I think criticism is a big part of the culture." (C6F)

> "Iranians take criticism very poorly. Whether they are the pastor or member, it doesn't make any difference what position they are in." (U9M)

> "So when you criticize someone, it is not taken well or welcomed. It's always taken as a personal attack. Not attacking the subject, but attacking me. Now I'm going to look bad in front of the others. It's taken personally." (U13F)

> "Constructive criticism doesn't have a lot of room in the Persian churches, because it goes back to communication—both sides haven't learned to criticize in love, so when people do criticize, it's to attack. The leaders get very defensive too. It's not constructive. It's attack or defense rather than a dialogue or talk to see what the problem is." (U13F)

Many wanted me to understand that criticism was a particular problem in the Iranian community. I asked to know the difference between the Iranian expressions of criticism and a Western expression of criticism. "We created the word *criticize*. We thrive on putting each other down so we can feel good about ourselves, but that's the root of criticism. We don't feel good about ourselves, so we have to criticize other people" (U3M).

Criticism is a trait found in every culture, but it is particularly grievous in an honor-and-shame culture. No one wants to look bad in the eyes of others. Any such criticism is considered defamation, a personal attack and shameful. Constructive criticism is a foreign concept; when it is attempted, it is often hurtful and a source of disharmony.

Hospitality. Hospitality is a core value of Middle Eastern culture. It is mentioned mostly as a strength of the Iranian church, and therefore not a potential source of disharmony. Yet seven people, or 14 percent of those interviewed, brought up hospitality as a cause of problems in the church.

"Iranians are very polite people. Because of that, they expect people to be polite with them. Being polite is one of the biggest virtues, along with your family always coming first above all. Hospitality is so important, which is great" (E5F). Hospitality is so important that if people were not included in expressing some aspect of hospitality, it causes problems in the Iranian church.

> "Our very first Sunday people got into fights about who is in charge of setting up the tea table and taking it down. Those bizarre and tiny things—friendships started exploding over those kinds of things." (U22M)

> "It is very important for Iranians to be welcomed and hugged, and to ask if there is anything we can do for them. This makes sure they are accepted by us. If you just shake a hand and say 'Sit there,' then it is not good enough for them." (E9M)

> "I think that if I had been accepted in a church in Norway, I'm not sure I would have left Norway. If I had an activity in the church, I might not have left." (E9M)

One person expressed the opinion that fear and mistrust of new attendees can taint the way people are accepted in the close-knit, smaller Iranian church.

> "At the English church, we were welcomed from the minute we first went to the church. I've really felt like this is the place where I feel at home and fit in. However, at the Iranian church, it took a while to fit in and to see the other people accept the fact that we were regular churchgoers." (E15F)

Can We Just Play Nice?

Hospitality is a core value found within the Iranian church. Hospitality and spending time together are a crucial part of the Iranian church experience. There are high expectations that hospitality and polite greetings should be normative. When they are not fulfilled, Iranians take offense. When they are met, Iranians feel at home.

Summary of the Interpersonal Component

Iranians are very social, and the Iranian church reflects this great value of spending time together. However, interpersonal relationships remain the area that creates the greatest challenge for the Iranian church. Communication—or the lack of it—creates miscommunication, resulting in tensions. People quickly cross personal boundaries in their relationships, creating hurt feelings. The cultural trait of using indirect communication creates further tension, and gossip occurs to fill in the lack of information.

Some pastors seem to be poor at communicating with the members and have difficulty with competitiveness and lack of trust among each other. Weak attempts at cooperation, combined with revenge, envy, criticism, and judgmental attitudes, create an unhealthy environment. Since Iranian culture is shame based, forgiveness is difficult, particularly for grave offenses. The interethnic tension, principally between CBBs and MBBs, has created splits within the Iranian church in the diaspora.

Conflict regularly develops, but the nascent church is not prepared or trained to deal with it. The normative leadership response is to hide or deny the existence of conflicts. Confrontation only leads to more conflict, with the typical result of people leaving the church. Rarely does reconciliation or resolution of the conflict occur. There is little if any memory in the Iranian culture of dealing with conflict positively.

5
All in the Family

Everyone comes with a family history. In some cultures family plays a limited role after the individual reaches adulthood, whereas in other cultures family plays a major role, not only in raising a child but also throughout the person's life. When family bonds are broken through one person leaving the boundaries of acceptable belief, norms, values, and practices, the consequences can be overwhelming. This is often the case for people from a Middle Eastern culture who make a dramatic change. One's religious belief is intractably linked to the family.

In this chapter, we will take a closer look at the family and its influence on the MBB's faith, and at areas to be considered in the discipleship process. These include marriage, nuclear family relationships, and extended family relationships, and how these areas of influence contribute to what is experienced in the MBB church.

Most Muslim societies are collectivist societies. On the positive side, they have strong, close-knit, and often multigenerational families. They value conformity. The values practiced by the family, the relationships between family members, and their attitudes toward society and modernity will dictate what is acceptable and unacceptable. The role of the extended family—such as uncles, aunts, and cousins—as keepers of the family and societal norms is more significant than what is found in individualistic Western societies. Opinions are predetermined by the group, and the individual's identity is expressed by the whole, whether that be the family, society, nation, or religion.

On the negative side, there are strong pressures on the individual to conform to the will of the family, the family to the clan, and the clan to the religion. Deviating from the family norm is met with great resistance. There is a great fear of isolation from the "in-group," for it is difficult to survive financially and socially outside the family and clan. Often the MBB will look to the church to fill the void left by broken ties with the family. Discipleship will need to address two different aspects: (1) helping the MBB transition into the new social and financial reality forced upon them when they became a follower of Christ (Matt 10:32–39); and (2) helping the fellowship minister to the emotional loss the MBB is experiencing.

Hofstede (1991, 32) confirms that dependent behavior in high power distance cultures[49] is taught from childhood. Respect for parents and other elders is seen as a basic virtue. Hofstede recognizes that dependence on seniors pervades all human contacts. Yet individuals in high power distance contexts carry a strong need for dependence in contrast to independence in low power distance families. The religious element only reinforces submission and dependency to the "in-group" of Islam; in fact, Muslims have formalized it in Islamic doctrine.

The family is an extremely important element in Iranian culture; family connections are still relied on in all classes for influence, employment, and security (Behjati-Sabet and Chambers 2005, 136). However, the traditional role of the family is often severed in the diaspora, thus altering the place usually dominated by family values and relationships.

Iranians use the word *gharibeh* for outsiders, which often carries with it a xenophobic meaning. There is a real hesitancy to trust others or be vulnerable, particularly regarding those outside the family. "Self-revelation often is seen as a sign of weakness, or at least of self-indulgence. The only people who can be truly trusted are family" (Sciolino 2000, 30).

> Iranians have described themselves as suspicious, distrustful, and somewhat cynical in their dealings outside the circle of family and close friends. In the midst of the 1979 Islamic revolution, Iranians were turned against one another and "ordered to spy on each other and report any misbehaviour." (Behjati-Sabet and Chambers 2005, 134-35)

Cynicism and distrust also typify the Iranians' dealings with government authorities and the Western world. Underlying all this is a sense of insecurity from years of political unrest and upheaval. In an atmosphere of survivalism, the family becomes the stabilizing force.

Behjati-Sabet and Chambers note that by 2004 some working-class or lower-class immigrants who arrived in the West were beginning to experience a loss of power in the family. This happened when their wives began to think about their rights and the children wanted the freedom experienced by their peers in the West. The extra stresses of adapting to Western society often trigger family violence. "For example, the husband may be unemployed or underemployed but his wife has been able to find a job. His loss of the traditional role of breadwinner and his dependence on his wife's income is an insult to his self-esteem" (ibid., 139).

---

49 Power distance is a dimension that relates to the degree of equality/inequality between people in a particular society. High power distance means that inequality between the boss and workers is expected. Low power distance means that greater equality of members is expected, no matter their position.

> Stresses associated with migration, that is, lack of extended family support, change in family roles, and financial problems, along with the general increase in the woman's awareness of their rights to independence, have led to interesting and steady increase in the rate of separation and divorce in Iranian families in Canada. (ibid., 140)

This stress on the family was reported by the Welfare Organization in Iran's Ministry of Public Health, which offers a portrayal of life in Iran, stating that "suicides [are] reaching epidemic scale" (Taheri 2008, 319).

> In 2007, there were more than 42,000 officially recorded suicides, compared with 1,612 in 1977. Before the revolution, divorce was rare in Iran and unknown in some rural areas. Now, over 30 percent of all marriages end up in divorce, according to the report. The main reasons for this "epidemic of divorce" are unemployment, poverty, drug addiction and depression. The number of drug addicts is estimated at around 4.5 million, a tenfold increase over the pre-revolutionary era… . The ministry's report warns that depression is becoming "a national disease." (ibid.)

The report goes on to estimate that between 10 and 12 percent of the population, almost fifteen million people, suffer from chronic depression. It cites "poverty, sociopolitical violence, domestic violence, unemployment, divorce, drug addiction, the feeling of lack of freedom, social disappointment, prostitution, inflation, discrimination, [and] violation of the rights of citizenship" as contributing factors (ibid.).

The impact family has on developing a person's cultural response is very great and very difficult to change. Much of a person's character is formed in the early years of childhood. What we learn from our parents we put into practice in our adulthood. The Bible advises parents to "train a child in the way he should go, and when he is old he will not turn from it" (Prov 22:6).

Behavioral responses are learned through household rituals and discipline during childhood and early adolescence. The discipline of children in the home, school, and madrasa can be cruel in Middle Eastern societies. Patai (2007, 36) reveals that the transition for male children from maternal pampering to the male world is harsh. The disciplinarian father is expected to counterbalance the compassionate, tender, loving mother and prepare the young adult for the harsh reality of life. This is often done with verbal threats and corporal punishment. The transition from adolescence to adulthood is painful.

Coming to Christ has serious repercussions for members of a Muslim family. One man said that his mother goes to the mosque and prays for him to become a Muslim again (E3M). Another avoids telling the family that he is a Christian since the relatives would put pressure on the mother (E7M). I asked if the relationship between a mother and her son is closer than between a father and his son.

The response was that in most cases the relationship is closer with the mother, and one respondent admitted that some Iranian mothers try to control their sons and never give up (E7M).

The family is obviously extremely important within the Iranian context. When an Iranian converts to Christ, there are repercussions for the larger family unit. Adding to the complication, the Iranian family unit is already fractured through the asylum process. Discipleship that is comprehensive will need to teach and model a new family in Christ. A lot of time and energy must be spent dealing with the fallout of the male's diminished role in the family, creating trust with those outside the trusted family, and countering the isolation that is deeply felt in American society, which functions more from an individual perspective than a collectivist mentality.

Childhood Education

Childhood education, both formal and informal, is instrumental in establishing patterns of behavior that children will continue into adulthood. Everyone brings with them the values they have learned in childhood. The topic of how children are raised surfaced on several occasions as an answer to unrelated questions—why it is hard to forgive, why Iranians are hypersensitive, pastoral judgment and control, fear in communicating, and additional remarks at the end of the interview. These individuals confirmed that the way a child is raised by his or her parents does shape adult behavior.

When asked why the Iranian church is unique in its problems, one person answered, "The way our parents raised us" (U3M). Another admitted that families didn't have the knowledge, books, or time to raise children in a proper way (E4F).

The positive view of how Iranians are raised shows a large number of Iranians getting good grades and gaining higher education. Yet it was quickly pointed out in the interviews that the motivation for higher education comes from parents wanting to gain a greater standing in the community through the honorable positions their children hold (U3M).

As I probed to better understand why Iranians are so "sensitive" or easily offended, one response again confirmed that it has to do with how children are raised. The remark "Iranian parents are more protective" (U2M) is understood to mean that the parents do not let their children grow up. Mothers were said to be the worst offenders and were accused of spoiling their children and not allowing them to take responsibility early in life. "I wish that Iranians would learn some parenting issues and boundaries" (U2M).

Fathers were mentioned as those who make all the decisions with the expectation that everyone will obey. This causes a "lack of experience" (U15F) on the part of children in making decisions. Children are told to submit to their father's decisions, and it is similar at school. The authoritarian and uncompromising way in which children are raised at home is reflected in their behavior at school and later on in their adult life (U10F). One consequence is an inability to resolve conflict. Children have never seen their parents calmly resolving conflict through communication (U9M), so any hints of dishonor at school often result in fights.

> "So there were a lot of battles in schools, because that was the only way we knew how to solve problems. There is no negotiation or discussion. It's always fighting. In church, we continue the same culture here." (U9M)

> "It's the Persian culture—that's how we are raised. It's part of the culture, not part of the church. When we come to church, we bring some of that to church. It takes time to grow and get over these things." (U13F)

Abuse of various kinds was mentioned as part of how Iranians are raised. "Abused by even their parents, society, school, home, between friends—so many different ways. If they start to talk, gradually you can find out where it is coming from" (E4F). Several used the term "baggage" in reference to the way they were raised. "We all have baggage, whether pastors, leaders, or members" (U12M).

Now that the family is being raised in the freedom of the West, with different cultural values, some of the values from Iran are out of their element. "That's one of the biggest problems of first-generation Iranian families raising their kids here; when you bring your kids to a guilt-based society, anything goes, because shame doesn't work anymore. There's no power to control them" (U3M).

Hofstede gives us a grid with which to understand the conflict of values found between cultures that operate within a high power distance index (PDI), such as Middle Eastern countries, and those that operate within a low power distance index, such as countries in the West.

Table 6.1. Conflict of values between high and low PDI (Hofstede 2001, 107-8)

Low PDI	High PDI
In the Family	
Parents treat children as equals.	Parents teach children obedience.
Children should enjoy leisure.	Children should work hard even if it is a burden.
Infertility is no reason for divorce.	Infertility may be a reason for divorce.
Children should respect rules of civil morality.	Informal lenience toward rule of civil morality.
Children should treat parents and older relatives as equals.	Respect for parents and older relatives is a basic virtue and lasts throughout life.

Low PDI	High PDI
Children are expected to be competent at a young age, especially socially.	Children are not seen as competent until at a later age.
Children play no role in old-age security of parents.	Children are a source of old-age security, especially to fathers.
Small enterprises are set up for job reasons.	Small enterprises are for family interest.
At School	
Teachers treat students as equals.	Students are dependent on teachers.
Students treat teachers as equals.	Students treat teachers with respect, even outside class.
Student-centered education.	Teacher-centered education.
Students initiate some communication in class.	Teachers initiate all communication in class.
Teachers are experts who transfer impersonal truths.	Teachers are gurus who transfer personal wisdom.
Parents may side with students against teachers.	Parents are supposed to side with teachers to keep students in order.
Quality of learning depends on two-way communication and excellence of students.	Quality of learning depends on excellence of teachers.
Lower educational levels maintain more authoritarian relations.	Authoritarian values are independent of education levels.
Educational system focuses on middle levels.	Educational system focuses on top levels.
More Nobel Prizes in sciences per capita.	Fewer Nobel Prizes in sciences per capita.
More modest expectations on benefits of technology.	High expectations on benefits of technology.

The respondents had a realistic perspective that Iranians bring Islamic baggage from their upbringing into their new life in Christ. Parenting classes and good mentorship for families struggling with conflicting beliefs in the host culture is another dimension of discipleship that will need to be explored. The respondents felt that beliefs they were raised with that are antithetical to the values of the Christian life are Islamic and bad, and these values were a contributing factor of making them angry. Though many mentioned that time is needed to outgrow the negative cultural values of the past, I suggest here that in order for the church to move from birth to maturity, there is a real need for a more proactive time of instruction and a place to talk out the areas that make them angry.

All in the Family

Dating, Marriage, and Divorce

The area of male-female relationships was brought up by ten people, or 20 percent of those interviewed, but not in response to questions about family. Most of the responses gave explanations of conflict in the church or reasons why people leave the church.

> "Life was difficult for many in our congregation. There were a lot of broken marriages, single parents, issues with raising their children in the new culture and adjusting to life in America. It was a heavy burden to have so many refugees for our little congregation and to be involved in meeting needs in a crisis so often." (U22M)
>
> "We have only a few married ladies in our church. Most of our ladies are single mothers and divorced. They don't want to be sad or questioned, and they don't invite you to their home." (U7M)
>
> "Divorce is a big problem among Iranians." (C3M)

Being single in the Iranian church can be difficult. The pressure is to be married. As one person expressed, "You are very good if you get married" (E4F). When couples start to date but then decide not to marry, the pressure placed on them can be unbearable.

The area of sexual innuendos is a problem, lying just under the surface, that the Persian church struggles with. "That's another repressed area in the Iranian culture. For example, so many of the jokes that men tell each other have sexual innuendos. There's a lot of below-the-waist jokes; so it's on their minds, but no one ever talks about it or preaches about it" (U22M).

Divorce is a common experience as a result of the inability to resolve interpersonal conflict. Male-female relationships in the church are a major topic of gossip and an area in which the nascent Iranian church struggles. Failed dating relationships are particularly hard, as they become fuel for discussions at church. When divorce reaches the pastor, it can be devastating for the young church. It is difficult for the new church, small to begin with, to address all the areas needing attention. However, dating, marriage, and a relatively healthy family unit are crucial in establishing a stable church environment. Hosting regional marriage seminars would go a long way in addressing this foundational part of any church.

Women's Issues

The interviewees agreed that women represent the majority of those attending church, and this has been my experience and observation as well. Most of the discussion on women's issues arose while conversing about conflict in the church and the question of freedom, rather than in the course of questions directly pertaining to the family.

The Burden of Baggage

Iranian women experience a lot of cultural pressures and expectations in regard to how they behave, dress, show hospitality, and respect others.

> "In Persian culture, there is a lot of pressure to be very formal in the way you address people and mingle at a social gathering. You are always aware of who is older, who is younger. There is a lot of pressure to look good as a woman, to have it all together. The meals you cook, the way you decorate your home, the way you educate your kids, who your friends are, who you are dating, not dating, and why you are not married. There's enormous pressure." (U1F)

Blame was placed squarely on Iran as an Islamic republic and its inability to define who women are, resulting in women becoming victims of a male-dominated society (E1M). The consequence is that women experience constant pressure within the Iranian community, which is only lifted when women spend time with non-Iranians (U1F).

Many interviewees were concerned about how some women dress for church, because Iranian women are very conscious of dressing up when going out. Jewelry, makeup, and clothes show status. Making a good impression, even when one does not have wealth, is an important cultural characteristic (E4F), and one respondent said that women are inappropriately drawing attention to themselves when they walk into church (U22M). This was explained as more common with new arrivals or new Christians than with those who have attended church for a while. There are individuals within the church who take it upon themselves to point out when clothing is unsuitable for church. Predictably, this correction is met with the retort that "church is not a mosque" (E4F).

Women's relationships with men, and in particular with their husbands, are an area of great concern in the church.

> "I view that in the marriage problems that we've had in our churches, an Iranian woman coming out of Iran is like a spring that has been pressed down all of her life by her husband, by society, the authorities—and now when she comes out to the West, that spring, that pressure, is gone; and the spring goes nuts. It explodes; bouncing up and down, hitting the windows. I've seen that kind of explosion, because there has been so much anger and grievances repressed from that kind of repressive culture. Now she comes to the West; she can call 911 and get her husband kicked out of her house because he smacked her or threatened her. The government in the West can take care of her; she is free to be herself. I've seen that kind of explosion in marriages, even people who have been married for twenty to twenty-five years, that just explodes. I believe that [there is] repression in Iran, then when they come out you see that side of a wild side of their lives." (U22M)

Young girls are particularly vulnerable when they experience the freedom of the West.

"I can just imagine that they come here, they let go of the headscarf, and they notice that 'People are giving me attention; men are giving me attention.' And I think this is something that I noticed in some of the Iranian girls that come here. They are often very, very, very hungry for attention and for love. Often girls crave more the other girls noticing them than even guys. And they latch on to that and they cling on to that. And that takes over everything. They experience problems in relationships because they are so desperate for love and attention and whatever, and this really affects their way of being in church." (E5F)

Older women who have gone through a divorce are not exempt. They go through a stage where they seek a more public role in the church, such as joining the worship team, with the desire that older men in the church will take note. "I want the older men in the church to see me" (E5F). It is a public way of seeking a marriage partner.

The problem is complicated in that "There are not enough intellectual, good, well-established Christian men in Iranian churches. You will often find women of any age who complain about that" (E5F). This is a major problem in all MBB churches regardless of ethnicity or nationality. One Egyptian MBB leader carries pictures of single MBBs wherever he goes and is trying to be a matchmaker for this community.

Women are looking for something new and different in the church, "where men and women are equal. It's wanting to feel like an equal, like they are respected in their youth, or as a woman, that you can contribute—wanting to be a peer among equals rather than feeling oppressed" (U1F). They understand that there are roles in Christian marriage and women are to respect their husbands. But the male hierarchy in the church reflects too much of the oppression experienced in Iran. It is hard for these women to enter the Christian community when the church mirrors life back in Iran, conjuring up "a lot of the negative feelings" that they tried to leave behind (U1F).

When considering areas of discipleship in the MBB community, the topic of women and their unique struggles is important, as the interviews indicate. If these concerns are left unaddressed, they will become a source of conflict within the MBB's life. One of the major weaknesses in Islam has to do with the identity and role of women in a male-dominated society, which has ramifications for the Iranian church. There are enormous pressures and expectations placed on Iranian women in terms of how they behave, dress, show hospitality, and respect others. The freedom of the West exposes the weaknesses in Iranian marriages.

Women crave attention, expressing this through the way they dress; and they desire to find a well-established Christian man, something that is in short supply. Women desire equality and respect, which have been denied them in a macho male-dominated society. This is particularly acute among single women.

The nascent church, which is often dominated by the male lens, will need to give space for women to biblically address some of the underlying insecurities they are experiencing. In addition, men need to biblically address the ways they themselves have been responsible for perpetuating inequality within the body of Christ.

Summary of the Family Component

In the interviews on the topic of family, the large extended family and its influence on those attending church in the diaspora was not mentioned as a concern. I was expecting more responses in this area than what were given. There could be several reasons for this. First, most families in my research sample were not living as extended families. Second, there was a higher number of single parents or divorced women, indicating that the family unit was broken. Third, family members who would influence the family were located in other countries or back in Iran, thus limiting the contact to only short visits.

The way children were raised in Iran was seen as significant in explaining current adult behavior in church. Overprotective parents, mothers who pamper their children, and authoritarian fathers are believed to stunt children's maturity.

Marital issues—including broken marriages, single parents, and child-rearing in a new culture—are problems the small, nascent church is ill-prepared to solve. The old traditional expectations and pressure placed on Iranian women follow them into the Iranian church in the diaspora. The freedom of Western society exposes marital problems, and women are often particularly vulnerable to the new role and identity they are given. The old male hierarchy found in some Iranian churches elicits visceral reactions from women, who are longing for greater equality in structure and relationships in the church.

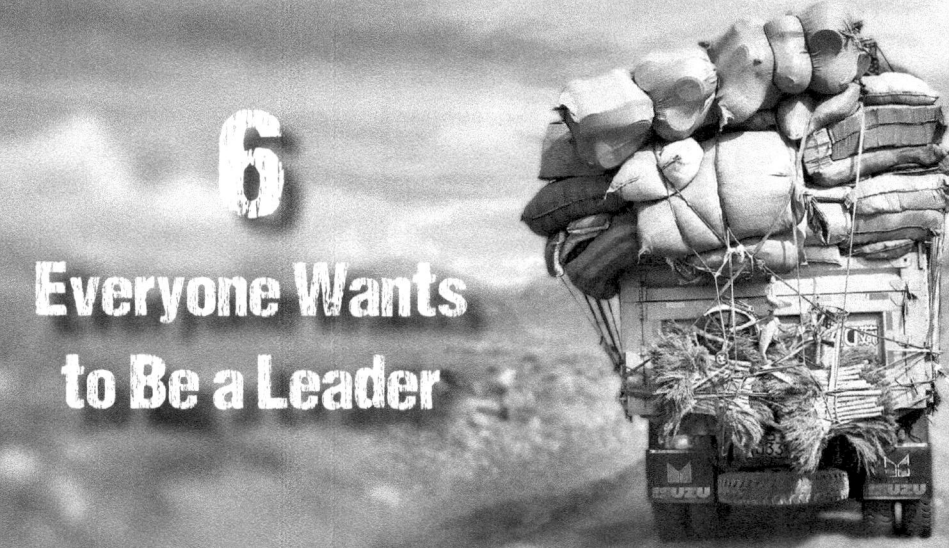

6
Everyone Wants to Be a Leader

Power is a very important dimension in any society; and along with money, Satan seeks to seduce people with its allure.. This chapter takes a look at power as expressed in leadership, institutional structures, giving, financial dependency, and use of finances, which all may contribute to the conflict experienced within the Iranian church in the diaspora. Hofstede's research shows that there is a strong relationship between a country's national wealth and the degree of individualism in its culture; citizens of wealthy countries are more individualistic (1991, 53). Power distance is defined as the extent to which a society accepts that power in institutions and organizations is distributed unequally.

Power is exercised in leadership, influencing the way structures operate and how people relate to one another. Our tendency is to mimic familiar patterns that we understand, perpetuating the existing power structure. Establishing new patterns of behavior in relationship to power is a complicated process. For instance, an MBB leader might be trained in a new dynamic of servant leadership, but those who serve on the leadership board may still filter the new behavior through the old pattern of power dominance and thus totally misunderstand the new structure. The problem is especially acute when people come from a cultural background that values concentrated power but are trying to establish a church that reflects the upside-down kingdom that Christ describes in the Bible.

High Power Distance and Collectivism

Middle Easterners come from a highly relational society with a tight social framework, in which people distinguish between in-groups and out-groups. Hofstede defines collectivism as "societies in which people from birth onwards are integrated into strong, cohesive ingroups, which throughout people's lifetime continue to protect them in exchange for unquestioning loyalty" (ibid., 51). The greatest insult in these societies is to go against lifelong loyalty to the in-group. The extended family protects the individual against hardships in life, but as a consequence the latter develops a practical and psychological dependency that is hard to break.

High power distance countries tend to be more collectivistic. Iran scores high on this dimension (score of 58), which means that people accept a hierarchical order in which everybody has a place and which needs no further justification. Hierarchy in an organization is seen as reflecting inherent inequalities, centralization is popular, subordinates expect to be told what to do, and the ideal boss is a benevolent autocrat (The Hofstede Center 2017). What About Iran? (https://www.hofstede-insights.com/country/iran/)

Hierarchy in a high power distance culture shapes the perceived roles within the organization. For example, Iranian power structures tend to be authoritarian; however, Iranians are most interested in reducing the power distance and increasing the future orientation aspects of the societal culture (Dastmalchian, Javidan, and Alam 2001, 548). Though the church may adopt the structure of the dominant low power distance Western church, with a board of elders with equal authority, old patterns often surface.

Interviews with pastors and lay leaders of the Farsi-speaking church confirmed that form and functionality often do not match. Pastors who desired to share power with the elders often found that the elders didn't fully understand the role they were to play. The elders took a passive role on the board, consenting to anything the pastor proposed. Conversely, elders wanting to share in the decision-making process of the church often found that the pastor was the sole authority, never sharing power with the elders. This misunderstanding of power sharing may be explained by the fact that there is no collective memory of how an egalitarian rule functions. The confusion over power sharing in the church is another element that needs attention to help the MBB church move toward stability.[50]

Research shows that the higher the power distance, the greater the inequality in power distribution. The opposite is equally true—the lower the power distance, the greater the equality between persons of power and subordinates (Hofstede 1991, 27).

Iran's ranking in power distance, though high, does not tell the whole story.

---

50 Pastors and church leaders of the host culture may need to take a proactive role in discipleship when partnering with an Iranian church plant.

The "should be" score on this dimension of culture is equally quite revealing, in that the desire of the society to alter this aspect of the culture is by far the greatest among all the dimensions of culture under study (the absolute difference between the "as is" and the "should be" scores is highest for power distance, and lowest for in-group collectivity). (Dastmalchian, Javidan, and Alam 2001, 540)

The following table compares the way structures are often formed based on their cultural values of power distance and will help to explain the leadership styles pastors and churches gravitate toward.

Table 7.1. Leadership differences between low and high PDI (Hofstede 2001, 98)

Low PDI	High PDI
All should be interdependent.	A few should be independent; most should be dependent.
Inequality in society should be minimized.	There should be an order of inequality in this world in which everyone has his/her rightful place; high and low are protected by this order.
Hierarchy means an inequality of roles, established for convenience.	Hierarchy means existential inequality.
Subordinates are people like me.	Superiors consider subordinates as being of a different kind.
Superiors are people like me.	Subordinates consider superiors as being of a different kind.
The use of power should be legitimate and is subject to the judgment between good and evil.	Power is a basic fact of society that antedates good or evil; its legitimacy is irrelevant.
All should have equal rights.	Power holders are entitled to privileges.
Powerful people should try to look less powerful than they are.	Powerful people should try to look as powerful as possible.
Stress on reward, legitimate and expert power.	Stress on coercive and referent power.
The system is to blame.	The underdog is to blame.
The way to change a social system is by redistributing power.	The way to change a social system is by dethroning those in power.
Latent harmony between the powerful and the powerless.	Latent conflict between the powerful and the powerless.
Older people neither respected nor feared.	Older people respected and feared.

The Burden of Baggage

Pastoral Leadership Styles

Lawrence Rosen's analysis of Arab social life reveals several characteristics of leadership and power that may inform the way pastoral leadership spends its time in the MBB church. First is the ability of men to move freely, forming attachments wherever they prove most advantageous (Rosen 2006, 164). Any attempt to restrict movement cuts deeply into their sense of justice, maturity, and legitimate authority. Second, mechanisms of internal leveling and moral equivalence maintain the even distribution of power. Leveling keeps power from flowing into too few hands for an extended period of time and dispels the felt disadvantage of hierarchy (ibid., 169).

Muller states that in shame-based cultures people criticize and question others to keep them from becoming too proud in the light of any success. He states, "Arabs are often quick to criticize leaders and pastors if they perceive that they are too ambitious and proud. They are sometimes publicly questioned or shamed, and often they leave the ministry" (2000, 54–55).

It was explained to me this way: "You heard the joke about a guy who had two buckets of crabs? One was covered and one was left open. A man asked him, 'Why is one covered?' 'I don't want them to get away.' 'Why is the other one open?' 'They are Iranian crabs—as soon as one gets too high, the others will grab him and drag him down.'"

The third characteristic is what Rosen calls the spirit of reciprocity. All obligations are interchangeable and subject to bargaining. Power is accumulated by getting people indebted with the expectation of reciprocity in quite different domains, to the advantage of the person in power. These cultural dimensions of leadership may form the roles, freedoms, and the vicarious relationships between the congregation and the pastor.

Rosen points out that election does not legitimize a leader in the Middle Eastern context, since anyone is free or morally equivalent to try their hand at developing a network of connections (2006, 169). The legitimacy of any leader lies in his ability to put together a network of dependents who owe him support, just as he must support them in turn through his much larger network of connections. This may help explain how the concept of freedom in the Middle East informs the understanding that may shape leadership and shed light on the independence exhibited in pastoral leadership.

The opposite of freedom is not tyranny but chaos (*fitna*) (ibid., 174). In order to avoid social chaos, Rosen proposes four freedoms important in the Middle East: (1) freedom of movement, understood as the ability to freely negotiate one's network wherever advantageous; (2) freedom of law, understood as freedom from having to follow a legal regime that is not locally responsive, which would subject one to potential chaos; (3) freedom of the local, understood as personal identity built upon tribal or local networks; (4) freedom of personality, protecting the right to privacy and confidential knowledge, particularly from invasive governmental controls (ibid., 174–77). These freedoms may also be exhibited in the fellowship and inform how social networking is done in the church. The pastor may spend more time establishing and maintaining this social network than ministering to the spiritual needs of the congregation.

Decision Making

Khalid Al-Yahya's study on power influence in decision making highlights both the actual decision-making method and the ideal or preferred decision-making style. Although Iran is a collectivist society, "The employees are as detached from their work organizations and have as individualistic a relationship with their work places as any individualistic nation" (Al-Yahya 2008, 395). His study reveals a shift from consultation, or authoritative, as the ideal decision-making behavior to an overwhelming support (60 percent of respondents) for the participative decision method (ibid., 396). Participation increases with the level of hierarchy.

Power sharing is resisted unless loyalty and commitment to the existing system are assured. Al-Yahya found some public officials "suspicious of employees who show great interest in additional power and responsibility because this may be an indication of a desire to exercise power for personal gain or to be a recipient of *wasta* (connection and patronage)" (ibid., 402).

Political systems in Muslim-dominated societies tend to be hierarchical. The males are to protect the family, the government is to protect its citizens, and the religious leaders are to protect the religion's adherents. This idea of protection can be found in every institution within society. A main characteristic of leadership pertains to the use of authority. Authority or power can be inherited (by being born into a family of privilege), or ascribed (by earning it and being recognized based on one's ability). The typical pattern of rule is autocratic (i.e., one-person rule) and paternalistic (i.e., the fatherly figure is wiser than and acts in the best interest of his protected figures), with little emotional interest. The powerful say that authority survives only where it is matched by obedience. These patterns are found within the church as well.

Decision making is placed under power, for often the person who has power is the decision maker within the church. I asked questions about the topic of decision making within the Iranian diaspora church. Seventeen people, or 34 percent of respondents, spoke on various aspects of decision making. According to the responses, there is a clash of cultures when it comes to decision making. The default setting is the pastor making all the decisions and letting the congregation discover the decision afterward. This style is particularly prevalent in the charismatic churches that claim a theocratic rule (U19M), which in actuality is a one-person rule. Iranians living in the West, however, are seeing group leadership elsewhere and desire more participatory decision making. The consequence of leaders resisting this trend is that people leave the church.

Though the church is structurally adopting the form of participatory leadership, functionally it may still be governed by one-person rule. This is due in part to confusion over the process and in part to cultural values of politeness (*ta'arof*) and honor and shame, resulting in people acquiescing to the ascribed leader.

Many indicated that the pastor makes all the decisions (C9M, U3M, U6M, C7M, C2M, U8M, U15F). "In this church, it is completely dictatorship" (U12M). Others put it this way:

> "Well, actually in the Persian church there is not structure. Eventually, the pastor makes all the decisions. [In] the churches that I served, I was always trying to bring other people into the decision—as we say, "the collective wisdom." But then there are other churches who say 'No, the church is not a democracy; it is a theocracy.' And by theocracy you don't usually hear God making decisions. Theocracy means the pastor makes all the decisions and they call it a theocracy." (U19M)

> "I think more and more churches over the past several decades, living in [the] diaspora, have moved to at least a structure of group leadership. Some smaller churches still have a one-pastor show. But some have developed the group team, but how it functions is another question. But I know some of my Pentecostal-charismatic friends—it's still one person who makes the call. In charismatic circles it's the person who is supposedly the man/woman of God who hears messages: 'God told me'; 'God spoke to me'; 'I have a prophecy.' The group deciding and discerning something is not encouraged in many of the Pentecostal circles." (U22M)

Decision making requires the pastor and the leadership team of elders to work together. Yet if the pastor has not been trained in this area, board meetings become another prayer meeting (U6M). If the pastor is insecure, open discussion of issues in the church can be reduced to the pastor accusing any member of the leadership team who voices concerns "of being a troublemaker, so quite a number left. There was a constant revolving door of people leaving, so the church would not grow" (U6M). Pastors in small churches have a particularly hard time finding mature believers to form a board because "there's a lack of mature leadership" (U14M).

In part, the confusion over leadership and the decision-making process can be attributed to a lack of collective memory of how to work together. One pastor said,

"When you look at the Persian church, the schema is the same as the American church. There is a pastor, board, and all the deacons. But none of them are used. Board meetings are not really that important. Board members don't take their jobs seriously. They usually want to please the pastor and say yes to whatever he says, even though he begs them, 'Please contradict me; let's brainstorm.' As I said, it goes back toward culture; we don't have a Christian culture. We care more about shame and honor than right or wrong. That's how I see it." (U19M)

Thankfully, there seems to be a conscious move on the part of some of the leadership toward a congregationally run church and away from the exclusive one-pastor rule (E3M, U22M, U5M). "After coming through that experience, I realized the importance of our having shared leadership. I realized the importance of being accountable to a group and valuing their opinions, their ideas, and feedback" (U6M).

Pastoral Calling

The main source of power in high power distance societies is family and friends, charisma, and/or the ability to use force (Hofstede 1991, 38). A charismatic or forceful person will often be recognized as a leader, though they may not be qualified as a mature Christian leader. These types of leaders resort to forceful control or intimidation to make people conform or take a certain direction. Open questioning of decisions in a meeting can easily be seen as dishonoring and defying the authority of the leader, provoking strong, defensive reactions.

Iranian history before Islam is filled with ancient kings whose names people still choose for their children. Though Iranians do not support the dictatorial system of their kings, they are proud of what they achieved (Bradley 2008, 45). There is still a cultural ideal of leadership based on these ancient rulers. If "the ruler shows he has 'charisma,' looks after the poor and gives justice to all, then he deserves obedience. If he breaks this contract, then he can be challenged" (ibid., 48).

Despots, tyrants, and secularists operate with the assumption that they know what is best and must make the decisions for those under them. Dependency, nepotism, paternalism, and hierarchical structures are familiar styles of leadership. In such systems, there is little place for the common person to have access to positions of power or to have a place to voice their opinions.

> In the Iranian concept of leadership, a leader possesses charisma because he is endowed with supernatural powers, or at least exceptional qualities, that set him apart from ordinary humans. He commands a special grace, an otherworldly quality that engenders trust, commitment, and an irresistible desire to follow. The reality that charismatic figures bearing a new dynasty often appeared during pivotal points of history to sustain the Iranian nation

reinforced the concept of the hero king. Thus monarchy became a function of personality, where authority flowed to the charismatic leader rather than being imposed by the institution of the throne. Furthermore, this ideal and expectation of charismatic leadership constitutes one of Iranian culture's defining characteristics. (Mackey 1996, 96)

Leaders within the Iranian community are held in high regard. Iranians are known to offer loyalty and devotion to people in authority. Shirin Ebadi (2007, 147) describes the extent to which Iranian society has created a cult of leadership:

> Unfortunately, Iranians are at heart hero worshippers.... They cling to the notion that one lofty, iconic figure can sweep through their lives, slay their enemies, and turn their world around. Perhaps other cultures also believe in heroes, but Iranians do so with a unique devotion. Not only do they fall in love with heroes, but they are in love with their love for them.

One interviewee put it very forcefully, criticizing the Middle Eastern conception of heroes: "You have to be very careful not to help feed Middle Easterners' emotions. They think with their emotions, not their logic" (U18M).

The standards for clergy within Islam, particularly in Iran, are fluid. Anyone could put on the mantle of a religious cleric. This self-appointment to the position of cleric may help explain the phenomenon of self-appointed pastors within the MBB Iranian Christian community. Taheri explains that

> Islam in general has never had an organized "church" with an easily recognizable clerical hierarchy. Almost anybody could grow a beard, don a turban and flowing robes, and claim to be a mullah. A survey by the Iranian Endowments Office in 1977 revealed that over 250,000 men claimed to be mullahs at the time. An astonishing 20 percent were categorized by the survey as "illiterate" or "semiliterate." Moreover, men could switch from a clerical career to other pursuits and back again at any time. (2008, 31)

The pastors' lack of quality theological or university education was mentioned often as a reason for pastoral problems (U22M, U2M, U6M, U11M, U20M, C7M, C8F, C9M, E11M, U4F, C1F, C2M, U8M).

> "Other problems that contribute are the lack of biblical education among elders, leaders, and pastors; lack of true understanding of biblical principles; lack of a spirit of obedience and unity, the spirit of working together, supporting each other, being humble, encouraging each other. Plenty of 'I did it my way,' as Frank Sinatra sang the song, or 'My way or the highway.' The second thing I mentioned was a lack of spiritual education, Christian education, doctrinal education." (C2M)

A frequent concern was how Iranians became pastors (C7M). One man floated between several churches before he "started his own church and became ordained on his own" (U22M). "Everyone wants to be a pastor or teach" (U17F). There is little collective memory of what a pastoral calling is, and few have ever read any books dealing with this subject. This causes problems, as one person explained:

> "That's another thing that I've noticed—they come to Christ, they are full of enthusiasm, and they love the Lord. People tell them, 'Why don't you become a pastor?' And they do—without the proper training. That can result in problems, not just theologically but managing people and dealing with people in a Christlike way." (U6M)

The Western church is just as culpable in the pastoral selection process. Sometimes Westerners naively encourage an Iranian believer to start a church without taking into consideration the training and education needed to pastor a church.

> "Iranians find an American church and say, 'I'm an ex-Muslim." And the church says, "Hallelujah, we have found a jewel here!' And they make him a pastor. That's it! You can lead a church. It's sad to see such things happening. Westerners get so excited, but it doesn't mean that he's ready for leadership. He needs to go through training. They praise him, and he even thinks he's something. Some take advantage of it. They think they don't need anyone else. God talks to them; they can lead a church." (U2M)

Without proper training for the pastor, the church will struggle. "The church may start with only five to ten people until they split. Lack of training, lack of leadership, is a major factor" (U2M). Alternatively, the pastor might manipulate the Bible to explain away the problems in the church (C1F). When individuals become self-proclaimed pastors, they "do not know exactly who they are" (E11M).

> "I am deeply critical of the pastoral leadership of the Iranian church. For the most part, our pastors are not educated [and] do not grow or gain new skills. That is also a problem with the house church movement in Iran. The pastors try to rule. I put a lot of the blame on the pastors in terms of many of our struggles in our Iranian church." (U22M)

Members of churches are frustrated when pastors are not properly trained (U16F). One shared that he suffered for years under self-proclaimed pastors who didn't know the Bible (U20M). "There is no way that [biblical teaching] is going to be passed on to these people who are spiritually hungry. They don't know how to grow themselves up. You need the leaders to guide them as shepherds" (U4F).

The lack of education and training is often reflected in the way the church is organized and the irrelevance of the preaching and teaching.

> "The church was very disorganized. I couldn't talk with the members, even those of my age. I felt like the teachings weren't something that was interesting for the young people. Sometimes I felt like I didn't even understand the pastor's preaching. It was disjointed and irrelevant. I just stayed because I had to, but [it was] not something I wanted to listen to." (C6F)

However, some interviewees recognized that pastors who have grown up in the church are more mature and have seen many of the problems before (E1M).

> "You can find pastors here who were pastors back there twenty to thirty years. They are experienced pastors." (C1F)

> "There are some who have wonderful training, are grounded, involved in 'Seminary on the Air,' to make sure the new converts in Iran and Afghanistan are properly trained." (U6M)

Patron-client relationships and the power structures of fellowships are another dimension of the power component. In the Islamic view of power, a person in power is often seen as a guardian leader (Beekun and Badawi 1999, 2). Patron-client social structures are omnipresent in the Middle East. "Iran is clientelistic and is composed of many autonomous parallel groups formed in patron-client bounds" (Alamdari 2005, 1298). Clerics function as glorified social welfare agents who gather money and dispense it. This gives the cleric independent power (Mackey 1996, 118).

Despite the hierarchical nature of Iranian society, it is difficult to determine where exactly a leader leads and the follower follows.

> Laymen look to their leader for guidance and pattern their behavior accordingly. At the same time, the cleric from his position of authority seeks to understand the will of his followers and then to shape his policies to reflect that will. As a result, religious leadership, unlike kingship, is circular rather than vertical. The leader both leads and follows and the followers both follow and lead. (Mackey 1996, 118)

Even in the diaspora, new patron-client relationships are sought to replace the old ones. "Hope is a key component of patronage and clientage" (King 2005, 321). Patron-client relationships influence normative ideas about migration and resettlement processes (ibid., 324). It is possible that this repositioning influences relationships in the church, explaining why so many people go to church for help and then leave once the need is met.

Church Structure

Church structure is also an area of concern. It is important to understand how the new community shapes its structures of power to its own ideas and interests. Armando Geller suggests that a type of neo-patrimonialism may develop in authoritarian systems in which the leader assumes power through patrimonial power. He suggests that this power is based on "authority, suppressed subjects and paid military organizations, by virtue of which the extent of a ruler's arbitrary power, as well as grace and mercy increases" (2008, 2).

There is a strong emotional dimension in hierarchical societies. People either adore or despise the leader, with equal intensity. Hofstede states that countries with higher power distance have more domestic political violence (e.g., politically inspired riots) than lower power distance countries, and that high power distance countries are characterized by strong right and left wings with a weak center, which he calls a reflection of the polarization between dependence and counterdependence (1991, 38). The center position (which is considered the ideal in Western societies) is seen as a position of weakness. There will be a power struggle of opinions, and the pattern of leadership that can quickly develop reverts to old patterns of overpowering the others to keep strong opinions in check.

Iran scored 59[51] in uncertainty avoidance, meaning Iranians like to maintain rigid codes of belief and behavior and are intolerant of unorthodox behavior and ideas (ibid., 113). Many Iranians are reluctant to compromise or to recognize the validity of others' points of view, but instead try hard to convert others to their opinion. It is often difficult for Iranians, especially men, to admit they may be wrong (Behjati-Sabet and Chambers 2005, 135).

A significant note for voluntary church organizations is that "Iranians had very little, if any, experience of participation in voluntary organizations in Iran, which could be carried over to the United States" (Min and Bozorgmehr 2000, 720).

> Compared to other new immigrant groups, Iranians have very few ethnic associations or organizations. The main explanation for this pattern is cultural. Voluntary associations were uncommon in Iran, and as such Iranians do not have the requisite experience to establish them. Even when they are formed, many of these associations fail in their infancy. (Bozorgmehr 1998, 24)

Ebadi affirms this propensity of Iranian organizations to fail. "As has been the tendency of organized Iranian political groups from the beginning of time, the movement splintered, and then its splinters splintered" (2007, 155). This was the experience of the political groups in July 1999 after President Khatami's government cracked down on any voice in opposition to or critical of the government. No one could agree anymore on tactics, let alone strategy. Global Leadership and Organizational Behavior Effectiveness (GLOBE) is a long-term program designed to conceptualize, operationalize, test, and validate a cross-level integrated theory of the relationship between culture and societal, organizational, and leadership effectiveness in sixty-two societies. Iran ranked twentieth from the lowest in the GLOBE sample, indicating that planning, investing, and future-oriented behaviors are not highly emphasized (Dastmalchian, Javidan, and Alam 2001, 541).

The first years of the Iranian Revolution, 1979–81, were dominated by power struggles. "Many of the groups went through radical changes and schisms as they

---

51 The uncertainty avoidance index is for fifty countries in three regions based upon the mean scores from two questions and the percentage score from the last question. See Hofstede 1991, 111-12, for details.

defined and redefined their range of political and ideological views, particularly their position on the future of Islamic leadership" (Spellman 2004, 24). The way the authoritarian clergy secured their power base was by eliminating the opposition forces. Schisms followed them into the diaspora. "The political divisions that existed between the leftist groups have continued in exile and there have been many schisms within the parties" (ibid., 29).

Yet Iranians seek to change these cultural traits. The most important "should be" cultural traits they desire to transform are their two weakest orientations. "In terms of the desires to change the culture, the data showed that Iranians are most interested in reducing the power distance and increasing the future orientation aspects of the societal culture (Dastmalchian, Javidan, and Alam 2001, 548). This too has followed Iran into the diaspora.

It is necessary to understand leadership and power structures to truly understand the MBB church in the diaspora. The need to create a network of dependents, along with the freedom to act independently, informs social networking. The political system of hierarchical structure, in which undisputed power is ascribed to the person in authority, often becomes the default mode of church leadership. Yet at the same time the complicated nature of the patron-client relationship blurs the lines between leader and follower. Middle Easterners' high score in uncertainty avoidance explains the desire of their leaders to maintain rigid codes of belief and behavior and, in general, their intolerance of other ideas. This rigidity is a defense mechanism against the perceived threats of trauma and humiliation.

So how does this work itself out in the church? Six people, or 12 percent of those interviewed, described the structure of power in the Iranian church. Much of this discussion followed from questions asking how the church makes decisions and how much control or freedom the pastor has. The respondents talked about their desire for positions of power and the disharmony that follows. "Power—everybody wants power" (U12M).

One man talked about two types of power. The first is the power of the pastor, who knows more than other people. The second comes from the national church or denomination from which the fellowship rents the facility. Fear of the denomination's power might play into the pastor's insecurities. "If they don't see I have more people here, they might take my salary or tell me to go because I don't have fruit here. So I try to not trust them" (C4M).

> "My experience of the Iranian church is [that it is] largely very top-down in the sense that the pastors are seen as a spiritual authority. The deacons and deaconesses and the elders of the church that I attended kind of upheld the view that the pastors are the spiritual authority and you have submitted to them. Throughout the years, trouble was initiated by men who have a lot of pride and had their own ideas about how things should be. Instead of

praying for the pastor humbly, they would stomp out and leave. Sometimes they would try to bring other people with them." (U4F)

One respondent expressed the opinion that power is not only exercised by the pastor; it can also be found among the older members of the congregation and the younger ones (E14F). At times, pastors are the sole power brokers in the church structure. Some individuals believe that they can do better than the pastor; so when the pastor maintains firm control, these power seekers leave the church. Another strategy is to undermine the pastor's influence, trying to unseat him through manipulation. This will be discussed more in the "Pastoral Leadership" section below.

Finances and Money

The area of finances is a source of disharmony in many churches, and the Iranian church is no exception. I raised the topic of finances, with special attention to collection, financial problems of attendees, and pastoral use and distribution of funds. Twenty-five people, or 50 percent of those interviewed, expounded on finances in the Iranian church.

Several people talked about how their Islamic background negatively influences the way money is viewed (U9M, U22M, U19M). "In Iran, the clergy, after the revolution, they take our money. There is corruption. Members are against it. They hear things on TV that there are pastors living in luxury, like Benny Hinn, and they compare that" (U18M).[52] Some feel that giving is optional and can be the cause of tension in church (C6F, U17F, U19M, U16F). "In Islam, they teach that you just give alms. When they see a minister, they think they should just give alms…. Here they don't have a clear understanding [of giving] unless they stay in the church for a long time" (U11M).

I asked how the pastor uses the money. The way money is handled and dispensed was viewed negatively (U20M, E17F, U14M). Some said that pastors required church members to give 10 percent (U22M, U7M), and that they would even give freewill offerings after the minimum offerings (E3M). Some pastors pushed their people to give so they could preach on TV (U8M). For the most part, it seems that financial accountability is not understood.

> "There is no accountability for the most part. For the most part, money is never talked about. People have no idea about the money they give every week: where it goes, how it's spent, how much the pastor takes for salary, or how much goes for other things. The pastor is usually in charge of the money and spends it how he wishes." (U22M)

---

[52] Benny Hinn, born Toufik Benedictus Hinn, is well known through his international crusades and media ministry. He is best known for his "Miracle Crusades" of faith healing, and his net worth is estimated to be $42 million.

In some churches finances were not a problem, for a variety of reasons. It could be because an American church paid the salary (U19M) or because the church was so small that finances were not a significant concern (C7M). "In our church finances haven't been a problem. We have been very open and given our members a good report of where our finances go. The money issue never became a critical issue in our church" (U21M).

Money, or the lack of it, takes a toll on pastors and ministries. They must seek alternative means for income, such as wives supporting them (U9M), or they must always rent facilities rather than have their own meeting space (U22M). Sometimes pastors have to spend their own money on church functions (E15F).

Money is a major area of concern for new immigrants. The lack of disposable income has a bearing on how churches function and are structured. "Most of the members are on social security or government aid. There are so many of these problems" (U16F). So many people have financial problems (E3M, U7M) and are insecure in their employment (E4F).

Helping people who attend church financially was mentioned as an area of concern. "Sometimes if they need some help, if you give them the help, they are there. The moment you say you can't do [it] anymore, it looks like you are slapping them in the face. They don't see that there is a limitation" (U8M). Often people ask for money to pay any and every bill, like cell phone bills (E1M, C9M, C7M). Since giving money to those in need is so complicated and such a source of disharmony in the church, there is a need for a clear policy on how to help people financially.

I asked if people knew how their churches used the finances. Some did not know where the money went. "I don't know; I'm sure the church is helping some people, but I don't know about this" (E3M, E2M, C6F, U17F). In other churches, there was a clear and transparent policy in regard to the money collected at church.

> "We don't have anyone taking a salary here. All we have, we collect an offering; the way we spend it is always [with] two signatures, even for five dollars. Every year we give the report to people so they know what we did. They respect that. For the same reason, they question our finances and our expenses less than in other churches." (U18M)

Tithing is not cultural for Iranians. Finances and the use of money are a source of disharmony, since there is no collective memory of Christian tithing. Instead, people's memory is informed by mullahs manipulating for funds; or tithing is understood as optional almsgiving. Financial scandals involving televangelists further erode the trust of new Christians, resulting in meager giving. Typically pastors have little or no accountability with the use of tithes collected, adding to the mistrust of the pastor. The lack of financial support leads to bi-vocational pastors who have insufficient funds for ministry; it is also a contributing factor to their poor options for further ministry education.

Further complicating the desire to tithe, many of the Iranians are refugees with little or no income. Refugees are seeking resources to pay bills, many of which are not for basic necessities. Yet not all Iranians are without income, for many arrived with large amounts of money to establish businesses in North America. The church will be in a better position if it has a written policy to guide the many requests for financial help.

Pastoral Calling and Education

The topic of pastoral calling and education was an area of concern mentioned by eighteen people, or 36 percent of the respondents. I asked questions about pastoral leadership, but calling and education were not included in the questions. The interviewees' answers reflected a perceived source of disharmony within the Iranian church in the diaspora.

The Iranian church is a growing first-generation church, but finding trained, seasoned pastoral leadership is the foremost concern. The low educational level of pastors was cited as the most glaring obstacle to the Iranian diaspora church's growth and maturity. Many pastors do not have theological or university education and, once appointed, have no concept of continuing education to grow in their knowledge. Some are self-appointed and self-ordained, seeking a title to bring them honor. Others are appointed by national churches that desire to have an ethnic ministry, so they hire a charismatic person who has a heart for evangelism but no training.

Iranians who desire to be ministers often fail to comprehend the complexities of pastoral ministry, including knowledge of proper theology, management of people, pastoral care, and knowledge of the community's needs. The result is division in the churches and pastors who are not equipped to minister to their congregations. Members know if someone can properly feed them the Word of God and minister to their needs.

Pastoral Leadership

Pastoral leadership issues are a growing source of disharmony in the burgeoning Iranian diaspora church. Twenty-eight people, or 56 percent of those interviewed, spoke about pastoral leadership. I pressed for clarification to better understand how leadership is understood and practiced.

"For the Farsi-speaking church, I would call the lack of leadership as the number one barrier. What we lack in Farsi-speaking churches is lack of management and Christian character, things of that nature. That's why there is a split—they don't know how to handle it" (U2M). One even called it "the blind leading the blind" (C2M).

Much of the blame is placed on church leadership (U20M, U16F, U1F, C6F, E19M). Some respondents thought that pastors focus on numbers, their position, and money instead of what they should focus on (C1F, E4F).

I shared that one of the strengths of the American church is that the pastor is usually vulnerable from the pulpit, and people respond well.

> "Yes, they like it when the pastor does that. It gives them a good role model. Some follow and some become more relaxed. If the pastor does that, then I can do it. But most Iranian pastors don't do that. Most Iranian pastors think that they have to be Superman and show no sign of weakness. That's the norm among Iranian pastors." (U21M)

Pastoral leadership often reflects high control and authoritarian rule, replicating a familiar system in Iran (U8M, U21M, U2M), as we have seen earlier. There is a variety of leadership styles within the Iranian church in the diaspora, some of which seem to be based on the personality and education of the pastor. On one side of the continuum is a pastor who has a great heart and is loved by the members but has little biblical or theological education. On the other side is a pastor who makes all the decisions irrespective of the members' wishes. It doesn't matter what the purported structure of the church is, since it is determined more by personality and education (U22M). Still others try to gain an advantage over people to hold their position.

Some interviewees mentioned insecurities as the driving force behind pastoral behavior; pastors do not want their members to grow beyond them spiritually (C1F, E2M). I pressed for clarification, since this type of behavior is common to human nature. The explanation was that Iranians live in fear (E2M). Since Iranians come from an authoritarian society, some find security in a strong pastoral role (U3M), and this trend continues today (U9M). Whether or not the pastor comes from a Muslim background is irrelevant (U16F, C6F), for this dynamic has existed in the Iranian church through the ages (U9M).

One variable to consider is that pastors have a limited amount of time available for ministry. Many Iranian pastors are bi-vocational and do not have enough time to respond to all the responsibilities of the ministry (E12F). They often become very possessive of the church (U11M) and limit contact with other churches (U15F). The result is tension between the leadership and the pastors.

When a pastor leaves, there is often a power vacuum, causing problems in the church (U21M, E7M). Pastoral leadership doesn't necessarily come with the title of pastor. There needs to be a vision for the church and the time given to developing a vision (C7M).

Pastoral care is an area that is lacking; there is little or no collective memory of how care is an integral part of the life of the church (C1F). A layman who became a pastor shared his story:

> "I was new, first of all, and I had no idea what I was doing. All I knew was use my gift of teaching the Bible. I had no model of what church should look like, and I didn't even know what was missing—and why these things failed. After failure after failure, I started asking why these things are happening. What is lacking? I was growing personally also over the years, the first few years. I came to the conclusion at the end of that, after seven times of failure, that 'OK, I'm good at teaching, but this community is not happening and needs to happen.' People need to have somebody who cares more for them and takes care of their problems that are in their lives, which I wasn't. I would give them a teacher's comment, but that would be it. So that was the conclusion I came to—something is lacking for these groups to become a community and a church. Then I realized that that is the role of the pastor. There is the teacher, pastor, evangelist, prophet; those fivefold became a little bit more clear, that you need all five to have healthy churches. I realized that I have a couple of them, but I don't have the rest." (U21M)

Qualified pastoral leadership is the most significant aspect of the growth and development of a church. The nascent Iranian church in the diaspora has a crisis of pastoral leadership. When the pastor does not understand pastoral care or ministry and does not have maturity in the Christian life, the congregation will struggle to grow in its faith and walk in Christ. Pastors too often understand leadership as being a boss and controlling people, even to the point of not allowing members to attend regional conferences. Though members might tolerate this type of behavior in the beginning, many soon become disillusioned and leave. Without a comprehensive understanding of pastoral ministry, some pastors revert to focusing on numbers or promoting their own interests instead of nurturing members to grow in their faith.

Lay Leadership

Leadership at the lay level is just as important as pastoral leadership. Lay leadership was mentioned by five individuals, or 10 percent of respondents, as a concern. I asked how someone stepping forward in leadership is viewed by the Iranian community.

> "As soon as they have a guy that they want to rise to leadership, the others would pull him down, so they were doing this in secret, trying to train some of the leaders." (U22M)

> "They'll ignore him or pull him down." (E2M)

> "The main problem of this church is they all want to be the boss. I haven't noticed it in American church that much. But in Persian church, they all want to be boss." (U17F)

The acceptable way for new leaders to emerge in the Iranian church is through servant leadership (E2M). "Young leaders spent a long time in the congregation on the same level as the other people, helping other people. You earned the right to be the leaders. But if someone is seen [as] wanting to move up the ladder a little too quickly, then a lot of those jokes and sarcasm come" (U22M).

One respondent summed up how critical it is to have mature leadership in the Iranian diaspora church:

> "If we can get a leader, we can have a really big church of Iranians. We talked to other leaders here as well and they all said, 'Well, we can send you someone, but would you be able to support them with a house and everything else like that?' We had an experience about one and a half years ago. Our church started to advertise in Elam, a training ministry based in the UK, for a new leader, an Iranian. We got someone. They got him in his house and everything, and it was all OK, and he was there for a year. His contract was there for a year. I can say that during that period, our church grew from thirty-five attendees to fifty-five or sixty-five in a period of one year." (E6M)

Lay leadership also faces obstacles to growth. Members try to keep others from taking on leadership roles without earning the position of leadership through service within the church. The desire everyone harbors to achieve status or position leads to competition and disharmony.

Summary of the Power Component

Power, leadership, decision making, and financial management are significant factors in the disharmony in the Iranian diaspora church. Both Iranian clergy and laymen seek to be in positions of power, often resulting in tensions that lead to splits in the church. The default setting for pastoral decision making reflects the strong authoritarian and dictatorial style of leadership in Iran, with little communication between pastor and congregation. Seeking to reflect the democratic leadership style of the host culture, the church may be egalitarian structurally, but functionally it remains under one-person rule, particularly in charismatic churches.

Biblical tithing is not usually taught or practiced; financial management creates suspicion and mistrust of the leadership. Since most churches are small and cannot afford to pay a pastor, many pastors are bi-vocational, so they do not have enough time to minister to people or to deal with complicated problems in the church. Many pastors are either self-appointed or selected by a national church, with little supervision for pastoral education, training, and mentoring, leading to further problems within the church.

Pastors with strong teaching or evangelism gifts sometimes neglect shepherding and caring for the people. The misuse of power, lack of leadership skills, poor decision-making models, and distrust over finances reflect the nascent nature of the church and are major sources of disharmony.

7
Conversion Is Like a Bomb Going Off

Religion powerfully shapes the values, traditions, and culture of a people. Even if individuals are not particularly religious, the cultural stream they swim in is highly influenced by the majority religion they are brought up in. Islam provides a matrix of belief that is manifested in behavioral practice more than doctrine (Weir 2001, 17). Therefore, in this chapter we will examine the religious influences on those raised in a Muslim-majority society, particularly in Iran. How does the Iranian religious background influence Iranians' understanding of Christianity, including religious identity, theological worldview, theological misunderstandings, and spiritual warfare? Does this background contribute to disharmony?

Religion is a major contributing force in shaping values. It shapes how a child is disciplined, determines what is right and wrong, and forms one's understanding of how God relates to this world and of human responsibility.

In our era there is a move toward religious nationalism in which religion is seeking to take control of every aspect of society. Religion already plays a large part in shaping cultural patterns; the two are intertwined, and it becomes very difficult to separate one from the other. In Muslim societies, Islam is defined as submission to Allah, and submission is the duty (*din*) of all Muslims. The Islamic religion has a large variety of expressions, but broadly speaking Islam is more concerned with orthopraxy (right practice) than it is with orthodoxy (right belief). Islamic theology describes Allah as distant and emotionally unattached to his creation. Allah's will is inscrutable to human beings and is above criticism. This understanding of Allah closely reflects cultural values of high power distance in Islamic societies. Therefore, some revisionists have argued that the God of Islamic theology is created after Middle Eastern cultural understandings rather than coming from divine revelation (Cook and Crone 1977; Wansbrough 1977).

The Burden of Baggage

Indian university professor Yoginder Sikand notes that madrasas have instilled in their students a dogged commitment to their own particular sect (*maslak*) or version of Islam, promoting sectarian strife. He corroborates his perspective with other academics reporting that sectarian prejudice in the madrasas has assumed extreme proportions. Even admitting sectarian differences will cause people to descend into hate-filled polemics. These madrasas focus simply on rules of medieval jurisprudence (*fiqh*) instead of issues of contemporary concern (Sikand 2006, 56).

Historically, Islam began as a minority tradition in its fledgling community of Mecca. Harsh persecution drove the emerging community from its birthplace to Medina, where it quickly took on a majority status with power. Traditional Islam divides the world into two domains: *Dar al-Islam* (those who believe in Allah and his prophet) and *Dar al-Harb* (those who either do not yet belong to Allah and his prophet or who refuse to join). These two divisions were the only two domains in early Islam. Reform movements of Islam, such as traditionalists, fundamentalists, and in particular neo-political groups, give heightened attention to these two categories. Modern leaders, such as al-Afghani, al-Banna, and Sayyid Qutb, and movements like al-Ikhwan al-Muslimin, Jamaat-e-Islami, and Hizb-e-Tahrir, or the current Islamist movements of al-Qaeda, the Islamic State (IS), Boko Haram, al-Shabaab, and a myriad of other sociopolitical entities involved in an Islamist agenda, hold strongly to this binary division in Islam.[53] However, to the average Muslim who is seeking to live life and provide for the family, this binary, polarizing rhetoric is destructive.

Yet the stream in which many Muslims swim has relegated non-Muslims in Muslim-majority societies to secondary citizens or worse. The term used for non-Muslims is *dhimmi*. Bat Ye'or defines the *dhimmi* category, historically, as the product of "the unequal agreements that regulated the relationship between the Muslim conquerors and the vanquished populations" (1985, 45).

Ye'or elucidates the treatment of non-Muslims through her penetrating analysis of history.

---

[53] Other categories are found with modern Muslim societies. *Dar al-Amn*, "the abode of order," is the state where the Islamic community within a nation is ruled by Islamic law; *Dar al-Sulh*, "the abode of treaty," is the state where Muslims are allowed freedom to live but not allowed to live by Islamic law; *Dar al-Kufur*, "the abode of infidel or unbelief," is the state where Muslims live in freedom but are greatly influenced by non-Islamic law; and *Dar al-Dawa*, "the abode of invitation to God," is the state where Muslims are commended to call non-Muslims to Islam. For further discussion, see Bennett (2005); Nasr (1990); Ramadan (2004); and Saeed and Saeed (2004).

> Certain purists reject documents coming from Europeans and only trust Arabic and Turkish sources, as if they were not even more biased. These sources speak through their ideological prism: the sanctity of the jihad, the justice of the dhimmi, the perfection of Islamic law. An unvarying stream, it provokes no dispute nor interrogation; a serene certitude, an ideal discourse, in which the vanquished exist only to serve with gratitude the cause of Islam. Dhimmi sources, on the other hand, present a violent cacophony, full of virulent mutual recriminations, a reflection of religious schism and sectarian fanaticism. (ibid., 258)

Al-Zawahiri and other Islamists hold to the doctrine of "loyalty and enmity," based upon surah 60:4.[54] Loyalty is to Allah and to fellow Muslims, whereas enmity and even hatred are directed toward infidels.

Farish Noor, a Malaysian academic, argues that Muslims need to overcome this enmity with critique of their own notions of identity and difference, something that the Muslim community has feared to do. "Pluralism in Islam has been frowned upon, suppressed, denied, and even hounded on the grounds that it would undermine the unity of the commune itself" (Noor 2003, 326). His proposition is as follows:

> The cause of Islam and Muslims has not been adequately served by the narrow and exclusive understanding of identity and difference on the part of some Islamist groups and movements. I have called for a different approach to the whole question of Muslim identity and its relation to the other: one that recognizes the internal differences and pluralism within the Muslim umma itself, one that problematizes its own identity while addressing the multiplicity and difference of the other, and one that seeks to identify the common threads that bind us to others. (ibid., 327)

The notions of predestination (*kadar* or *taqdir*) and decision (*kada*) have greatly shaped Islamic understanding of unexplained events into an uncompromising fatalism (Hughes 1995, 472–74; Houtsma et al. 1987, 605; Van Donzel et al. 1978, 119–22; Bearman et al. 2000, 364–67). Major teachings reflecting this fatalism are expanded in foundational works of the Hadith.

Research on Iran done by Behjati-Sabet and Chambers reveals that the deep-rooted cultural belief in fate (*taqdir*) remains strong in all classes. Secularization among the educated is eroding this concept, however, and it is more likely for individuals in the diaspora to assume responsibility for their own lives. At the same time, the sense of pride and competitiveness may cause many MBBs in the diaspora to suffer greatly from a sense of lost status and social rank. "Moreover, many Iranians in the West, in part to satisfy their pride, struggle to conceal losses,

---

54 "There is for you an excellent example (to follow) in Abraham and those with him, 'When they said to their people: "We are clear of you and of whatever ye worship besides Allah: we have rejected you, and there has arisen between us and you, enmity and hatred for ever, unless ye believe in Allah and Him alone."'" For a fuller treatment of this topic, see Ibrahim (2007), 66–115.

which they are expected to accept gracefully, and, as a result, develop various psychosomatic disorders" (Behjati-Sabet and Chambers 2005,135).

Darrow Miller expounds on three barriers to risk in what he calls zero-risk societies bound by fatalism. The first barrier is the lack of a compelling vision. The second is a mentality that idealizes the past, which is understood as an overly conservative stance in which the past is held as sacred. "Whole societies are held in thrall to the tradition of the elders" (1998, 231). Hall and Hall note that Iran, India, and East Asian nations are past-oriented countries (1990, 17).

The third barrier to risk that Miller identifies is fatalism. Others include fear of failure, fear of losing face, fear of the unknown, fear of the future, and simple selfishness. His antidote to risk is repentance, which he says results in worldview change. However, repentance is only one ingredient of change, exemplified by table 8.1.

Table 8.1. Comparison between fatalism and faith (Miller 1998, 230)

MINDSET	
FATALISM	**FAITH**
Fear of failure	Courage to risk
I can't do it	All things are possible
I am a victim	I'm a responsible person
Resign myself to my fate	Rebel against the world
Life happens to me	Life is what I make it
Man is like a pebble in a still pond; he does not move the water, the water moves him	Man is like a pebble thrown into a still pond; his impact creates ripples that go on forever
Dependent/Responder	Interdependent/Initiator
Tradition/Unchanging	Progress/Innovative
Bureaucratic	Entrepreneurial
"We" Centered	"They" Centered
Luck (Fail)	Hard Work (Achieve)

The identity of a person who has come to faith from Islam, a religion that has a polemic against Christianity, is an area of concern. Confusion concerning the Christian life, values, and behavior can cause tensions. It is important to consider whether confusion and identity issues are also part of the reason for disharmony in the church.[55] Kathryn Kraft (2007, 180) identifies some identity challenges that occured with some of her respondents:

---
[55] It is beyond the scope of this study to investigate issues surrounding identity. I refer the reader to Kathryn Kraft (2007).

Conversion Is Like a Bomb Going Off

Conversion is in and of itself a form of social deviance, and so the feelings of anomie which accompany deviance may therefore be expected to be experienced by converts. As they have broken one of the greatest taboos of their community, that against apostasy, they have rejected the social norms and arrangements which provided their lives with some stability, and they may no longer know what is expected; their act of making their own choice leads to uncertainty.

When Muslims come to Christ, there will be tensions. One area that may need attention is problem solving. A better understanding of the cultural tendencies will help the discipler navigate the labyrinth of cultural reactions to change. Disciplers act as negotiators and change agents, much like managers or leaders in business. Therefore, "Knowledge of each group's culturally endorsed leader behaviors would be beneficial to all individuals involved in substantial intercultural interactions" (House et al. 2004, 7).

Many Muslims now leaving Islam are coming out of an environment of "toxic faith," which is defined by Stephen Arterburn and Jack Felton as "a destructive and dangerous relationship with a religion that allows the religion, not the relationship with God, to control a person's life" (1991, 31). The common characteristics of religious addicts are having rigid parents, experiencing disappointment, having low self-esteem, and being victims of abuse (ibid.). People with low self-worth often feel alienated and isolated and have the need to belong and be accepted. People from an abusive background crave attention and are vulnerable to being victimized again by a father figure.

Various forms of toxic faith express themselves with compulsive religious activity, often driven by the desire to earn favor with God. Toxic faith produces laziness, which manifests itself when a person forfeits personal responsibility and desires God to fix his or her self-defeating behavior instantly (ibid.). It is easy for MBBs to fall into this behavior because of the Islamic concept of fate (*taqdir*).

Tat Stewart, who returned to Iran as a missionary in his adult life, outlines ten falsehoods about God from his years of ministry experience with Iranians that he feels MBB leadership needs to confront biblically (2005):

1. God is sovereign, so I am not responsible.
2. God is not immanent, so I cannot know Him.
3. God is both the source of good and evil; therefore, I am on my own to live a holy life.
4. God does not love me as I am, so I must earn His love through good works.
5. God is against those who disobey Him, so I am encouraged to take revenge on those who are against me.
6. God never humbled Himself to reach out to mankind, but sent others (prophets), so it is a weakness to show humility and be vulnerable.
7. God never provided a clear way to be reconciled to Him, so I have no real hope of eternal life.

8. God never provided a way to be reconciled to Him, so I have no way to be reconciled to others.
9. God is Almighty and does whatever He pleases to serve His own purposes, so I am free to use whatever means I can to advance my own good.
10. God did not provide a means for human nature to be changed, but rather provided a way for sinful human behavior to be sanctified, so I have no real hope of ever really changing.

Another characteristic of toxic faith is extreme intolerance. The Middle Eastern historical view is that a leader is a person who has a strong opinion. Honor/shame values, hierarchical societies, and the historical examples of unswerving dictatorial leaders feed this perspective. Leaders, in their rigidity, reject other believers rather than accept them. They routinely judge others and find the negative in their lives. From a position of superiority, they put others down for what they believe and for how they manifest their faith. They want to control the lives of others, especially their beliefs (Arterburn and Felton 1991, 42).

Hope and faith play an important role in moving beyond subjective feelings based on fear. Hope is recognized in the social sciences as a higher cognitive process (Bar-Tal 2001, 604). "Hope requires conviction about the not yet proven, courage to resist the temptation to compromise the vision, and transformation of present reality in the direction of greater aliveness" (ibid., 604–5). The role of healing deep wounds in the discipleship process, as explained in Charles Kraft's theory of healing (1993), may be an important element in bringing healing to the whole church.[56] Duane Elmer's principles for managing conflict (1993) are helpful, particularly that of using a biblical model of mediators, although Elmer is more concerned with mediation between Western workers and national workers.[57]

Understanding the role of the church and the individual in the kingdom of God is important for changing the perspective and giving hope. Understanding the multiple dimensions of the church in light of spiritual, social, and economic needs is also foundational. The unique church community is to be understood as a covenantal community, and individuals "are not free to reject one another" (Hiebert 2008, 281), but are to be committed to each other. The church will become more stable and healthier when individuals learn how to live in community.

---

56 For a fuller discussion on the topic of deep healing, see chapter 4's discussion under "Forgiveness." See also C. Kraft (1993); Anderson (1990); and Travis and Travis (2008).

57 Elmer's work on conflict (1993) is foundational. His cultural insights into conflicts and their cultural frame of reference are astute. His references to values in handling conflict remind the reader that conflict is far more complex than first understood. He is thoroughly biblical in his approach to conflict, and his suggestions in developing a positive strategy in dealing with conflict are culturally sensitive. Wisley and Wisley (2006), quoted in chapter 4, draw heavily upon Elmer's insights on conflict.

Religion is a powerful force within Iranian society, shaping values and worldview. Post-revolution Iran was particularly shaped by Khomeini's doctrine of *Velâyat-e-Faqih*, which infused Iranian politics with Islamic law and justice. Although MBBs may have rejected Islam theologically, Islam has permeated common cultural expressions culturally. The values and characteristics of interpersonal communication, trust, power structures, and conflict resolution in Iran and other Islamic societies comprise the collective memory of the Middle Eastern community in the diaspora, providing a backdrop for the sources of disharmony in Iranian diaspora churches.

Spirituality

Responses on the topic of Iranians' spiritual life shows a vibrant community that believes in the supernatural dimension as an important part of the Christian experience. Seventeen people, or 34 percent of those interviewed, spoke about how Iranian Christians understand spirituality.

There is a zealous pursuit in the spiritual realm to live the Christian life, a greater intensity than what is found in the Western church. This intense spirituality is uniquely shaped by the impact of Sufism on the Persian worldview. "When it comes to knowing God's will for your life, they believe in getting a direct leading from God. You have to either hear it from the Lord or see visions from the Lord, or you have to have a strong feeling about something" (E2M). This tendency to experience a supernatural encounter often defies any sense of logic or rational thought. In their passion for a mystical connection with God, new believers often miss the more rational side of the faith.

For various reasons, the Iranian church seems to be vulnerable to the message of hyperspirituality, even to the point of pretending and faking the spiritual life (U22M). Much of this seems to be confusion over how the Holy Spirit works in the life of the young believer (U3M, C1F). It is easy for Iranians to depend on a spiritual authority figure, like the pastor, for their spiritual life (U3M). Some of the interviewees told of people trying to measure spirituality by, for instance, looking for signs of the Spirit on people's faces (C4M) or evaluating spirituality by how someone prays (E3M).

Emotions are considered an important ingredient in the life of the believer. "It is easy for Iranians to get caught up in emotions and fail to listen to the Holy Spirit (U3M), or to fool the leadership of the church with their expression of zeal (U6M). It can be hard to counter someone. As one respondent said, "When someone says, 'God told me this,' it's very hard to trump that" (U19M). A particular problem is knowing how to respond to people who claim the leading of the Holy Spirit when this "leading" does not seem wise (C7M, U15F, U15F).

Practical issues in life are seen through the grid of emotional spirituality. This includes finding a marriage partner, finding jobs, making purchases, and planning one's future based on hyperspirituality in trying to discern God's will, possibly reflecting the Islamic teaching of fate (*taqdir*). Blame was placed on the Iranian church fathers, who fed this mentality in their sermons by using stories like that of God telling Abraham's servant to go find a wife for his son, thus portraying this kind of leading as normative (E2M).

Confusion over the role of the Holy Spirit in the life of the believer, coupled with the hypersensitivity discussed earlier, creates a situation in which some pastors and church leaders must deal with the fallout of people offended when the Holy Spirit convicts them during their preaching. People get upset, believing the pastor is dishonoring them by talking about them and shaming them publicly in the sermon (U21M).

In summary, the spiritual life of many Iranian Christians is vibrant, with the expectation that God directly speaks to or visits the believer. They pursue a living relationship with a personal God, and the spirit world is alive to them. The pitfall is that they are vulnerable to hyperspirituality through imitation (*taqlid*), trying to duplicate what they see in meetings. Spirituality is determined by the degree of emotion expressed in a meeting and God's direct intervention in their lives. Often this spiritual hype precludes believers' ability to reason with each other, because they believe God directly speaks to them. Disharmony ensues, resulting in people getting offended and leaving the church. Conviction by the Holy Spirit is misinterpreted, further complicating the life of the believer.

Teaching and Bible Knowledge

The process of understanding Christian doctrine takes time, particularly when a person comes from another religious tradition such as Islam, which already has a framework of monotheistic doctrine. Some respondents described conversion as a bomb going off in the mind. The ensuing "reconstruction" of right doctrine and belief is confusing and all-consuming, as this leader explains:

> "The problem with the Muslim is to sort through a theology that is quite crowded. You don't know what to do with that all the teaching you have from the past. For me, as a Muslim, my mind and soul were filled with so many things. I needed to carve out space to think.
>
> "First and foremost was the teaching of God himself. As Muslims, we had a common monotheistic understanding of God. Now the teaching of the Trinity devours everything in our theology. What is this? From the very beginning, we are trying to understand this new concept of the oneness of God. It consumes your energy and your patience–first to correct what is wrong and then try to discover the correct understanding of God. This was our first challenge.

> "Second was to define the concept of Jesus. The question we wrestle with is discovering Jesus as the Son of God. How do you define that? It is quite a challenge. These were our questions. It takes time for Muslims.
>
> "The result of the conversion bomb going off [is that] not all the doctrinal differences are discoverable at first. Our task as new believers is to find out what should be kept of the old and what should be thrown out. Throwing out everything is not an option. It was more complicated than that." (E1M)

The default setting of most people, and in particular those from a Muslim background, is a religious works orientation (U21M). The tendency is to simplify the world into black and white, reflecting the familiar simplistic binary division of the world in Islamic teaching. In the same way, sin is reduced to a list of do's and don'ts (*halal* and *haram*). "In a Muslim context, sins of the flesh are adultery, drinking, eating pork, dietary rules, and lying" (E1M). The biblical teaching about sin is much more nuanced, revealing that every part of humanity's thoughts, actions, and intentions is immersed in sin. The drift toward the default works theology needs constant theological attention.

The Christian teaching about love resonates greatly with Muslims whose theological understanding is works based. Those who have known oppression, hardship, and abuse respond favorably to God's message of love. However, the obsession with love can take on another dimension of becoming enthralled with God, almost as if he were a human lover. "It's a very emotional relationship with God. It's all about God's love for me" (E5F).

Some pastors and teachers expressed concern that a new believer has a different lens through which they interpret the Bible. They accept teachings they understand, but other teachings just as important are overlooked. For example, though stealing and adultery are wrong, envy may be considered OK (U18M).

Another theological area of misunderstanding is atonement. "One of the theological issues that I don't believe has touched the Iranian heart a great deal is the doctrine of atonement. Iranians give lip service to it, but the theme of why did Jesus have to die on the cross, the shedding of his blood for atonement for my sins, eludes them" (U22M). The Christian concept of the atonement goes against the Islamic teaching that no one can die in the place of another, so MBBs sometimes have an underlying, perhaps unevaluated, resistance to the idea.

Grace is another doctrine that is difficult for Iranians to grasp.

> "Grace—it's a Christian pillar. That concept is foreign to Persians. They can't relate to it." (U1F, E1M)

> "It could be faith. It could be grace. It could be forgiveness. It could be the concept of God. It could be the atonement. It could be the Trinity. Or it could be anything. The fatherhood of God is hard. People hear that, but experientially it is so far from where they come from." (U21M)

Others recognized that there needs to be time to absorb the new doctrines and biblical teaching (E8F). Often seminars or conferences are places where more theologically trained teachers can delve into these foreign doctrinal concepts in more depth (E14F).

In reaction to the dead formal religious orthodoxy of the Iranian church in Iran, the diaspora churches often emphasize the charismatic or Pentecostal expression of faith. The problem comes when there is little collective memory of how this dynamic Christian life is lived out (U22M, U20M), as we noted above in the discussion of hyperspirituality. Several pastors shared that Pentecostal doctrines and teaching cause confusion in the nascent MBB church (U22M, U20M). "Within Pentecostalism there's a lot of phony practice—if you're not speaking in tongues, then you aren't a believer, certainly not an effective believer" (U6M).

What new believers find most confusing are the doctrines that vary from one leader to another (U16F). All too often, untrained pastors pull verses out of context to support their personal leanings (C1F). Many respondents recognized that there needs to be better Bible teaching that builds their character (U2M, C2M).

On the positive side, many believe that the church does address points of conflict (E3M, U5M).

> "Iranian Christians are growing in theology, morality, and maturity. I have witnessed very mature reactions in the church to people who have fallen into these traps, such as adultery. It's not just personal growth that you are seeing; it's communal growth." (E1M)

Biblical knowledge and teaching are foundational to the Iranian church in the diaspora. When the teaching is haphazard or incorrect doctrine is taught, disharmony will arise. The lack of biblical maturity leads many new converts into confusion over what are perceived as doctrinal contradictions. MBB converts need time to absorb the new doctrines, values, and worldview. As MBBs grow in their new life in Christ, those who disciple them should give attention to Islamic doctrines that need to be dismantled and others that need to be reconstructed. These doctrines include God, Jesus, the atonement, sin, grace, and faith.

Two particular areas of concern were mentioned to help mature the Iranian church: (1) teaching that highlights the interconnectedness of Scripture (i.e., Bible survey) and (2) specific teaching against the extreme emotionalism so prevalent in Pentecostal expressions of the faith. What is evident from this section is that the more time is given to grounding people in the Word, the more it will shape people's character. The tendency of MBBs is to move toward legalism, which needs to be resisted. As the Iranian church in the diaspora matures, it will grow in theology, morality, and maturity.

Discipleship

Much of what is discussed in this book relates to discipleship. Though the questions did not specifically address that topic, it did come up in conversations. Discipleship is another area in which the church struggles, and shame may be a key factor in this, drastically limiting people's scope of concern, involvement, and action with regard to others.

> Some psychological researchers argue that while guilt is a moral emotion insofar as it tends to be externally orientated, other-directed, empathic, and oriented to reparative action, shame has many of the opposite features. It focuses attention acutely upon the global self and its own self-consciousness, not upon particular acts or possible courses of action. It blocks out awareness of other people and their feelings and needs, except insofar as these impinge upon the self. It inhibits empathy because the self is too engaged in its own internal processes and particularly its own sense of feeling bad. Finally, and as a consequence, shame actually induces a sense of powerlessness and paralysis. Thus any action that might be taken to remedy offence, to effect reparation, or to improve the situation of others, is not taken. (Pattison 2000, 125-26)

Pattison concludes that shame needs to be superseded by guilt if people are to live together in a way that enhances mutual life and well-being. "What is required for society to be more moral, in the sense of being more respectful and other-regarding, is more guilt and less shame" (ibid., 129). He goes on to suggest that self-preoccupying chronic shame might be minimized so that other-regarding guilt might have a more prominent place (ibid.).

Pattison proposes that chronic shame needs to be recognized and diagnosed. Shame is often concealed by conditions such as depression, anger, or sadness. Therefore, it must be acknowledged and owned before it can be healed (ibid., 166). Pattison moves from the personal to dysfunctional shame in society. He states that shame plays an enormous part in shaping social life and maintaining social control, which he calls "negative and dysfunctional" (ibid., 171). First, societal shame helps to define and defend the boundaries of groups, creating a powerful incentive to conformity and social control. Second, scapegoating is a common feature of many groups and organizations, a way of transferring blame onto a victim in situations where the self or the group may be exposed and found wanting (ibid., 174).

Taheri argues that Muslim societies historically have transferred blame, exemplified by three phobias: women, Jews, and America (2008, 106).[58] Jews, for instance, are blamed for many major events in the past three thousand years.

---

58 I would expand this understanding beyond Iran to generally include all Muslim communities.

"Blaming the foreigner for one's own shortcomings has always been popular in Iran" (ibid., 180).

> The feeling of victimization in light of sanctions against the Iranian regime burrows in the mind of every Iranian trips the powerful images in the Iranians' collective psyche—courage against injustice, martyrdom in service of the will to survive. (Mackey 1996, 391)

Societal or group shame has the advantage of undermining people psychologically from within by building upon individuals' propensities to shame. "Shamed people, like depressed people, may be unhappy but they are also malleable, quiescent and biddable. There are, then, considerable advantages from some perspectives to the social promotion of group and individual shame" (Pattison 2000, 175). Shame is the default setting in the MBB church and informs much of the behavior.

Disciplers within a chronic shame-based culture may need to introduce the concept of guilt within a redemptive, Christian worldview.

> Over the past few decades, a great deal of clinical interest has focused on the differences between the experiences of guilt and shame... . Guilt, which is a very important ingredient for a spiritually mature and emotionally healthy life, must be clearly distinguished and separated from shame. Again, it is important to separate these two experiences for this reason: While guilt is the partner of judgment, shame is the mate of judgmentalism. Even after they have been embraced by God's grace, some still need some help in distinguishing appropriate guilt and shame. (Cooper 2006, 81)

Marcus Warner (2007, 2-4) sorts ineffective discipleship into one of four categories, which I have illustrated with examples from the Iranian church:

1. *Discipleship by osmosis:* A person attends church faithfully and then is asked to serve. If the person serves faithfully, they get asked to lead. If they lead faithfully, they become an elder. The result is that the person settles into a relatively lifeless routine. Many Iranian churches lack any specific training to help new believers grow. "Some people still don't know how to pray" (E14F).

2. *Church-focused discipleship:* The focus is to keep the church running. Everything from membership and evangelism to spiritual gifts and small groups is designed to assimilate people into the church. Spiritual maturity is often neglected. MBB churches can become so singularly church-focused that they do not want their members to attend other churches.

3. *Head-focused discipleship:* This is academic training, often through a Bible college or seminary. Often the heart is not addressed in this type of training. Iranian pastors often either lack academic training and equipping in discipleship or tend to operate on the principle that Bible knowledge is what is needed.

4. *Behavior-focused discipleship:* The focus is behavior, which often promotes the view that God loves us but cannot affirm or accept us because of our behavior. This form tends to reduce the Christian life to categories of right and wrong, creating a very legalistic form of Christianity.

Warner concludes that effective discipleship should include a heart-focused walk with God.

> Heart-focused discipleship teaches perspectives and practices that lead to intimacy with God, freedom from bondage, and growth in maturity. These perspectives and practices are anchored in grace and emphasize the importance of living in the Spirit with a functional awareness of the spiritual battle that provides the context of our journey. (ibid., 6)

Some missiologists advocate a form of discipleship called "radical obedience-based discipleship."[59] The general idea is for new disciples to read Scripture with observation questions and obedience questions, on the premise that obedience is the essence of discipleship and is central to the gospel that Jesus taught. However, this method complicates the discipleship process in that many MBBs do not come from a culture that reads books (U3M).

> "You can't say, 'You're supposed to have quiet time with the Lord.' You teach them, but you can't force them to do it. It's a decision they have to make. They have to be spoon-fed all the time. They don't read a book or have some quiet time with the Lord, or pray and be patient with the Lord. That's why a lot of them don't grow in their faith." (E15F)

Through the interviews it became apparent that discipleship is not on the agenda in Iranian churches, and the discipleship process needs more time and individual attention (U1F). A common theme that emerged in discussing discipleship was that MBBs "come with no Christian background" (C8F, C7M), so they have a difficult time following through with Christian disciplines such as reading the Bible, praying, and attending church (U4F, C8F, C7M). Discipleship is complicated by the fact that new believers have little or no understanding of the Bible, and the influence of the Qur'an and Islamic philosophy hasn't faded away yet. MBBs still filter what they hear of the Bible through their own background (U19M), and in some cases they are even taught wrong things (C9M, U1F).

Part of the confusion of the post-conversion "reconstruction" expresses itself when new Christians get sidetracked by trying to find answers to questions that are not foundational to the Christian life and doctrine (E5F). The Christian faith, personal growth, and behavior in the church are totally new areas for the believer.

---

59 There is a growing body of literature on this; see, for instance, Steve Smith (2011), who advocates obedience-based discipleship. The idea is to put obedience into the DNA of the believer from conversion onward. The church-planting and disciple-making movements have proliferated as churches have caught the vision of learning obedience in each stage of growth.

It is important to recognize that there is a transitional period; some have to reach a theological cul-de-sac before they are ready to move on to the most important teachings of the Bible and the Christian life.

The concept of mentoring was mentioned as a way to disciple others. In one church it started with students who had to speak to a mentor about their spiritual lives; eventually it was introduced to the entire church (E5F). What they wanted was someone to guide them (E4F) and be good role models (E5F). They did not want just top-down teaching or event-based gatherings, but a more robust and interactive discipleship (U4F). Another insight was that churches should foster the relational side of disciples by including them in the home life of a strong believer. Discipleship is very much a way of life (U1F).

One person suggested, "I would do spiritual formation—how to fast, pray, commune with the Lord. I've seen more lives changed by meditation on the Word than five thousand hours of discipleship classes" (U3M). Though churches may be small, it is important to address the needs of the people. Another suggestion was to have one class for newcomers and another for the ones who have been around a longer time (E15F).

Discipleship also needs to be developed at the leadership level, as one pastor explains:

> "At the leadership level, I try to bring godly community values. I talk about Iranian culture that slips into the church, and if left alone it will destroy the church. So we work with ta'arof, forgiveness, and gossip. The pastor's work is to root it out from the church and diminish its influence. But in the leadership, you go to the next level. You expect your leaders to be more godly and throw away ungodly ways. They know that gossiping is not of God. Though leaders may lapse and gossip, they have a commitment not to do it and ask for forgiveness when they do. Biblical leadership must keep each other accountable. On the leadership level we agreed that if we see any of the leaders acting contrary to the Bible, we are to confront each other. Even with that agreement, our cultural background means that confrontation wasn't often. It was always late and soft, even among leaders. We knew that we shouldn't allow that culture to settle into the leadership." (U21M)

Another complication with discipleship is that so few resources are available in Farsi (U19M).[60] One way to overcome this lack is to look to the national church for resources for discipleship and Bible study materials. But these resources may not be sensitive to the deeper cultural issues in the Muslim background (E6M).

When it comes to leadership and accountability, Iranian pastors can gain valuable help by establishing an accountability relationship with a Western pastor. One respondent suggested that the accountability should cover topics such as the

---

60 I asked about the resources to which U19M referred, and most that he has are in English. Elam Ministries is translating good Christian books into Farsi, but there are limited resources written by Persian Christians.

use of their time, preaching topics, vision for the church, direction, attendance, and if people are leaving. The Western pastor could even ask the congregation if they love their pastor. This type of accountability is invaluable, especially for those new in the ministry (U20M).

Another avenue for help in discipleship is to look to the Christian ethnic community to understand how they do discipleship. For example, the Armenian church's experience can help the Persian church in this area.

> "They had entrusted me to the hands of these teachers, and they put me through the discipleship courses—that was the procedure of [bringing] a newcomer to the church before they baptized them… . Yes, we went through this discipleship course, and of course the teachers would report back to the pastor of the church and they would have meetings with the pastor of the church." (E2M)

Teaching children should be part of the vision for discipling the first-generation church. Parents must recognize the importance of language learning and their children connecting with peers in the new culture. A good example was one person taking his children to an American church for an earlier service so that in the evening they could be in Persian church (U3M).

There are other sources that are comprehensive and can greatly aid the Iranian church in growing healthy churches. Deeper Walk International[61] presents a more nuanced understanding of discipleship. Their approach encompasses four essential elements of heart-focused discipleship: building on a grace foundation, walking in the Spirit, emotional healing, and spiritual warfare—all areas Iranians struggle in. These areas take into consideration the effects of disgust and shame, sadness and despair, and anxiety and anger.

To achieve growth and health in the MBB church in the diaspora, a comprehensive and culturally relevant discipleship teaching needs to be developed. A major obstacle to growth is the cultural and educational aversion to reading, which is a reason for the lack of spiritual growth among some pastors. Bi-vocational pastors are faced with dividing their time between the personal discipline of self-feeding through the Scriptures and responding to the urgent needs of those seeking help in the Iranian community.

Discipleship in the diaspora must take into account the unique aspects of the Iranian context—dynamics such as *ta'arof*, forgiveness, and gossip, and the need to put on new behavioral norms instead of reverting to former cultural forms. The leaders need to take into consideration that the new believers have no collective memory of Christianity, so discipleship should begin with the very basic teaching of the Christian life and doctrine, allowing time for the new information to be assimilated.

---

61 This teaching can be found at http://www.deeperwalkinternational.com/.

The discipleship process must allow new believers to ask nonessential questions and gently help the disciple to understand core Christian doctrines and teachings.

The national church, with its long history of discipleship, is a great resource for the MBB church in the diaspora. A solid mentoring and teaching strategy is vital in the early life of the new Christian.

Summary of the Religious Component

Many of the issues I expected to be raised in this section were not mentioned in the interviews. Although Islam was most often blamed as a central factor for the negative behavior and values, the respondents did not give specific examples of how this influenced them. The areas I probed in the questions—such as spiritual warfare, fate, persecution, and doctrinal issues—were not prominently addressed in the interviews. However, respondents indicated that the spirit world is alive, reflected in the fact that many believe God speaks directly to people and visits us in this world. Since many Iranians are relatively new Christians, it stands to reason that they would have limited knowledge or teaching on the Holy Spirit.

The conversations revealed that Iranians are often open to the gospel but are also susceptible to "hyperspirituality." Spirituality is often understood to mean worshiping in a lively way, praying ardently, and seeking demonstrations of the Holy Spirit.

MBBs are frequently overwhelmed with new doctrines that are similar to their Islamic training yet profoundly different. Time is needed to process their new faith. New concepts such as the atonement, grace, Pentecostal theology, and Christology are difficult to assimilate into their worldview. The lack of pastoral training and the bi-vocational nature of most pastors' roles may be responsible for the haphazard approach to discipleship. The national church can play a significant role in mentoring pastors and providing training not found within the Iranian church.

In conclusion, there is a great need for discipleship that allows time for questions. Programs that are built on personal reading or content-heavy formal teaching do not reflect the Iranian relational culture. Mentoring is far more relational and effective as a methodology of discipleship.

8
Where Do We Go from Here?

The language-specific church is an important part of life for any first-generation believer. The Iranian's first impression of the church is overall very positive, whether first exposed to the national church or the Farsi-speaking church. The church is a place of peace and is very attractive to the new attendees. Most respondents described the church in familial terms, expressing deep emotional attachment to the church and its members, indicating that it had become a surrogate family. The Iranian MBB church's greatest strengths are its passionate worship, generous hospitality, and rich fellowship, which are experienced multiple times throughout the week.

New arrivals see the Farsi-speaking church as a safe place to get help as they transition to life in a new country. The church, and especially the pastor, is overwhelmed with the needs of this wave of new immigrants and asylum seekers. Established churches already have language skills and familiarity with the culture, making them a natural place for newcomers to seek help. However, the small fellowship and bi-vocational pastor are unable to meet all the demands.

The Iranian church can take several steps to alleviate this pressure. First, Western countries have Christian immigration organizations, such as World Relief, to help the church. Building relationships with these outside agencies is vital for the Iranian church to share the load of meeting needs that otherwise would tax all their time and resources. In addition, a strong relationship with a national church will provide another source of help for the refugees' needs—although language skills might be an issue for non-Persians—freeing the Iranian pastor to do the work of the ministry.

Acts 6 addresses a similar situation, in which the apostles were unable to do the spiritual work of ministry because the physical needs of the outsiders, in particular the Hellenist widows, were being overlooked. The widows, much like the Iranian refugees, did not have a support system to care for their immediate physical needs. Therefore the apostles appointed seven men to supervise the distribution of food. Three criteria were used to select helpers: they must be ethical, having good character; spiritual, being filled with the Holy Spirit; and practical, possessing the wisdom to manage the equitable distribution of goods to the needy widows. These same criteria should be used in selecting helpers from the national church to assist Iranian pastors in ministering to the myriad needs of immigrants, from getting official documentation to distributing furniture.

Second, due to the economic realities of new immigrants, the Iranian church is dependent upon the Western church for facilities. The danger is for MBBs to succumb to the patronage of Western institutional policies, as illustrated by the story C9M told about a denomination that dictated the size and location of the church, or the story U19M shared about being asked by a megachurch to translate the pastor's messages so the church could have a "Persian outreach." James Plueddemann warns,

> Despite a genuine desire to be egalitarian, churches in high-power-distance and wealthy countries are subtly tempted to see themselves as patrons in a partnership relationship with churches in less wealthy countries. Leaders in poorer churches may even desire and appreciate the junior partner role. Frank discussions about power distance need to take place at the beginning of the partnership relationship. (2009, 104)

The Iranian church is in its infant stage, in which leaders and members are relatively new believers. "Unlike other Muslim populations which have converts to Christianity, Iranians don't have an ethnic church they can look back to, a church to which their ancestors belonged. This marks them apart from groups like the Berbers and Palestinians" (Miller 2012, 5). Therefore there is little or no collective memory of how to structure a church.

The Iranian church needs time to create its own distinctive structure and history. "On the explicit level of beliefs, people become Christians but it often takes years, even generations, before the worldview of their church is transformed" (Hiebert 2008, 32). The unique aspect of the Iranian church in the diaspora is that it is creating its own history in the midst of a radical paradigm shift. Iranians are being exposed to another worldview by living in the diaspora, and Iranian Christians are learning to see reality through a new lens—that of Scripture. It is imperative that Iranian Christians study Scripture through their worldview and learn to apply it to their unique situation and not resort to imitation (*taqlid*)

Where Do We Go from Here?

of Western Christianity. The Iranian church must resist the Islamic tendency of religious reductionism, in which Christianity becomes a set of black-and-white rules, and discover the expression of the church that is unique to Iranian culture. A strong Bible program must be included in the church strategy for the second generation.

The Iranian church and other MBB churches need to develop a vision and strategy that looks beyond survival of the language-specific church and take into consideration the future of their children. This involves more than just designing activities to keep them busy, but developing an organized biblical curriculum in the national language. The children's cognitive language skills will be established through the language of the educational institutions they are attending, not the language spoken at home. Church leaders should seek to disciple and teach the next generation of Iranian Christians in the language of their new homeland. Workers from the national church are a great resource that the Iranian church can draw from.

We have seen that every person is unique and complex, and just telling new believers to read Scripture without a fuller understanding of the personal obstacles they face will not suffice. Having a better appreciation of a convert's background plays an important part in assessing the needs for personal growth. There are several areas I would like to highlight.

Backward-Looking Culture

As stated before, Iran ranks twentieth from the bottom in the GLOBE sample, indicating that planning, investing, and future-oriented behaviors are not highly emphasized (Dastmalchian, Javidan, and Alam 2001, 541). One Iranian blogger expresses this backward-looking propensity in the following way: "The future never seems to hold a candle to the past" (Ghahremani 2011). This cultural characteristic influences several aspects of the Iranian church.

First, the backward-looking perspective makes it harder for Iranians to forgive. The past still influences the present, even if the present seems far removed from what was. Revenge as a response to past offenses is, unfortunately, a part of the Iranian church experience. When someone is hurt, the visceral reaction is to respond in like fashion. The pastor and teachers will have to emphasize the Christian teaching that the cycle of violence and hurt must stop, and the best way to make it stop is to resist the natural cultural tendency to always view a person from past encounters. Revenge is to be left up to God.[62]

---

62 Regular teaching is needed on passages such as Matthew 5:38-48, Romans 12:9-21, and Colossians 3:12-17, in which we are admonished to leave room for God to avenge. Our task is to live at peace with everyone as far as it depends on us.

Second, the collective memory of the past remains strong in Iranians' consciences. Culturally and religiously, Iranians are reminded of the injustices of the past. E14F described memory as being scarred, so forgiveness takes time to learn and implement. For the church to move forward, it needs to consciously create a new collective memory around Christ's work on the cross that reinforces the concept of forgiveness. This can be done through drama or other cultural forms, such as poetry extolling the virtues of Christ and his forgiveness. By instilling the virtues of Christ and his forgiveness, the idea to capitalize upon is that the church is called to suffer with Christ through forgiving and accepting one another.

Third, the backward-looking perspective limits the ability of Iranians to move into new patterns of leadership. Iranians are interested in reducing the power distance. Pastors who rely on a hierarchical church structure in which power resides in the pastor, who exercises unquestioned control, may actually violate an intrinsic Iranian cultural value of reducing power distance. Reducing power distance is possible in Western society and reflects the cultural milieu in which the church is birthed in the diaspora. Although the cultural value of desiring a more cooperative leadership approach to church polity is the intent, there is little collective memory to know how to implement and function under such a system. This is equally true for the pastor as well as the lay leadership. Over time, however, disharmony is bound to result in more experimentation, and trial and error will eventually help establish an MBB governance form that reflects the new desired egalitarian patterns of church polity but also retains a Middle Eastern cultural familiarity of leadership.

A transitional period is necessary during which both the pastoral and lay leadership are trained in more cooperative styles of leadership while acquiring the knowledge and skills to implement these methods. Both the pastor and the lay leaders need mentoring and accountability from an outside body to help the church move in this structural direction.

Fourth, the backward orientation may well elucidate the lack of vision churches experience and the lack of discipleship and other future-looking ministries in the church. Mature second-generation MBBs, on the other hand, are concerned about the future and the direction of the church. They are frustrated by churches in survival mode and often leave in desperation for a church that actually has a vision for the future. Pastors who maintain the old paradigm of control and power will have trouble keeping the loyalty of the congregation, which desires a future-looking ministry.

To summarize, the economic reality of new immigrants, the lack of pastoral education, poor vision for the future of the church, and the existence of power distance in the Middle Eastern MBB church are major obstacles to achieving a growing, vibrant church.

Where Do We Go from Here?

Moving forward, the MBB church will have to make proper pastoral training and goal setting for ministry needs an ongoing part of the mentoring process of Iranian pastors. Iranian pastors need help in church-planting strategy from someone who has cross-cultural experience. To achieve a future-oriented ministry, a partnering church or denomination needs to help the Iranian church set six-month to four-year goals. It may be difficult to ask the pastor or congregation to look to the future when there is little or no collective memory in this domain, coupled with the reality of working from a survivalist mentality. Possible ways to move the conversation forward are to ask for a history of the church over the past several years and to follow up by asking how to move the church in a different direction.

Another dimension of creating a vision for the Iranian church is to address the cultural value of individualism and the inability to work together (Min and Bozorgmehr 2000, 720). Forbis recognizes this inability to work together as a cultural characteristic (1981, 91), and this was corroborated by comments from U14M, U13F, U18M, and E9M. The propensity for individualism and the lack of unity are sources of disharmony and a hindrance to creating a future-oriented church ministry. Collectivistic societies tend to be only narrowly collectivistic, pitting one extended family or clan against another, for trust is only found with those who are near, such as family. Honor-and-shame societies, discussed next, interpret events, circumstances, and relationships through an egocentric lens. Time is needed to mature from egocentric individualism to a "global-centric" mentality, as Plueddemann illustrates in figure 9.1. "Babies do not abruptly grow into adults, and the worldview development of leaders is also gradual" (Plueddemann 2009, 120).

Iranian pastors must recognize their need for each other, move past their insecurities, and create authentic and open relationships with other churches if they desire to create a future-oriented ministry. The spiritual leaders in the Iranian community should take the leadership initiative by reaching out to new and inexperienced pastors. Plueddemann's diagram illustrates the shift in thinking that must take place.

The Burden of Baggage

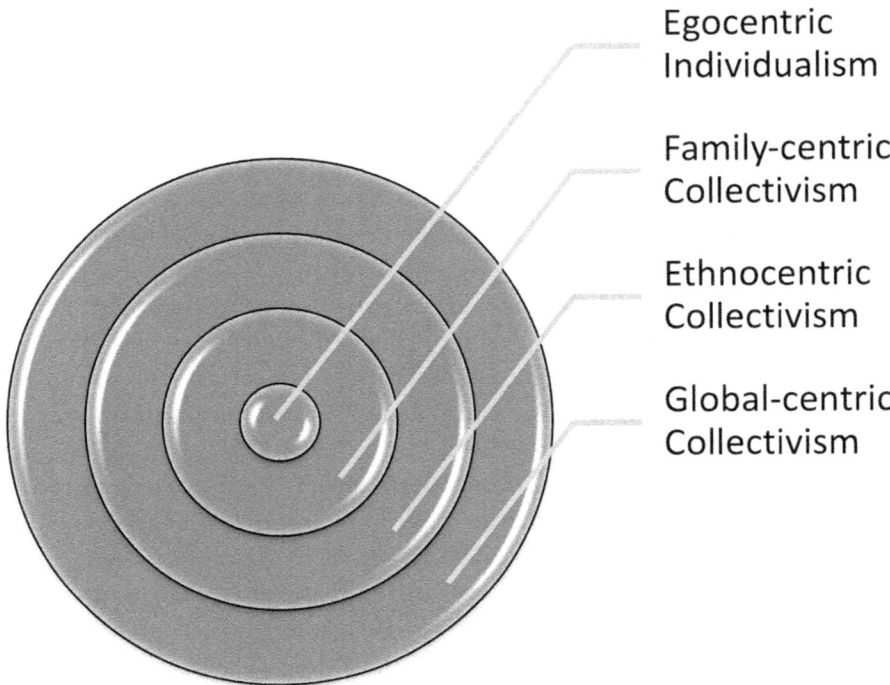

Figure 9.1. Individualism and collectivism horizons (Plueddemann 2009, 212)

Honor and Shame

The single most pervasive dynamic that influences the Iranian church on multiple levels is that of honor and shame. Iranians and other Middle Easterners struggle with overcoming the shame that shapes their worldview. The honor-and-shame paradigm interprets events, circumstances, and relationships through the lens of self-perception. In other words, the initial response is to filter everything through the issue of how others will perceive the event or conversation.

Church teaching must shift the emphasis away from the self as perceived by the community in terms of honor and shame, instead encouraging people to give up their honor through humility, and refocus the attention on God and loving others. To use Pauline language, the church is to "put off your old self, which is being corrupted by its deceitful desires; to be made new in the attitude of your minds; and to put on the new self, created to be like God in true righteousness and holiness" (Eph 4:22–24; see also Col 3:8–10).

The inability to distinguish between minor and major offenses, something that many respondents referred to, has roots in honor and shame. Any kind of shame creates a hurt or wound. The cultural heritage of Islam, and in particular Iranian

Shi'a Islam, coupled with the imagery of the Iranian Revolution with its cult of martyrdom and death, celebrated this shame. The church needs to reformulate the understanding of God, religion, and the human condition. "With some courage and imagination," Pattison suggests, "theology has the possibility of engaging with human hurt and healing in new and creative ways, enabling rather than imposing meanings, symbols, and images that enlighten rather than imprison" (2000, 300). What are some steps to help make this a reality in the lives of MBBs?

First, Pattison proposes that we focus on the fundamental goodness and value of creation and of humanity. There is a sense in which God has been creating and redeeming the world and its inhabitants since the beginning of time in a single movement. Insofar as people exist and participate in life, they contribute to the godly creative activity. As they join in the work of creation, they manifest aspects of the image and likeness of the Creator (ibid.). This kind of positive, holistic view of creation and human life is a powerful antidote to the morbid celebration of destructiveness, death, alienation, and stain found within Shi'a Islam. It also addresses the self-perception of shame, the sense that the individual is flawed in his or her innermost being and therefore is without hope for change.[63]

Second, Pattison's advice is to focus salvation away from the suffering of lost individual victims. The exaltation of victimhood can be death-promoting and life-denying. The Shi'ite continual exaltation of victimhood should be reimaged, with resurrection to life in Christ overcoming the death-dealing alienation of shame. The victory found in "Christ the Victor" and "Christ the Healer" theology should be common themes.[64]

Third, Pattison recommends that we teach and stress the biblical view of God's character. God is not a despot or super-father in the mold of Middle Eastern dictators. The image of God within Islam is essentially of one who is distant and authoritarian, demanding blind obedience and submission from his followers. MBBs' understanding of God needs to be reconstructed so that they can see him as a closer and more compassionate figure. The whole Bible is full of the love and compassion of God and his faithfulness to his creation, as seen in the covenants and in the person of Jesus Christ. The restoration of sonship (Luke 15:11–32) and the removal of shame through the adoption motif (John 1:12–13; Rom 8:15–17; Gal 3:26—4:7; Eph 1:3–14; 1 John 2:28—3:10) are themes that should be taught and emphasized.

In Islam, God's face is hidden from humanity. The Islamic understanding of God as "closer to us than our jugular vein" is used not as a consolation but as a

---

[63] Sandra Wilson identifies the effects of shame as leaving a person feeling uniquely and hopelessly flawed, and therefore different from and worth less than other human beings (2002, 9-10). For a more in-depth discussion, see her book.

[64] The work of Christ on the cross can be explained in various manners. For a fuller discussion of the doctrine of the atonement, see Beilby and Eddy (2006) and Mischke (2015).

tool of shame, for he knows us and judges us for our mistakes.⁶⁵ The concepts of God calling us friends (John 15:13–15) and of us being his chosen people (Deut 7:6; Col 3:12; 1 Pet 2:4–12) are powerful. In addition, the motif found in Johannine theology of our adoption and the removal of our shame as children of God speaks to the concept of self-shame by conferring on us an honor that comes from God and is ascribed, not earned.⁶⁶ Jesus reveals the possibility of courteous, respectful, inclusive relationships that overcome shame. He removed shame from individuals, such as the woman caught in adultery (John 8:1–11) and Zacchaeus with the crowd (Luke 19:1–10).⁶⁷

It is hard for Middle Easterners to analyze honor and shame objectively, for they feel the reality of it. Once people have sufficiently accepted the fact that God wants to move them from shame to honor, we can theologically reorient their deep feeling of honor and shame away from an egocentric individualism to a focus on Christ's love, humility, and self-giving love for others. U22M suggested that this requires proper, culturally relevant theological training for Iranian pastors.

Falsehood

Twenty-two people, or 44 percent of the respondents, expounded on some aspect of falsehood. Lying was mentioned as a significant aspect of Iranian culture, expressed through the cultural concept of ta'arof, which is tied to honor and is a source of disharmony.

The inclination to lie in order to guard one's honor needs to be replaced with a focus on a standard outside oneself, in addition to strong accountability groups in the church. God reoriented the newly formed nation of Israel at Mount Sinai through the Decalogue (Ex 20:1–17; Deut 5:6–21). In a moral sense, the Decalogue and Levitical laws brought an outside measure to morality that was guilt-based. The laws prescribing regular offerings for intentional and unintentional violations and other daily, weekly, monthly, and yearly sacrifices (Lev 5; Num 28) helped to reorient the Israelites away from their own honor to the guilt laws established by God. No longer was one merely shameful when the violation was made public,

---

65 Surah 50:16: "It was We who created man, and We know what suggestions his soul makes to him: for We [Sounds like the Trinity! Not even close they would argue] are nearer to him than (his) jugular vein." Yusuf Ali's commentary states, "Allah created man, and gave him his limited free-will. Allah knows the inmost desires and motives of man even better than man does himself. He is nearer to a man than the man's own jugular vein. The jugular vein is the big trunk vein, one on each side of the neck, which brings the blood back from the head to the heart. The two jugular veins correspond to the two carotid arteries which carry the blood from the heart to the head. As the blood-stream is the vehicle of life and consciousness, the phrase 'nearer than the jugular vein' implies that Allah knows more truly the innermost state of our feeling and consciousness than does our own ego."
66 Jerome Neyrey speaks of ascribed honor, in which value is given to a person in public based on one's family, bloodline, and heritage. Achieved honor is the value or worth given to a person based on what one has accomplished (1998, 15–16).
67 Kenneth Bailey's works on the parables (1980, 1983, 2008) highlight Christ's redemptive work in restoring honor and taking on people's shame.

but now—according to God's standard—the person was still guilty of sin, whether it was intentional or unintentional, known or unknown.

I am not advocating that the Middle Eastern worldview become only a guilt/innocence one, but that the notion of guilt be added to the current shame/honor paradigm.

Boundaries

The atmosphere in post-revolution Iran, and the unrest in other parts of the Middle East, has encroached on boundaries to the extent of pressuring children to betray their parents, which creates distrust on all levels (Taheri 2008, 89). This systematic violation of normative boundaries has resulted in societies with little or no understanding of where healthy personal boundaries lie. The result is a tendency to two extremes: either living with no boundaries or putting up impenetrable walls that do not allow others into one's life.

The domain of boundaries helps explain some of the disharmony experienced in churches. Several interviewees expressed that Iranians are "quick to express our feelings to each other" (E19M) and "quick to get close" (U18M, C5M, U9M, U10F, E2M). As Sandra Wilson writes, "The personal boundaries are either too permeable, allowing everything and everyone in, or impermeable, creating walls around us to keep everything and everyone out" (2002, 129). To help the church move forward, healthy boundaries need to be explored in the discipleship process. All too often pastors have fortress-like boundaries, creating an oppressive control reminiscent of Islamic regimes.

Many Iranians come with a naïve understanding that the Christian life is perfectly open and forgiving to the point of being lax. People are quick to get close and share intimate information without discretion or keeping a safe distance. The respondents expressed frustration that Western Christians have walls and are more reserved in what they share. This confusion over boundaries is normative for individuals and cultures that experience chronic shame. Wilson's table on boundaries can help the church identify overdependent extremes and inform the church of healthy boundaries.

The Burden of Baggage

Table 9.1. Table of healthy boundaries (Wilson 2002, 130)

Healthy Boundaries and Overdependent Extremes		
Too Permeable (Inappropriate)	**Permeable (Appropriate)**	**Impermeable (Inappropriate)**
I talk at an intimate level at the first meeting.	I don't overwhelm people with personal information. I allow time for trust to develop.	I don't ever open up, even to people I know to be trustworthy and caring.
I am overwhelmed and preoccupied with a person and his or her needs.	I am able to keep relationships in perspective and function effectively in other areas of my life.	I don't let myself even think about another person I'm interested in.
I can fall in love with a new acquaintance.	I know love is based on respect and trust; these take time to develop.	I don't let loving feelings ever develop for anyone.
I let others determine my reality.	I believe my perceptions are as accurate as anyone else's.	I am unwilling to listen to others' perceptions.
I let others direct my life.	I make decisions for myself based on God's leading of my choices.	I refuse to consider the opinions of others.
I don't ever notice when others invade my personal boundaries.	I notice when others try to make decisions for me, are overly helpful, or don't consult me about planning my time.	I never allow anyone to help me or give me ideas and suggestions, even when it is helpful and appropriate.
I sacrifice my values if I have to in order to be close to other people.	I am not willing to "do anything" to maintain a relationship. I have biblical values that are not negotiable.	I am never willing to change anything I do to please anybody.

Henry Cloud and John Townsend's book *Boundaries* (1992) is an excellent resource I have used to help explain what healthy boundaries look like.[68] In addition, some form of accountability structure needs to be introduced; perhaps a denominational superintendent or a healthy Western church can establish a strong relationship with the MBB church to help them through the labyrinth of relationship violations toward healthy interpersonal relationships, where boundaries are established and honored.[69] This mentoring relationship would require leaders

---

68 They have additional resources on their website, www.cloudtownsend.com.
69 Not all Western churches are healthy, but there are healthy churches with cross-cultural experience that can help. Denominations typically have a church health division to help transform stagnant churches into thriving churches. See examples at https://acts2journey.com/; http://growinghealthychurches.com; and http://go.efca.org/ministries/reachnational/church-health-transformation.

Where Do We Go from Here?

in the Western church with cross-cultural skills and experience to recognize inappropriate boundaries and help mentor MBBs toward healthier ones.

The Interpersonal Component

Interpersonal relationships are the area that the Middle Eastern church struggles with the most, their greatest challenge. Middle Easterners are very social people; therefore their churches reflect the great value they place on spending time together. However, miscommunication results in tensions. People quickly cross personal boundaries in their relationships and offend others. Gossip can grow out of indirect communication as a way to fill in the lack of information. Pastors are sometimes poor at communicating with their members and even lack trust among themselves. Meager attempts at interchurch cooperation, combined with revenge, envy, criticism, and judgmental attitudes, create an unhealthy environment in the church and present a negative example that can lead to disharmony in the broader body of Christ.

Conflict arises regularly, but the nascent church is not prepared or trained to deal with it. The normative leadership response is to hide or deny the existence of the conflict. Confrontation only leads to more conflict, and people eventually leave the church. Rarely does reconciliation or conflict resolution happen. There is little or no collective memory in Middle Eastern culture of dealing with conflict positively.

Conflict Resolution

Conflict and conflict resolution, as the areas of greatest weakness, require special attention. My recommendation is that a written protocol for how to proceed in conflict resolution be in place before the fellowship begins, and regular teaching on conflict resolution must be part of the church's curriculum and membership classes. It may be helpful to remember that conflict resolution is the goal of Western intervention, while conflict control or reduction is the goal of Middle Eastern intervention.

There are several obstacles to conflict resolution—in several areas. First, individuals involved in the conflict usually take a zero-sum attitude, in which everything is seen as being at stake in the outcome of the conflict and one's identity is directly tied to it. Strong beliefs are normative in the Middle Eastern experience; when one party believes the other to be misled and in need of correction, there is little that can be done. Mistrust and suspicion of outsiders, in particular of Westerners' methods, is normative. Recognition of the legitimacy of differences in beliefs and interests is a basic assumption of conflict resolution, but in Middle Eastern cultures it is often considered a weakness. I recommend that leadership model the reality that "agreeing to disagree" does not make the other an enemy, but rather that harmonious relationships are possible even with a diversity of opinions, where grace abounds (Eph 1:7–8; 4:32; Col 3:12–14; 1 John 4:7–21).

Second, honor and shame influence how conflict is viewed. In the moral dimension, shame/honor cultures are unable to distinguish between minor offenses, which are to be overlooked, and major offenses, which are to be handled immediately. The best way to resolve a conflict is simply to overlook the offenses of others (Prov 17:14; 19:11; Eph 4:2; Col 3:13; 1 Pet 4:8) (Sande 1997, 72–73). The Bible speaks about going beyond retribution, for God himself will judge (Rom 12:17–21). The focus of Scripture is breaking the cycle of violence and revenge with forgiveness (Matt 5:21–26, 38–48). Christians are called to not be overcome by evil but to overcome evil with good (Rom 12:21). In their teaching on conflict resolution, leaders must include a fuller understanding of the process of true reconciliation. The expanded teaching should include three necessary attitudes toward conflict (Wisley and Wisley 2006, 9–10):

- Conflict is inevitable (Job 5:7; Eph 4:26–27; 1 Pet 5:8).
- Conflict is an opportunity to grow and build stronger relationships (Rom 6:1–5).
- Conflict has a greater purpose than its immediate pain (2 Cor 1:8–9).

Teaching also needs to include the four obstacles people face when handling conflict, formulated by Wisley and Wisley (ibid., 39–46):

Category 1: Boundaries, or lack of them.

1. Complainants—People who allow others to violate their personal boundaries mainly because they don't want to "hurt others' feelings." The fear of abandonment or rejection leaves the gate open when it should be shut, then blames others for coming in. Treatment is awareness of this tendency and accountability.

2. Avoidants—People who shut the gates when they should let others in. The result is loneliness and isolationism. It takes committed friends who are willing to be patient and persistent to pursue the leader until a time when they are open and vulnerable, usually at a time of failure.

3. Controllers—People who don't respect others' boundaries. There are two forms: aggressive and passive. Aggressive controllers tell people how to think and how to live. Passive controllers use guilt and manipulation to get people to do their bidding. They need to be very forcefully challenged in order to change.

4. Nonresponsives—People who don't respond to others' needs or problems. They don't last long in ministry and require significant psychological coaching or therapy.

Category 2: Pride—a sense of superiority, a haughty attitude shown by people who believe they are better than others.

Category 3: Gossip and Slander—speaking about or listening to personal information about someone else, when one or both people are not involved in the problem or the solution. Slander is defaming someone else or speaking about someone with malicious intent.

Category 4: Manipulation—arranging things, people, and circumstances in order to promote one's own ideas. It involves deception, fraud, lies, and being a false witness. Flattery is part of manipulation as well.

The third obstacle to conflict resolution among MBBs is a lack of accountability. Accountability is a key ingredient in conflict resolution; where there is little or no sense of accountability, perhaps due to protecting the honor of the family and avoiding shame, there is little possibility of resolving the conflict. Often people fail to take responsibility for their actions and behaviors as they rely on outside help. The values of protecting honor and avoiding shame must change at the core through humility and the recognition that we are all sinners, and are capable of being wrong. Denial for the sake of saving face does little to address the real issues, particularly when wounds and consequences are still very much alive in people's collective and individual psyches. This leads to the mentality of victimization. In a collectivistic society, people may not recognize their own part in victimization. Therefore, people taking accountability for their actions is a key ingredient in conflict resolution.

Fourth, there needs to be teaching on the legitimacy of the other person in the conflict. If peace is understood as a superficial pacification without true justice, there will be no real peace.

Forgiveness

Forgiveness is an essential ingredient in conflict resolution. Wisley and Wisley define forgiveness toward another person as "an act of releasing the consequences for an offense they have committed against you and [ceasing to be] angry and resentful toward their behavior" (ibid., 72). Christians should forgive for the following reasons (ibid.):
- God has forgiven us, which is the ground of all our human forgiving (Eph 4:32).
- Christ tells us to forgive those who wrong us (Luke 17:3).
- We should forgive for the sake of being reconciled with the person who wronged us (Luke 15:11–32).

Minor offenses should be overlooked and forgiven, and the matter put behind us. When an offense is too serious to overlook, forgiveness may need to be approached in two stages: positional forgiveness, which is unconditional and a commitment one makes to God (Mark 11:25; Luke 6:28; Acts 7:60); and transitional forgiveness, which is conditional on the repentance of the offender

(Luke 17:3–5) (Sande 1997, 190–191). The progression from the offense to reconciliation includes the following components (Wisley and Wisley 2006, 85):
- Event—what has happened.
- Hurt—the initial stage, where the process of learning to forgive begins.
- Hate—the natural consequence of hurt if the one who is hurt can't forgive.
- Healing—the condition that occurs as one's hate is transformed by forgiveness.
- Reconciliation—healing provides the soil out of which new relationships can flower and bloom.

Acceptance of one's role in the conflict is another dimension of forgiveness. God is not to blame, nor is the community. A community is made up of individuals who are each accountable to God (Gen 4:6,7; Ps 14:1–3; Rom 3:9–18). Listening genuinely to others (Jas 1:19–21) is also important in forgiveness. Irani correctly notes that often "listening is drowned out by arguments in the never-ending struggle to get one's point across first" (1999, 3).

The pastoral role of caring for and nurturing individuals through the trials of life is a dimension of ministry that eludes most MBB pastors. There are several reasons for this blind spot. First, personal information has often been used against enemies in Iranian culture, and trust is a key ingredient if pastors are to care for their congregations effectively. This research has revealed that pastors who are friendly one year might have a grievance with the same person the following year.

Second, nurturing through pastoral care is often not understood by either the pastor or the members. Training in pastoral care should be informed through pastoral passages in the Old Testament (Ps 23; Jer 23:1–4; Ezek 34) and in the New Testament (John 21:15–19; Acts 6:1–4). In order to gain confidence and trust, pastors need to give time to listening and responding sympathetically and devoting undivided attention to the members under their care. Trust should be established during the first few visits, and once this is achieved the member is more likely to become loyal to his or her pastor.

Returning to the topic of forgiveness, another dimension is forgiving in word and deed (Col 3:12–14). Without forgiveness, there is no hope of lasting reconciliation. Wilson notes that forgiveness and reconciliation are closely related but not the same (2002, 160). Teaching on forgiveness must include teaching on boundary setting so that past abuses are not perpetuated after forgiveness. The biblical material on forgiveness through the story of Joseph in Genesis 37–50 and Jesus' parable in Matthew 18:21–35 should be part of the regular teaching. The following are a few principles for forgiveness (adapted from Wilson 2002, 162–68):

- Forgiveness is a realistic view of the hurt and hurters (Gen 50:20).
- Forgiveness is releasing the right to get even.
- Forgiveness requires admitting that forgiving is not merely difficult; it is humanly impossible (Gen 41:51).
- Stop cultivating bitterness (Heb 12:15).
- Be specific about the hurts and about forgiving the offender.

Humility is an important ingredient for conflict to be resolved. The parties in conflict must acknowledge unhealed wounds, as well as the emotions, viewpoints, and needs attached to them; humility does not pass blame to avoid shame and save face. Burying the wounds will never lead to peace. One valuable service would be a prayer and counseling ministry of healing for Iranians to overcome the political trauma many of them have experienced in Iran, coupled with the trauma of chronic shame. U9M said it best:

> "We are people that carry a lot of hurts and probably a lot of wounds with us. As you carry these wounds, as soon as people get anywhere close to you, you start hurting—let alone they touch you. Even though it might be just a casual touch not even meaning to hurt you, but still they touch you and you still hurt. That's why people are sensitive: because they have a lot of wounds that are not healed." (U9M)

When U21M started a prayer ministry in his church to heal the wounds from the egregious power struggle in the church, the church stabilized and began to grow.

John and Anna Travis talk about three types of deep-level healing prayer: breaking prayer, healing prayer, and deliverance prayer. Breaking prayer is largely based on Neil Anderson's *Bondage Breaker* (1990), which "deals with breaking spiritual bondage and is characterized by renunciation and repentance... . Breaking prayer is helpful in starting the process of inner healing, or in resolving issues which present themselves once the process of prayer for healing is under way" (Travis and Travis 2008, 108).

Healing prayer is asking the Lord to heal deep emotional pain. "This generally takes place as the one seeking healing (the prayee) and the one leading the prayer time (the pray-er) go together before the Lord in prayer, asking God to remind the prayee of any incident(s) where the prayee's heart was wounded" (ibid.).

Deliverance prayer is ordering out demons from the life of the person, praying with the authority given to us in Christ. Travis and Travis suggest that breaking prayer and healing prayer occur first, making the deliverance more straightforward. They conclude, "In short, deep-level healing is not an end in itself; rather, it is part of the larger divine plan of seeing biblical truth and allegiance to God made real in every human life" (ibid., 111).

Communication

The interviewees expressed frustration in the area of communication. They used terms like "superficial" (U19M), "delicate" (U18M), and "walking on eggshells" (U1F). They shared about their desire to avoid conflict and the shame they feel when they have to say no. Part of this communication style comes from high-context culture (Hall 1976), in which communication is indirect to avoid shame. Middle Easterners' communication patterns can also be understood in light of honor and shame. The unwritten rules intended to conceal family/societal imperfections are:

> Rule 1: Be blind to negative things happening in the family.
>
> Rule 2: Be quiet about secrets such as abuses in public or in the home. This often accompanies children into their adult lives.
>
> Rule 3: Be numb to feelings and personal boundaries.
>
> Rule 4: Be careful since your world isn't very safe. Trust is at the heart in this rule.
>
> Rule 5: Be good, which is a code word for perfect. (Wilson 2002, 42-50)

Communication will improve when several factors are addressed. First, the four obstacles people face when handling conflict should be replaced:

- Replace unhealthy boundaries with healthy boundaries (Mark 1:21–45; John 17:4) (Scazzero 2003, 132–51);
- Replace pride with humility (Jas 1:9–10);
- Replace gossip and slander with words that edify (Eph 4:29–32; 5:4)
- Replace manipulation (Rom 16:17) with concern for others (Rom 12:9–17; Phil 2:3–4).[70]

The second factor to address is broken trust. Trust will be restored when authentic, transparent, and positive relationships are established. Third, as MBBs experience healing of past wounds through breaking, healing, and deliverance prayer, they will be more receptive to conflict resolution and forgiveness.

The Family Component

The topic of women and their unique struggles featured prominently in the interviews and revealed a source of concern within the Iranian church in the diaspora. The area of male-female relationships was brought up by ten people, or 20 percent of the respondents, and women-specific issues were singled out by seven people, or 14 percent, in the interviews. One of the major weaknesses in Islam is the inferior identity and role of women in a male-dominated society,

---

[70] This list is a combination from several sources. Wisley and Wisley (2006, 41-49) list four hindrances to managing conflict: pride, gossip, manipulation, and culture. Scazzero (2003, 147-51) lists boundaries as a particular area of concern for emotionally healthy churches. My research shows that boundaries are an area in which Iranian MBBs struggle.

which has ramifications for MBB churches in the diaspora. Enormous pressure and many expectations are placed on Middle Eastern women in how they behave, dress, show hospitality, and respect others. Many women crave attention through their appearance and desire to find well-established Christian men, who are in short supply. Women desire equality and respect, which have been denied them in a macho male-dominated society. This is particularly acute among single women. Mature women from the host culture can greatly help the new believing women understand their role as Christian women and their place within the church.

The traditional large extended family and its influence on those attending church in the diaspora was not mentioned explicitly as a concern. However, the topic of family influence surfaced in other forms. Interviewees saw the way children are raised in the Middle East as significant in explaining current adult behavior in church. Overprotective parents, spoiling mothers, and authoritarian fathers are believed to stunt the maturity of children. Marital issues, including broken marriages, single parents, and child-rearing in a new culture, are problems the small, nascent church is ill-prepared to resolve. The traditional expectations and pressures placed on women follow Middle Easterners into the MBB church in the diaspora. The freedom of Western society exposes marital problems, and women are particularly vulnerable in the new role and identity they are given. The old male hierarchy found in some Middle Eastern churches creates visceral reactions from women, who are longing for greater equality in church structure and relationships.

My recommendation is for mature Christian women to establish mentoring and accountability relationships with those new in the faith. A healthy relationship with the national church can provide mature Christian women with cross-cultural experience, and these can mentor newer believers in parental discipline, marital issues, life and job skills, and discipleship where needed. There are many valuable conferences and much good teaching on DVDs that can help equip the teachers in the church to deal with male-female relationships, marriage, and raising children. Though these materials reflect a strong Western bias, the scriptural teaching is solid and can be incorporated into the church until Persian materials are developed.

The Power Component

Power, leadership, decision making, and use of finances are important factors to better understand in order to address the sources of disharmony in the Middle Eastern diaspora church.

Both clergy and laymen seek to be in positions of power, which often results in tensions, leading to splits in the church. The default setting for pastoral decision making reflects the strong authoritarian and dictatorial style of leadership in the country of origin, with little communication between pastor and congregation. Although the church seeks to reflect the democratic leadership style of the host culture—structurally egalitarian—functionally it remains under one-person rule, particularly in charismatic churches.

In the area of money, tithing is an unfamiliar concept to those from a Muslim background, creating suspicion about the use of finances. And since most churches are small, many pastors are bi-vocational. They need more time to minister to people and to deal with complicated problems in the church.

Many pastors are either self-appointed or selected by a national church, with little supervision for pastoral education, training, and mentoring, leading to problems within the church. Those pastors with strong teaching or evangelism gifts may neglect shepherding and caring for the people.

To summarize, misuse of power, lack of leadership skills, poor decision-making models, and distrust over finances are significant sources of disharmony, reflecting the nascent nature of the church.

Power Structures

Responses to the topic of power were deeply informed by the lack of trust within the community. Six people, or 12 percent of those interviewed, described the structure of power in the Iranian church, but many did not know precisely how the structure worked. Middle Eastern power structures tend to be authoritarian, and in the church this is particularly evident in charismatic congregations. As mentioned previously, Iranians are most interested in reducing the power distance aspects of the societal culture. MBBs come from a political context in which leadership is often exercised through the use of power to squelch dissentient voices. Forceful rulers impose their will upon the people. These patterns of governance invade church polity.

I recommend that the MBB leadership seek to understand the diversity in church polity and work toward a structure that is God-honoring and includes giving legitimacy to the voices and opinions of others. It is easy for MBB fellowships to slip into familiar structures of power and lose sight of the royal priesthood of all believers (1 Pet 2:4–12).

Donna Hicks has noted that intolerance of uncertainty and ambivalence is a way of measuring egocentrism. "The more one steadfastly holds onto beliefs, especially when there may be disconfirming evidence, the more egocentric (embedded in one's own perspective) is one's understanding of the world" (2001, 135). The interviews in my research revealed rigidity when conflict happens, particularly with the clergy; this may be a form of anxiety avoidance. Leadership styles range from weak victim to strong rescuer, as seen in the table 9.2.

Table 9.2. Personal responsibility and overdependent controlling styles (Wilson 2002, 133)

Weak Victim (Underresponsible)	Human Adult (Responsible for Self)	Strong Rescuer (Overresponsible)
I am so weak I am a "wreck."	I have strengths and weaknesses. I am a human being.	I am so strong I am a "rock."
I have no responsibility for anyone or anything.	I am responsible for myself and to others.	I am responsible for everything/everyone.
I can't change anybody.	I can change only myself.	I can change everybody.
I need someone to take care of me all the time.	I can take care of myself most of the time. I trust God to care for me at all times.	I will take care of you all the time.
Everything is "too much" for me.	Some things are "too much" for me, but nothing is ever "too much" for God.	Nothing is "too much" for me.
I desperately need you.	I desperately need God, and I long for relationships.	I desperately need to be needed.

Special attention must be given to pastoral leadership. Duane Miller notes that

> there is the individual context of each fellowship or congregation, which calls for pastoral creativity and flexibility.... This represents, among other things, a flexible approach to organization, as the community is neither a "'congregation," nor is it bound by denominational affiliation, and yet it does not cease to meet and, at times, fellowship with Iranian Christians from neighboring cities. (2012, 5)

Pastoral leadership is a major concern. I recommend that denominations or churches partnering with an MBB who desires to be a pastor regulate the process. Formal biblical training, pastoral internship, and accountability must be included in any partnership. Areas of specific weakness revealed in this study, such as the lack of biblical knowledge, personal insecurities reflected in Middle Eastern culture, a tendency toward one-person rule in church polity, or little or no understanding of pastoral care, must be addressed. In light of the loose, independent structure of Iranian churches, one Iranian leader in Canada (C2M) shared his ideas for cooperation among Iranian leadership in a five-point draft:

1. Leadership starts meeting monthly to get to know each other and build trust among each other.
2. Leadership conducts monthly interdenominational meetings, regardless of particular theological distinctives. These monthly meetings would show the

Muslim world in Toronto that we can put our differences aside and celebrate our unity in Christ through concerts, conferences, and worship services.
3. Leadership encourages each other by joint congregational meetings so our people can get to see the larger body of Christ.
4. Church leaders work together to organize special conferences to help our members grow in their walk in Christ.
5. Create annual events with the Assyrian, Armenian, and Arabic-speaking churches to discuss mutual problems they face.

The interviews revealed the propensity of MBBs toward hero worship and the idea that one person will come and make everything right. Furthermore, this study demonstrated that shame creates a desire for perfectionism, creating unrealistic expectations. "Perfectionism is an unhealthy pattern of thoughts and behaviors we use to conceal our flaws" (Wilson 2002, 88). The perfectionist proclivity shows itself when new believers think that when people become Christians they are to be perfect, inevitably leading to disappointment and disillusionment.

In order to address this inclination, I recommend teaching and preaching that includes the truth about who we are in Christ, including the dual teaching of how Jesus brings honor to us through salvation (John 1:12–13; Eph 2:6) and the fact that every Christian still carries around "this body of sin" (Rom 7–8; 1 John 1:5–10). In other words, God knows we are more sinful than we realize, but he loves us more than we can imagine. However, maturity does not happen immediately after teaching doctrine applied to specific areas of concern. It is a process. A mature church leadership that has built open and vulnerable trust relationships, combined with time for new members to form authentic relationships, will move the congregation toward maturity.

The Religious/Theological Component

The Iranian church in the diaspora has some good resources available in the domain of theology, including Christian missionary literature that deals with theological misunderstandings. Seventeen people, or 34 percent of respondents, spoke about how Iranian Christians understand spirituality. There is a zealous pursuit in the spiritual realm to live the Christian life. Nineteen people, or 38 percent of those interviewed, mentioned that Bible knowledge and theological teachings in their particular church are an area of concern.

The Middle Eastern worldview conceives of a spirit world in which God speaks directly to people and visits us in this world. Many MBBs are relatively new as Christians and have little knowledge or teaching on the Holy Spirit. Iranians are open to the gospel, but the flipside is that they are susceptible to the hyperspirituality of those who appeal to emotions. Spirituality is often understood to mean passionate worship, praying ardently, and seeking demonstrations of the Holy Spirit. In addition, MBBs are often overwhelmed with new doctrines that are similar to, yet profoundly different from, their Islamic training. They need time to process their new faith. New concepts such as the atonement, grace, Pentecostal theology, and Christology are difficult to assimilate into their worldview.

The lack of pastoral training and the fact that most pastors are bi-vocational may be responsible for the haphazard approach to discipleship. The national church can play a significant role in mentoring pastors and providing training not found within the Iranian church. Therefore there is a great need for discipleship that allows time for questions to be answered. Programs that are built on personal reading or content-heavy formal teaching do not reflect the Middle Eastern relational culture. Mentoring, as a relational approach, is far more effective as a methodology of discipleship.

Theologically, U22M noted that the doctrine of the atonement does not touch the Iranian heart. "Shame does not respond to forgiveness" (Cooper 2006, 83).

Table 9.3. Differences between guilt and shame (Cooper 2006, 82)

Guilt	Shame
Healthy guilt is specific about negative actions taken, rather than labeling itself.	Shame exaggerates what it has done, labeling itself negatively, rather than its behavior.
Healthy guilt focuses on specific things to change and resists clobbering with a totalistic judgment.	Shame attacks with all-or-nothing thinking and global generalizations.
Healthy guilt opens the path to self-forgiveness and is encouraged to accept its frailties. It sees the worthwhile person underneath the unhealthy behavior.	Shame does not respond to forgiveness.
Healthy guilt involves the sharing of failure and regret with trusted friends.	Shame drives itself into isolation, loneliness, and feelings of unique depravity. It hides from others and itself.
Healthy guilt stays with the modest agenda of looking for specific change, without threatening its own worth.	Shame does not motivate toward constructive change; it immobilizes in inactivity.
Healthy guilt lets go of grandiosity and unrealistic standards.	Shame is often linked to an ideal standard.
Healthy guilt sees the pointlessness of self-punishment and understands that it is a block to self-acceptance. It makes amends and leaves it at that.	Shame encourages some form of self-punishment in an irrational attempt to "atone" for what has happened.

MBBs tend toward legalism. There are at least two elements involved in this propensity to legalism. First, MBBs come from a religion based on legal righteousness. Islam is concerned more with orthopraxy, whereas Christianity is focused on orthodoxy. The second element is a shame-based concept of God. Coming from a chronic shame-based society, Iranians will struggle with feeling acceptable before God.

> All shame-based religious systems project expectations that distort and deny truth.... In shame-based religious systems, expectations of participants don't match the truth of spiritual growth and human imperfection.... And if they are shame-based Christian religious systems, sincere but problem-laden believers feel different and less than the mythical perfect Christians who are purported to fill the pews.... And this sense of shame leads to perfectionistic pleasing and performing to earn the right to live with, and relate to, God and other Christians. Thus, shame-based churches become extended family reunions. (Wilson 2002, 144)

Wilson's comparison of the characteristics of shame-based versus God-directed service is very helpful in understanding motivation in ministry.

Table 9.4. Shame-based versus God-directed service (Wilson 2002, 146)

Sanctified Overdependency (Self-Protective Manipulation)	Compassionate Service (Christ-Centered Ministry)
Motivated by self-protection and energized by self-effort.	Motivated and energized by the Holy Spirit of God.
Characterized by legalistic and joyless works.	Characterized by a sense of peace and purpose.
People become statistics or a project to be "won" or "fixed."	People are seen as being the same as I am, needing to be lovingly led to Jesus Christ as Savior and "fixer."
I enjoy serving most when the task is a monumentally big deal.	I enjoy all service in which Christ calls me, even if it appears small.
I demand external validation through public attention and appreciation and become resentful if I go unnoticed.	I can accept attention, but I don't demand it; I can remain unnoticed without growing resentful.
Serving is the primary source of my identity and sense of worth in the church.	My service is the outgrowth of an identity based on being a loved, redeemed bearer of God's image.
In the name of "Christian love" I bail out others, not expecting them to take personal responsibility for themselves.	I take responsibility for myself under Christ's lordship and let go of others to do the same.
I jump in and take care of others without waiting to be asked.	I give help appropriately when asked (emergencies excepted).

Where Do We Go from Here?

As the "server," I feel and appear competent and powerful (like a savior). The "served" feels and appears incompetent and weak (like a victim).	"Server" and "served" have attitudes of mutual respect whereby neither feels nor appears incompetent, for we both realize our roles might be reversed next time.
I use my business for God to numb painful feelings and distract me from unmanageable parts of my life.	My active serving is balanced with quiet times of prayer, Bible study, and meditation on Scripture, when I reflect on my total lifestyle.
I often feel burned out and bitter because I don't take care of my health and I'm unable to set limits.	I can say no to requests of others for I recognize my own limitations and need for healthy self-care.

Both emotional and spiritual maturity were mentioned throughout the interviews. I recommend that MBB churches in the diaspora take Peter Scazzero's emotional/spiritual health inventory (2003, 60–66) to objectively diagnose the level of believers' emotional maturity.[71]

Many of the categories identified in the interviews can be summarized in the early church's identification of the eight deadly thoughts of Evagrius of Pontus (345–99),[72] which were later reduced and reordered by Gregory the Great (540–604) into the seven deadly sins.[73] These seven sins are pride, envy, anger, sloth, avarice (greed), gluttony, and lust. They deal with attitudes, emotions, and states of mind that condition behavior in ways that are destructive to us and to those around us. The eight deadly thoughts describe the internal battle of the Christian with external demonic forces, with an approach to combat moral evil. Learning to overcome the sinful will of the individual is of the utmost importance in engaging moral evil. The goal is to move from moral evil to recovery and is described as moving from the outer (defilement) to the inner (guilt) (Tsakiridis 2010, 7).

Evagrius' list adds acedia, described as boredom or restlessness, which I have redefined as depression, a characteristic of some MBBs encountered in the research. Acedia, along with its remedy, should be added to the list of deadly sins to address the depression that some Iranians in the church experience.

---

[71] Scazzero's emotional/spiritual health inventory can be accessed at http://files.stablerack.com/WebFiles/80878/spirtualandemotionalmaturityinventory.pdf.

[72] The eight thoughts are gluttony, fornication (lust), avarice (greed), sadness, anger, acedia (listlessness or indifference, leading to despair), vainglory (envy), and pride. Evagrius addressed the external and internal nature of temptation, which is common to all. He wrote to encourage the spiritual journey of fellow monks; hence his categories do not necessarily mirror the same attitudes, emotions, or state of mind of those outside the monastic contemplative life. For more on this topic, see George Tsakiridis (2010).

[73] The contemporary church in North America has popularized the seven deadly sins, which have become a recognized part of moral theology. Billy Graham recorded seven consecutive broadcasts on *The Hour of Decision* in 1955, preaching on the seven deadly sins; these were then published in his book of that title (1955). The seven deadly sins have appeared in various writings, from religious to social sciences publications. For a popular treatment of the same idea, see Anthony Campolo (1987).

Working in the Middle Eastern culture, I added a ninth category of lying. Each thought is accompanied by a corresponding remedy or antidote.[74] I recommend that MBB pastors preach about these nine deadly sins, allowing them to address some of the more pressing moral and interpersonal disharmonies without being seen as using the pulpit to single out individuals.

Creating a context in which these weaknesses can be addressed is essential. It cannot happen in a large church meeting or Bible study. The group is too large to create the intimacy and vulnerability needed for individuals to open up and allow others to see the personal struggles they are going through. Familiar examples of the kinds of programs where trust and vulnerability are forged are addiction-recovery programs like Alcoholics Anonymous (AA) or Narcotics Anonymous (NA). These twelve-step programs are built on elements that can be incorporated into the church.

Three essential elements are needed in these groups. First is a community of trust. In a culture where anyone outside the family unit is viewed with suspicion, this is a major hurdle. Gossip destroys trust. The second element is a community of vulnerability. In a culture where private information is used in leveling others or to gain an advantage over someone, vulnerability is not achieved quickly. The third ingredient is a community of accountability. Forging a trust relationship for the building up of each other and holding each other accountable in the safe place of the small group and not outside the group requires discipline and wisdom.

For these groups to be successful they must remain small, between five to ten persons, and gender-specific—men with men and women with women.

Discipleship doesn't happen by osmosis. Teaching and preaching should include a three-step process. The Pauline model, as mentioned earlier, is to put off the old, renew our minds, and put on the new (Eph 4:22–24; Col 3:9–10). The putting off, the first step, goes beyond just correcting bad behavior (Col 3:5–9) and also addresses worldview assumptions out of which we act—which are often shaped by our culture, religion, and family values. Many of them have been mentioned in this book.

The second step is renewing of the mind, or repentance (Rom 12:1–2; Jas 3:13–18). To use Evagrius' terms, we develop virtues that redirect our emotions and passions to that which is good. The spiritual life is about developing virtues that can move our emotions and passions away from the default setting of the old nature and putting on the new self. Our old life is self-absorbed. It is all about how others perceive us. The old self puts on a mask to be seen as good in the eyes

---

[74] I have modernized the list to truth or integrity (overcomes lying), fasting (overcomes gluttony), chastity (overcomes lust and impurity), generosity (overcomes greed), meekness (overcomes anger), wisdom (overcomes depression or melancholy), diligence (overcomes indifference and laziness–acedia), happiness (overcomes envy), and humility (overcomes pride).

of others, while all the time we know that we are empty and broken. When our focus is ourselves, it becomes impossible to put on the new self. We can't make ourselves become something new.

The teaching of God's Word, along with the transforming power of the Holy Spirit, will move us away from a culture that is destructive and leaves irreparable relationships. Our worldview needs to be reconstructed to a new way of life that is Christ centered. Repentance redirects our life from being oriented against God to seeing ourselves within the broader purposes of God's love. Instead of using ourselves as the lens through which we interact with this world, we see everything through Christ. The apostle Paul gives us an example of what a renewed mind meditates upon in Philippians 4:8–9.

The third step is to put on the new self, which addresses our new lifestyle in Christ (Ps 15; Rom 12:9–21; Gal 5:22–25; Col 3:12–17). What is put off in step one must have its corresponding antidote, something that we must put on. That is why Evagrius and those who write about the seven deadly sins all provide the contrasting remedy to the sin. Therefore it is important that all three steps be included in the teaching, preaching, and small groups. If we just put off the old and put on the new without renewing our mind, we inevitably will return to our old behavior. All three steps are important to help new disciples understand the process of transformation and how to live a life that is pleasing to God.

9
Conclusion

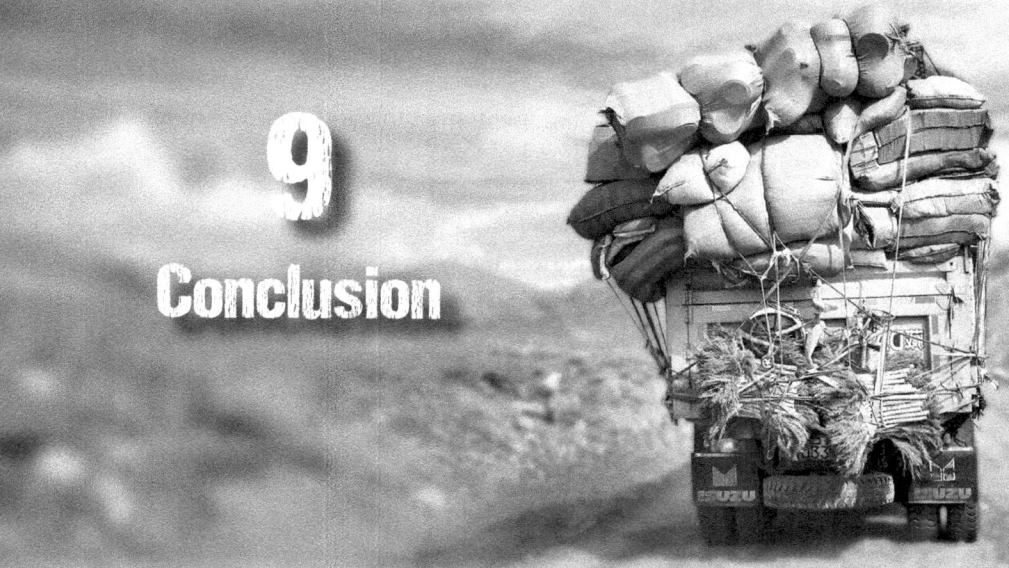

This book was written for the purpose of taking a closer look at the developing Iranian MBB church in the diaspora. The church experience of all interviewees who visited a church was, initially, extremely positive. They described it as a place of peace, hope, and love, something they had not experienced up until this time. The church is a place where new arrivals come to get help and where the culturally familiar greetings and hospitality are a welcome sight amid the harshness and upheaval of leaving home.

The language-specific church has a very important role to play in God's kingdom. The MBB church has spawned in an environment of hospitality, a theistic worldview, and a thirst for an authentic religious experience. MBBs are using their passion for God to witness to their compatriots who are coming to faith in Jesus Christ. Out of this context the Iranian church has been birthed in the diaspora.

It is important to remember that the Iranian MBB church is growing out of a culture that lacks a collective memory of the church. The collective memory is marked by the revolution of 1979 and its aftermath, in which Shi'ite Sufi Islam has dominated. Likewise, Middle Easterners who have gone through the Arab Spring are a people who have suffered greatly, and many have had their hopes crushed. Many deal with PTSD, having been spiritually, emotionally, and sometimes physically wounded. The hope for a normal life was crushed under oppressive Islamic regimes. In Iran, despair has given birth to high alcoholism, drug use, and suicide rates. Since it is out of this context of broken people that the church is born, the church naturally reflects this brokenness.

The Burden of Baggage

After all the particular struggles mentioned in this book, the question I hear is, "Is there hope for the MBB church?" Yes. God's redemption stops the cycle of revenge, hatred, and shame. God loves the church and intends for her to be his bride. Christ will present us spotless before the throne of God. God's message of peace, forgiveness, and reconciliation between God and humanity restores life to broken individuals. God is in the ministry of restoring life to a valley of dry bones (Ezek 37:1–14). He lifts us up out of the slimy pit of despair and sets our feet on a firm place to stand (Ps 40:2). This is the power of the cross of Christ. If the church is left on her own, she will not survive. But we have the power of the Holy Spirit (John 14:25–30; 16:5–15), the gifts of the Spirit (Rom 12:6–8; 1 Cor 12:4–11; Eph 4:11–13; 1 Pet 4:10–11), and the fruit of the Spirit (Gal 5:22–25) to help the church.

The particular challenge for the MBB church is the inclination to deny the weaknesses or to fail to confront the problem people. Confrontation is foreign in an honor/shame culture, which values relationships above all things. Moving the church away from a shame-based way of doing ministry into a more God-directed service model requires a major shift in worldview, something that may take a generation or two to happen fully. Changing the leadership style from an overdependent controlling style to one of instilling personal responsibility is equally difficult in the first generation. But it is important for the health of the leadership on a pragmatic level; and, more importantly, it reflects God's upside-down kingdom rule, exemplified in Christ (Matt 18:1–5; Luke 22:24–27).

Each culture has its own history that shapes a people's collective experience and their own peculiar set of challenges. I have taken a look at the specific struggles of the MBB church in focusing upon the Iranian church in the diaspora. Again, the purpose is not to expose the faults of the Iranian church to the world, but to give a voice to the many MBB believers who desire to be a part of a mature, growing church. I asked both pastors and lay people to describe their experience of the church, which was a mixed bag of both good and bad, as it is in every church. The unique set of challenges documented in this book will help the leaders of the MBB church to identify common areas of weakness and move the infant church on to adolescence and maturity. Creating healthy boundaries and moving away from the overdependent extremes requires boldness and emotional security. Developing healthy transparency and vulnerability is countercultural, but the rewards outweigh the discomfort of venturing into uncharted territory.

It is not my intent to bring dishonor to the MBB church through this study. I have great love and respect for what God is doing among the Iranians and other MBB communities throughout the world. It is my desire that this research be a mirror held up to the MBB church so that they can begin to prioritize and analyze

Conclusion

what is happening to move the church from infancy to adolescence, and on to adult maturity. Thankfully, we do not build alone. God has given his Holy Spirit to lead, guide, and empower the church. Jesus promises this:

> And I tell you that you are Peter, and on this rock I will build my church, and the gates of Hades will not overcome it. I will give you the keys of the kingdom of heaven; whatever you bind on earth will be bound in heaven, and whatever you loose on earth will be loosed in heaven. (Matt 16:18-19 NIV)

Appendix A
Research Methodology

The initial purpose of this research project was to investigate, describe, and explore the nature of conflicts within the nascent Iranian Christian church, examining the factors that lead to tensions. The research question that was investigated was, "What are the sources of disharmony in Iranian churches or fellowships in the diaspora?"

Thirty-one of the respondents were male and nineteen were female. The age ranges were (a) 15–24 (4); (b) 25–34 (6); (c) 35–44 (10); (d) 45–64 (29); (e) 65+ (1). Forty-two respondents, or 82 percent, came from a Muslim background; seven, or 14 percent, came from a Christian background. Three of the Christians were second-generation Iranians raised in the Farsi-speaking MBB church, whose parents became Christians from a Muslim background. Three of the Christians were pastors of Farsi-speaking churches and held significant leadership roles in the MBB churches. Only one of the pastors was American by nationality, but he grew up in Afghanistan. The seventh Christian came from an Orthodox Christian background in Iran, became a believing Christian in Iraq, and was attending an MBB Farsi-speaking church at the time of the research.

The distribution of respondents who left Iran in different time periods is as follows: 1960s (1); 1970s (9); 1980s (16); 1990s (11); 2000s (10). These numbers do not reflect the actual number of people attending Farsi-speaking churches. Since my research was limited to those whose language proficiency was adequate to understand the questions and respond in English, my interviews reflect only those who have left Iran and have had enough time to learn English. The years that they have been Christians also reflect this variable.

Selection of Interviewees

For the purposes of this research, I have limited my sample to the English-speaking countries of England, Canada, and the United States. I first contacted two key Iranian leaders who are widely recognized as leaders and itinerant speakers in the Iranian community in the diaspora. I requested their help in selecting other key Iranian leaders within each of the preselected countries to explore the possibility of interviewing Iranian Christians for the purpose of this research. Methodologically, I chose to use convenience sampling as opposed to systematic sampling. I specifically asked some people to be interviewed, but most people who gave responses volunteered. The purpose of the research was to collect stories of Iranian Christians, preferably from a Muslim background, in the broadest sampling possible.

Pilot Study

My questions were submitted to the two Iranian leaders based in the United States, who gave input on the selection of questions and their evaluations. Modifications were made based on their input. I also sought input from a clinical psychologist who has a family practice counseling Muslims and MBBs on family and marriage issues.

Then I visited three Iranian Christian leaders in a country outside my research parameters and presented them with the research questions. Their responses were very affirming. They stated that these questions framed issues that they were dealing with but did not have the opportunity to explore. The questions addressed areas that needed to be investigated, but the pressures of ministry and cultural limitations did not allow the pastors occasions to share their stories. One of these leaders remarked that the questions revealed that I understood their community and brought up issues that needed to be investigated.

I was concerned that the research questions would open wounds or sensitivities without bringing closure to the process, and that the interview process might encourage gossiping or cause problems because of the sensitivity of the Iranian community. I mitigated this risk by assuring each interviewee that no names would be mentioned in the dissertation and that any specific information that might identify a particular person or situation would be masked. The self-selection, along with guided input from key community leaders, minimized this potential problem. With these assurances, along with the human rights protocol, the interviews flowed freely.

I discovered that it was cathartic for the people to share their stories. They expressed gratitude that I cared enough to investigate this area and seriously consider their stories and concerns. They all expressed interest in the findings

Appendix A: Research Methodology

and recommendations, hoping that the research would produce solutions and direction for the Iranian church in the diaspora.

Data Collection and Recording

I personally interviewed all fifty respondents and recorded them on a digital voice recorder. My wife and I transcribed the audio recordings. It was necessary to edit the transcribed texts for several reasons. First, spoken English is structured differently than written text, thus editing took into consideration speech patterns in order to correctly transcribe the content. Second, most of the interviewees were native Farsi speakers, meaning that their English-language skills varied from poor to excellent. In order to make use of the interviews, we needed to focus on the conceptual meanings of the conversations instead of merely providing word-for-word transcriptions. Therefore, the transcriptions were done by me and my wife, who have worked among Iranians since 1985. Some of the responses would stray into personal history that was not relevant for the scope of the dissertation, so these parts were not included in the transcriptions. The purpose was to collect rich personal stories of disharmony between attendees and between attendees and leadership.

The interviews were meant to explore problem areas of behavior, beliefs, and worldview that lead to disharmony; how individuals and leaders deal proactively or reactively with problems within the church or fellowship; the experience of dealing with interpersonal relationships; and possible creative ways of discipling aimed at transforming problematic behavior, beliefs, and worldviews. In the interview process, I redirected the conversations back to the purpose of the study. At times it was not possible to redirect the conversation, so some material was not included in the transcriptions. To ensure accuracy in the transcriptions, we listened several times to the context to document the intent of the interviewees correctly and meet the parameters of the study.

Analyzing Data

The audio recordings were transcribed into 484 pages of text, and we coded the interviews with the qualitative data analysis software NVivo. The categories that were identified and analyzed came from the topics the interviewees determined as sources of disharmony in the Iranian church. The categorization of the interviews is my own. The coding began with the general categories and grew into eighty-three subgroups. For example, background codes were helpful in building a profile of the interviewees. The category of conflict was broken down into subgroupings, which were helpful in organizing the major heading of conflict.

In order to protect the anonymity of each interviewee, several precautions were used. First, I purposely did not record the name of the person interviewed.

Second, I used the digital voice recording identification number DS 400** to be the sole indicator of the file for each recording. Third, I created a code for each person interviewed. The first letter (E, C, or U) indicates the country where the interview was conducted. The number (1–22) indicates the order in which I interviewed someone out of all the interviewees in that country. The last letter indicates gender (M or F). Therefore, in the code E1F, E indicates that the interview took place in England, 1 indicates the first person on my list from that country, and F indicates that this person is female.

I considered personalizing each interviewee by creating a pseudonym but ruled against it for several reasons. First, since I did not use the name of the individual on the tape, I did not want to risk using the person's real name by mistake. Second, there might be the tendency within the Iranian community to try to figure out who said what, and other believers might try to connect the remarks with a real person they know with the same name as the pseudonym, thus causing needless tension. There needed to be a system by which the region or country and the gender could be identified to the reader, but so that no link to any person could be made. Thus I am using this simple system that identifies the country, another source, and gender.

Limitations

Several factors limited the scope of this research. Truthfulness is an extremely important ethical quality and is manifested strongly in personal relationships. Yet communication styles often use metaphors and verbal exaggeration in order to describe a matter, make a point, express an emotion, or contrast two ideas or events (Abi-Hashem 2008, 131). Knowing that exaggeration and embellishment are part of the communication style of Iranians, I sought to ask questions from multiple points of view to ensure accuracy. The interviews are straight renderings of the personal stories; they reflect the interviewees' personal perception of what they have experienced. I tried to keep the stories about their personal situations, as opposed to generalizations. When generalizations were made, I asked for a personal story to illustrate the point being made.

Language proficiency was a major limiting factor. Establishing a trusting and safe environment is foundational for Iranians, as high-context individuals, to openly share their thoughts. Since I am outside the community, I gained more trust. Being non-Iranian helped. I used my limited knowledge of Farsi whenever possible to establish connections with my interviewees.

Some of the interviewees viewed the interview process as a way of publicly sharing their particular grievances in a public forum. Even though the questions were predetermined to cover a variety of areas of the post-conversion experience, at times the response was focused upon the particular injustice the respondent experienced or on the singular weakness they felt needed to be rectified. But the uniformity in the nature of the responses was a good indicator that those who preselected themselves were not just disgruntled members. The variety of questions probed areas other than their particular grievances, so the interview was not dominated by their agenda.

I have taken into consideration the weaknesses expressed and have attempted to give a clear and accurate account of the Iranian church in the diaspora. The interviews have given greater insight into the state of the Iranian church in the diaspora and the challenges facing this nascent community.

Appendix B
Interviews

Number	Gender	Age	Religion	Residence	Left Iran	Years Xian	Years in Church	Other Churches	Place of Conversion
400052	M	45-65	Muslim	UK	1997	26	26	1	Iran
400053	M	35-45	Muslim	UK	1997	18	10	Several	Iran
400054	M	35-45	Muslim	UK	1998	9	6	Several	UK
400055/56	F	45-65	Muslim	UK	1988	16	16	1	UK
400057	F	15-25	Christian	UK	–	9	24	1	UK
400058	M	25-35	Muslim	UK	2000	8	8	1	UK
400059	M	45-65	Muslim	UK	1976	1	2	1	UK
400060	F	35-45	Muslim	UK	2003	7	6	1	Iran/UK
400060	M	45-65	Muslim	UK	1989	20	13	Several	Norway
400061	F	15-25	Muslim	UK	2005	5	2	Several	UK
400062	M	35-45	Muslim	UK	1996	15	8	Several	Germany
400063	F	45-65	Muslim	UK	2000	6	2	2 months	UK
400063	M	25-35	Muslim	UK	2009	1	7 mos	unknown	UK
400064	F	65+	Muslim	UK	1982	27	-1	Many	UK
400065	F	15-25	Muslim	UK	2004	6	6	1	UK
400066	F	45-65	Muslim	UK	1995	5	3	British	UK

The Burden of Baggage

Number	Gender	Age	Religion	Residence	Left Iran	Years Xian	Years in Church	Other Churches	Place of Conversion
400067	F	35-45	Muslim	UK	1979	20	20	1	Iran
400068	M	35-45	Muslim	UK	2000	9	11	Several	UK
400069	M	25-35	Muslim	UK	2009	8	6	Several	Armenia
400070	F	35-45	Christian	USA	USA	30	10	unknown	USA
400071/72	M	45-65	Christian Orthodox	USA	1987	40	24	1	Iran
400073/74	M	45-65	Muslim	USA	1969	40	12	House church	USA
400075/76	F	25-35	Muslim/ Christian	USA	–	17	3	Many	USA
400077	M	45-65	Muslim	USA	1991	31	21	1	Iran
400078	M	45-65	Christian	USA	1971	50	12 + 1 ½ yrs	12	Afghanistan
400079	M	45-65	Muslim	USA	1984	7	3 mos	6 mos in each	Dubai
400080	M	45-65	Muslim	USA	1987	5	8 mos	Several	USA
400081/82/83	M	45-65	Muslim	USA	1972	29+	7	Several	USA
400081/82/83	F	45-65	Muslim	USA	1978	28	7	Several	USA
400084	M	45-65	Muslim	USA	1980	27	4	91-03	USA
400085/86	M	45-65	Muslim	USA	1986	27	12	Many	Iran
400087	F	25-35	Muslim	USA	1997	18	11	1year 6 years 11years	USA
400088	M	45-65	Muslim	USA	1973	26	20	1	UK
400088	F	45-65	Muslim	USA	1983	20	20	1	Japan
400089/90	F	45-65	Jewish	USA	1979	42	5-6 1 ½	2	Iran
400091	F	35-45	Muslim	USA	1980	15	12/3	Several	USA
400092/93	M	45-65	Muslim	USA	1973	24	6	Several	USA
400094	M	35-45	Muslim	USA	1994	18	10	2	Iran
400095/96	M	45-65	Muslim	USA	2001	31	2	Several	Iran
400097	M	45-65	Muslim	USA	1979	31	24	Several	USA

Appendix B–Interviews

Number	Gender	Age	Religion	Residence	Left Iran	Years Xian	Years in Church	Other Churches	Place of Conversion
400098/99	F	25-35	Muslim	CAN	1997	14	7	Several	USA
400100/1	M	45-65	Christian	CAN	1988	15	9	Several	Canada
400102	M	45-65	Muslim	CAN	2000	6	6	1	Canada
400103	M	45-65	Christian	CAN	1992	29	4	Several	Iraq
400104	M	45-65	Muslim	CAN	1989	30	5	Several	Iran
400105/6	F	15-25	Muslim	CAN	1996	11	3	Several	Germany
400107	M	45-65	Atheist	CAN	1983	25	4	Several	Canada
400107	F	45-65	Muslim	CAN	1984	14	4	Several	Canada
400109	M	45-65	Muslim	CAN	1981	8	2	Several	Canada
400112	M	35-45	Muslim	USA	1984	27	4	Several	Portugal

Appendix C

Research Questions

I did not ask every question, but used the questions as a guide when the topics came up, so as not to prejudice the discussion. I began with a general question, such as "What are the doctrinal concepts that Iranians struggle with in church?" The questions that followed were built upon the response. If religion was mentioned in the discussion before, I referenced that remark and asked for more clarification. Satan, spiritual warfare, and fate were not mentioned in most of the discussions. On the few occasions when I referenced these subjects, they did not engender much discussion.

Personal Background Information

What city are you from in Iran?

Age: (a) 15–24 (b) 25–34 (c) 35–44 (d) 45–64 (e) 65 or older   Gender:

When did you leave Iran?

What religious background do you come from? (Muslim, Armenian, Assyrian, Baha'i, Jew, Zoroastrian, other)

What country do you currently live in?

What country were you in when you made a conscious decision to follow Christ?

How long have you been a follower of Christ?

How long have you been in your present church?
   What is the ethnic or racial mix of the church you currently attend?

Have you been in other churches? Did you leave a different church to join this one?
   Was it a Farsi-speaking church? Why did you change from one to another?

The Burden of Baggage

Questions concerning the Emotional Component

IQ[75]1.1: What has church meant to you? What has been your involvement in church?

IQ1.2: Every church has newcomers visiting. Can you tell me your story of when you started attending this church? How long did it take before people accepted you as being a fully participating member of the church? How did you know they accepted you?

IQ1.3: Some people say it is easier to trust non-Iranians than other Iranians. How deeply can you trust another Iranian? How do you know that you can trust a fellow Iranian? (Story)

IQ1.4: I have heard that there are religious police and civil police in Iran. Society and family have rules about what you can and cannot do. Islam has many rules. Do you know of someone who became a Christian to get away from all the rules and control? Should Christians have rules? Can you tell me a story of someone who is confused between freedom and rules?

IQ1.5: Can you describe a time when someone in the church was discovered to be living in sin? What did the leaders or the people in the church do? Tell me how the situation was handled. If not, how should the church handle this situation in the future?

IQ1.6: When someone is caught doing wrong, describe the process that actually takes place. If the leaders confronted the person, how did the person and their family react?

---

75 IQ means "interview question."

Appendix C–Research Questions

Questions concerning the Interpersonal Component

IQ2.1: Church attendance—Can you give me a history of how your church has grown? Is there any particular group of people who have trouble in being faithful attending church every week? Do you know of any situation in which someone has left the church community? Can you tell me a story of when someone or yourself left your church?

IQ2.2: Every country has customs in communicating. If your church has non-Iranians attending, do they understand the cultural way Iranians communicate when they talk? Can you give me an example? Can you tell me a story of when people misread what the other person is saying?

IQ2.3: The Christian community is supposed to get along with each other. Can you give me some stories of people getting offended in church and what happened?

IQ2.4: Have you ever been criticized by someone from church? How did you respond to the criticism? How does the leadership of the church respond to criticism? What do you think is the best way to deal with criticism?

IQ2.5: Forgiveness—How does the Iranian community view forgiveness? How do people in your fellowship view forgiveness? When do you know you are forgiven without any strings attached?

IQ2.6: People like to talk about others. Do you try to hide things from others to protect yourself? Can you explain why or why not?

IQ2.7: Every church has conflict. Some churches have more problems than others. How would you describe the way your fellowship handles conflict? Please explain.

Questions concerning the Family Component

IQ3.1: How did you find your husband or wife? Is your husband/wife a believer?

IQ3.2: Raising children is a great responsibility.
Are boys and girls disciplined differently or disciplined the same way in your culture?
When should the child be held responsible for his/her actions?

IQ3.3: Whose responsibility is it to discipline your children?
Whose responsibility is it to watch and control the children when you are in church?

IQ3.4: How much influence does your larger/extended family have on how you live your Christian faith?
Can you talk with them about your Christian faith?
Do they know you are a Christian?

IQ3.5: Can you tell me what role or influence your husband's mother has on you, on your husband, and on any family decisions?
Does she cause problems in the home or at church?

IQ3.6: Sometimes women marry at a young age in Iran.
Can you tell me some stories of families like this and how they integrate into the church?

Appendix C—Research Questions

Questions concerning the Power Component

IQ4.1: Every church has a way to make decisions.
Can you describe how your church makes decisions?

IQ4.2: The pastor of a church has an important job.
How much control or freedom does the pastor have to do his job in your church?
(1) Total freedom.
(2) Pastor needs to report at annual meeting.
(3) Pastor needs to report monthly to church board.
(4) Pastor needs to ask the board before he does anything. Please clarify.

IQ4.3: Sometimes groups or cliques form in a church.
Tell me about some of the groups in your church.
Do these groups cause problems in the church?
If so, in what ways?
Do people leave the church because they don't feel accepted by a group in the church?

IQ4.4: From an Iranian perspective, how do people in the church view someone who steps forward to take on more leadership responsibilities or positions? Please explain.

IQ4.5: The country of Iran has a history of violence. Often refugees have suffered physical and emotional abuse or oppression.
Can you give me a story in which past abuses affected how people interact with the authority in the church?

IQ4.6: The use of money in the church can be a problem.
Who collects and holds the money in your church?

IQ4.7: New arrivals to this country seem to have financial problems. In your church, can you tell me how money is used for the needs of new arrivals?
Are there any problems associated with money?

IQ4.8: When people come to the pastor for money, should the pastor have freedom to use and spend money?
Is it good to set limits on the way the pastor spends ministry money?
How do you think the church's money should be used? Explain.

Questions concerning the Religious/Theological Component

IQ5.1: Sometimes bad things happen to us, or some unforeseen problem comes into our lives.
How do you understand what is happening to you at that time?
Can you describe your response?

IQ5.2: Since becoming a follower of Christ, explain how you identify yourself to your family.
Do you have a different identity with people in the church?
What do you say to others about where you came from and what you used to believe?

IQ5.3: What Christian teachings do you find difficult to understand?

IQ5.4: Satan is our enemy and seeks to destroy us.
Describe some of the spiritual conflicts that you experience now as a follower of Christ.

IQ5.5: What are the strengths of the Iranian church and what are the weaknesses of the Iranian church?

Appendix D
Distribution of Interviewees

	United Kingdom	Canada	United States
Male	10	6	15
Female	9	3	7
Clergy	4	3	10
Laity	15	6	12
Conversion in country of residence	11	5	12
Conversion in Iran	4	1	7
Conversion in another country	3	3	4

Appendix E
Suggested Readings of Cultural Commentaries

Bailey, Kenneth E. 1973. *The Cross and the Prodigal: Luke 15 Through the Eyes of Middle Eastern Peasants*. St. Louis: Concordia.

———. 1980. *Through Peasant Eyes: More Lucan Parables, Their Culture and Style*. Grand Rapids: Eerdmans.

———. 1983. *Poet and Peasant* and *Through Peasant Eyes: A Literary-Cultural Approach to the Parables in Luke*, combined ed. Grand Rapids: Eerdmans.

———. 1992. *Finding the Lost: Cultural Keys to Luke 15*. St. Louis: Concordia.

———. 2003. *Jacob and the Prodigal: How Jesus Retold Israel's Story*. Downers Grove, IL: IVP.

———. 2008. *Jesus Through Middle Eastern Eyes: Cultural Studies in the Gospels*. Downers Grove, IL: IVP Academic.

———. 2011. *Paul Through Mediterranean Eyes: Cultural Studies in 1 Corinthians*. Downers Grove, IL: IVP Academic.

Campbell, Barth L. 1998. *Honor, Shame, and the Rhetoric of 1 Peter*. Atlanta: Scholars Press.

deSilva, David Arthur. 1995. *Despising Shame: Honor Discourse and Community Maintenance in the Epistle to the Hebrews*. Atlanta: Scholars Press.

———. 2000. *Honor, Patronage, Kinship and Purity: Unlocking New Testament Culture*. Downers Grove, IL: IVP.

Elliot, John Hall. 2007. *Conflict, Community, and Honor: 1 Peter in Social-Scientific Perspective*. Eugene, OR: Cascade.

Laniak, Timothy S. 1998. *Shame and Honor in the Book of Esther*. Atlanta: Scholars Press.

Neyrey, Jerome H. 1998. *Honor and Shame in the Gospel of Matthew*. Louisville: Westminster John Knox.

Glossary

Definitions come from a variety of sources. The primary ones are Hughes (1995) and Esposito (2003). Persian word translations come from personal correspondence with an Iranian translator in Canada.

Asheghetam—Persian phrase word meaning "I love you." The noun *ashegh* means "lover," or "someone who is in love."

Ashura—Literally, "the tenth," which is the tenth of the month of Muharram in the Iranian calendar. Ashura is the only day of Muharram observed by Sunni Muslims, being the day on which it is said that God created Adam and Eve, heaven and hell, the tablet of decree, the pen, life, and death. In the Shi'ite community, it commemorates the slaughter of Imam Hussein.

bâzâri—Small shopkeepers and the merchant sector, often the traditional middle class of Iran. They joined forces with the ulama and were a powerful force in influencing policies and politics in Iran.

caliph—Term adopted by dynastic rulers of the Muslim world, referring to the successor of Muhammad as the political-military ruler of the Muslim community.

Chap chap bé man négah kard—Persian phrase literally translated, "He (or she) looked at me left left," meaning "from the corner of his (or her) eyes."

Dar al-Harb—Literally, "the abode of war"; nations or regions of the world that are hostile to Islam. In some schools of thought a defensive war should be waged to protect Islamic interests.

Dar al-Islam—Literally, "the abode of Islam"; situation in which a country is ruled by Islamic law.

dhimmi—Arabic term best translated as "protected person"—a non-Muslim under the protection of Muslim law. Adult male dhimmis are required to pay a tax on their income and sometimes on their land. Restrictions and regulations are often applied.

din—Way of life for which humans will be held accountable and recompensed accordingly on the day of judgment. It can also be used for "religion."

Doosat daram—Persian phrase that means "I love (or like) you."

fatwa—A published opinion or decision regarding religious doctrine or law made by a recognized authority, often called a *mufti*.

fitna(h)—Literally, "rebellion, strife." Any sedition or rebellion against the rightful ruler is *fitnah*. Widespread fitnah is one of the traditional signs of the impending Day of Judgment.

gharibeh—Persian word in reference to a foreigner, outsider, stranger, alien, one who is not from your background, traveler, someone new to a place, or merely someone unfamiliar. It can also be used by "insiders" to refer to "outsiders," reflecting xenophobia.

hadiths—Reports of the words and deeds of Muhammad and other early Muslims. The Hadith, as a collection of such reports, is considered the second-most authoritative source of revelation next to the Qur'an.

Khoda(h)—Persian word for the Supreme Being, or God.

Power distance—A dimension of culture that relates to the degree of equality/inequality between people in a particular society.

Hijra—the migration or journey of the Islamic prophet Muhammad and his followers from Mecca to Yathrib, later renamed by him to Medina.

Hizb-e-Tahrir—Islamic Liberation Party, founded in Jerusalem in 1953 by Taqi al-Din al-Nabhani and former Muslim Brothers to revive the Islamic nation and purge it of vestiges of colonialism. It seeks to establish the classical model of the caliphate. Its focus is exclusively on the political and intellectual sphere.

ijtihad—Literally, "effort"; the intellectual effort of trained Islamic scholars to arrive at legal rulings not covered in the sacred sources. In the Sunni world, the door to *ijtihad* was closed in the ninth century. In the Shi'ite world, however, it has never closed.

Ikhwan al-Muslimin—Muslim Brotherhood, founded in 1928 in Egypt by Hasan al-Bana. It is the parent body and main source of inspiration for many Islamist organizations in Egypt and several other Arab countries, including Syria, Jordan, Kuwait, Sudan, and Yemen, and in some North African states.

Jamaat-e-Islami—Pakistani Islamic revivalist party founded by Mawlana Abu al-Mawdudi in 1941 in pre-partition India. It has developed extensive contacts in the Islamic revivalist movements in the Middle East.

jizyah—A tax formerly levied on non-Muslim adult males who were able to pay it, provided that they belonged to a religion recognized as divinely revealed—that is, "people of the book." Its practice is based upon surah 9:29.

MBB—Muslim-background believer, some prefer believer from a Muslim background (BMB) or Christian from a Muslim background (CMB).

madrasa—School or establishment of learning where the Islamic subjects and sciences are taught.

maslak—Islamic term meaning a particular sect or version of Islam. Each school (madrasa) claims authority from the Qur'an, the Hadith, and Islamic jurisprudence (*fiqh*) to support their claim of leadership. They include, but are not limited to, Dar ul-Ulum, Deobandis, Shi'as, Barelvis, Ahl-i-Hadith, and Jamaat-e-Islami.

mullah—Title used to identify a religious functionary, cleric, learned man, or someone with a religious education. Mullahs are the principal interpreters of Islamic law for Shi'ites.

Glossary

Noruz—Iranian New Year, celebrated on the first day of spring.

Safavid dynasty—A dynasty that ruled Persia from 1501 to 1722. The Safavids made Twelve-Imam Shi'ism the state religion, thereby establishing the basis for internal unity but tending also to isolate Persia from its Sunni neighbors, as well as laying it open to the tensions inherent in Shi'ism.

Sira of Muhammad—The biography of Muhammad and the Rightly Guided Caliphs (saints following Muhammad). The Sira is often considered the third-most authoritative source for Islamic practice and laws.

ta'arof—Persian word referring to the flattery and false modesty used to make another person feel good and to preserve a degree of social harmony.

taghdir—From the Arabic *takdir*; a decree existing in the divine mind from all eternity. Synonyms are "predeterminism," "fate," and "destiny"—as determined and fixed.

taqiyeh—Literally, "guarding oneself." A Shi'a doctrine of dissimulation. A pious fraud whereby the Shi'a Muslim believes he is justified in either smoothing down or in denying the peculiarities of his religious belief in order to save himself from religious persecution.

taqlid—Literally, "to hangaround the neck." In religious terms, it means blind imitation of the past. In law, it is the reliance upon the decisions and precedents set in the past. Often considered the opposite of *ijtihad*. In many modernizing Islamic societies today, the word has become pejorative, implying what is old-fashioned and retrogressive.

ulema—Plural of *alim*, meaning "one who knows"; learned; a scholar. Those learned ones who have been trained in religious sciences of the Qur'an, the Hadith, *fiqh*, etc. They formulate Islamic theology and issue fatwas.

Velâyat-e-Faqih—Rule or guardianship of an Islamic jurist, or reign of Iran's mullahs. The concept derives from the historical understanding that the exclusive right of interpretation of Islamic law belongs to religious scholars. It became the form of Islamic government when Khomeini came to power in 1979.

yekdadeh—Persian word meaning "solo," "single," "one."

Yeki bood yeki nabood—Persian phrase used in children's stories, the equivalent of "Once upon a time."

References

Abi-Hashem, Naji. 2008. "Arab Americans." In *Ethnocultural Perspectives on Disasters and Trauma: Foundations, Issues, and Applications,* edited by Anthony J. Marsella, Jeannette L. Johnson, Patricia Watson, and Jan Gryczynski, 115–74. New York: Springer.

Abu-Lughod, Lila. 1985. "Honor and the Sentiments of Loss in a Bedouin Society. *American Ethnologist* 12, no. 2: 245–61. http://www.jstor.org/stable/644219.

Abu-Nimer, Mohammed. 1999. "Conflict Resolution in an Islamic Context." *Peace and Change* 21, no. 1: 22–40. https://www.researchgate.net/publication/229801843_Conflict_resolution_in_an_Islamic_context_Some_conceptual_questions.

———. 1996b. "Conflict Resolution Approaches: Western and Middle Eastern Lessons and Possibilities." *The American Journal of Economics and Sociology* 55, no. 1: 35–52. http://www.jstor.org/stable/3487672.

———. 1998. Conflict resolution training in the Middle East: Lessons to be learned. In *International Negotiation* 3: 99–116 http://www.jstor.org/stable/3487672.

———. 2001. Conflict Resolution, Culture, and Religion: Toward a Training Model of Interreligious Peacebuilding. *Journal of Peace Research* 38, no. 6: 685–704. http://www.jstor.org/stable/425559.

Ahmed, Akbar. 1992. *Postmodernism and Islam: Predicament and Promise.* New York: Routledge.

Alamdari, Kazem. 2005. "The Power Structure of the Islamic Republic of Iran: Transition from Populism to Clientelism, and Militarization of the Government." *Third World Quarterly* 26, no. 8: 1285–301.

Al-Ashqar, Umar Sulaiman. 1998. *The World of the Jinn and Devils.* Boulder, CO: Al-Basheer.

Al-Attas, Seyd Muhammad al-Naquib. 1979. *Aims and Objectives of Islamic Education.* London: Hodder and Stoughton; Jeddah, Saudi Arabia: King Abdulaziz University.

Alexander, Claire E. 2000. *The Asian Gang: Ethnicity, Identity and Masculinity.* Oxford: Berg.

Alexander, Jeffrey C. et al. 2004. *Cultural Trauma and Collective Identity*. Oakland: University of California Press.

Al-Yahya, Khalid O. 2008. "Power-Influence in Decision Making, Competence Utilization, and Organizational Culture in Public Organizations: The Arab World in Comparative Perspective." *Journal of Public Administration Research and Theory* 19: 385–407.

Anderson, Neil T. 1990. *The Bondage Breaker*. Eugene, OR: Harvest House.

Arterburn, Stephen, and Jack Felton. 1991. *Toxic Faith: Understanding and Overcoming Religious Addiction*. Nashville: Oliver-Nelson Books.

Azumah, John. 2001. *The Legacy of Arab-Islam in Africa: A Quest for Inter-Religious Dialogue*. Oxford: Oneworld.

Babbie, Earl. 2007. *The Practice of Social Research*. Belmont, CA: Thomson Wadsworth.

Bailey, Kenneth E. 1973. *The Cross and the Prodigal: Luke 15 Through the Eyes of Middle Eastern Peasants*. St. Louis: Concordia.

———. 1980. *Through Peasant Eyes: More Lucan Parables, Their Culture and Style*. Grand Rapids: Eerdmans.

———. 1983. *Poet and Peasant* and *Through Peasant Eyes: A Literary-Cultural Approach to the Parables in Luke*, combined ed. Grand Rapids: Eerdmans.

———. 1992. *Finding the Lost: Cultural Keys to Luke 15*. St. Louis: Concordia.

———. 2003. *Jacob and the Prodigal: How Jesus Retold Israel's Story*. Downers Grove, IL: IVP.

———. 2008. *Jesus Through Middle Eastern Eyes: Cultural Studies in the Gospels*. Downers Grove, IL: IVP Academic.

———. 2011. *Paul Through Mediterranean Eyes: Cultural Studies in 1 Corinthians*. Downers Grove, IL: IVP Academic.

Bar-Tal, Daniel. 2001. Why Does Fear Override Hope in Societies Engulfed by Intractable Conflict, as It Does in the Israeli Society? *International Society of Political Psychology* 22, no. 3: 601–27. http://www.jstor.org/stable/3792428.

Ba-Yunus, Ilyas. 1988. Al Faruqi and Beyond: Future Directions in Islamization of Knowledge." *The American Journal of Islamic Social Science* 5, no. 1: 13–28.

Bearman, P. J., Th. Bianquis, C. E. Bosworth, E. Van Donzel, and W. P. Heinrichs, eds. 2000. *The Encyclopaedia of Islam*. Leiden, Netherlands: Brill.

Beekun, Rafik, and Gamal Badawi. 1999. "The Leadership Process in Islam." http://makkah.files.wordpress.com/2006/11/ldrpro.pdf.

Beeman, William O. 1986. *Language, Status, and Power in Iran*. Bloomington, IN: Indiana University.

Behjati-Sabet, Afsaneh, and Natalie A. Chambers. 2005. "People of Iranian Descent." In *Cross-Cultural Caring: A Handbook for Health Professionals,* 2nd ed., edited by Nancy Waxler-Morrison, Joan M. Anderson, Elizabeth Richardson, and Natalie A. Chambers, 127–61. Toronto: UBC.

Beilby, James K., and Paul R. Eddy. 2006. *The Nature of the Atonement: Four Views*. Downers Grove, IL: IVP Academic.

References

Bennett, Clinton. 2005. *Muslims and Modernity: An Introduction to the Issues and Debates.* New York: Continuum.

Bozorgmehr, Mehdi. 1998. "From Iranian Studies to Studies of Iranians in the United States." *Iranian Studies* 31, no. 1: 5–30. http://www.jstor.org/stable 4311116.

Bradley, Mark. 2008. *Iran and Christianity: Historical Identity and Present Relevance.* New York: Continuum International.

Campbell, Barth L. 1998. *Honor, Shame, and the Rhetoric of 1 Peter.* Atlanta: Scholars.

Campolo, Anthony. 1987. *Seven Deadly Sins.* Wheaton, IL: Victor.

Cloud, Henry, and John Townsend. 1992. *Boundaries: When to Say Yes, How to Say No to Take Control of Your Life.* Grand Rapids: Zondervan.

Cohen, Robin. 1996. "Diasporas and the Nation-State: From Victims to Challengers." *International Affairs* 72, no. 3: 507–20. http://www.jstor.org/stable/2625554.

Cook, Michael, and Patricia Crone. 1977. *Hagarism: The Making of the Islamic World.* New York: Cambridge University.

Cooper, Terry D. 2006. *Making Judgments without Being Judgmental: Nurturing a Clear Mind and a Generous Heart.* Downers Grove, IL: IVP.

Dastmalchian, Ali, Mansour Javidan, and Kamran Alam. 2001. "Effective Leadership and Culture in Iran: An Empirical Study." *Applied Psychology: An International Review* 50, no. 4: 532–58. http://www.fhfulda.de/fileadmin/Fachbereich_SW/Downloads/Profs/Wolf/Studies/iran/Iran.pdf.

De Bellaigue, Christopher. 2012. "Talk Like an Iranian." *The Atlantic,* August 22. http://www.theatlantic.com/magazine/archive/2012/09/talk-like-an-iranian/309056/.

De Dreu, C. K. W., J. C. H. Blom, L. Hagendoorn, D. J. M. Hilhorst, K. E. Giller, J. Potters, and G. A. Wiegers. 2007. *Conflict: Functions, Dynamics, and Cross-Level Influences.* Amsterdam: Netherlands Organization for Scientific Research.

De Silva, David Arthur. 1995. *Despising Shame: Honor Discourse and Community Maintenance in the Epistle to the Hebrews.* Atlanta: Scholars.

———. 2000. *Honor, Patronage, Kinship and Purity: Unlocking New Testament Culture.* Downers Grove, IL: IVP.

Ebadi, Shirin. 2007. *Iran Awakening: One Woman's Journey to Reclaim Her Life and Country.* New York: Random House.

Elliot, John Hall. 2007. *Conflict, Community, and Honor: 1 Peter in Social-Scientific Perspective.* Eugene, OR: Cascade.

Elmer, Duane. 1993. *Cross-Cultural Conflict: Building Relationships for Effective Ministry.* Downers Grove, IL: IVP.

Esposito, John L. 2003. *The Oxford Dictionary of Islam.* New York: Oxford University Press.

Forbis, William H. 1981. *Fall of the Peacock Throne: The Story of Iran.* New York: McGraw-Hill.

Foster, George M. 1965. "Peasant Society and the Image of Limited Good." *American Anthropologist* 67 (April): 293–315.

Friedman, Ray, Shu-Cheng Chi, and Leigh Anne Liu. 2006. "An Expectancy Model of Chinese-American Differences in Conflict-Avoiding." *Journal of International Business Studies* 37, no. 1: 76–91. http://www.jstor.org/stable/3875216.

Garrison, David. 2014. *A Wind in the House of Islam: How God Is Drawing Muslims around the World to Faith in Jesus Christ*. Monument, CO: WIGTake Resources.

Geller, Armando. 2008. "Power Structures, Small World Networks, and Conflict in Afghanistan." http://www.psa.ac.uk/journals/pdf/5/2008/Geller.pdf.

Ghahremani, Zohreh Khazai. 2011. "Yeki Bood Yeki Nabood: Our Culture—Assaulted as It May Seem—Still Maintains Its Profound Beauty." *The Iranian*. http://www.iranian.com/main/2011/feb/yeki-bood-yeki-nabood.

Good, Byron J., Mary-Jo DelVecchio Good, and Robert Moradi. 1985. "The Interpretation of Iranian Depressive Illness and Dysphoric Affect." In *Culture and Depression: Studies in the Anthropology and Cross-Cultural Psychiatry of Affect and Disorder*, edited by Arthur Kleinman and Byron Good, 369–428. Berkeley: University of California.

Goode, Reema. 2010. *Which None Can Shut: Remarkable True Stories of God's Miraculous Work in the Muslim World*. Carol Stream, IL: Tyndale House.

Graham, Billy. 1955. *The Seven Deadly Sins*. Grand Rapids: Zondervan.

Greenlee, David H., ed. 2013. *Longing for Community: Church, Ummah, or Somewhere in Between?* Pasadena, CA: William Carey Library.

Hall, Edward T. 1976. *Beyond Culture*. New York: Anchor.

———, and Mildred Reed Hall. 1990. *Understanding Cultural Differences: Germans, French and Americans*. Yarmouth, ME: Intercultural.

Helmick, Raymond G., and Rodney L. Petersen, eds. 2001. *Forgiveness and Reconciliation: Religion, Public Policy, and Conflict Transformation*. Philadelphia: Templeton Foundation.

Hesselgrave, David J. 1980. *Planting Churches Cross-Culturally: North America and Beyond*. Grand Rapids: Baker.

Hicks, Donna. 2001. "The Role of Identity Reconstruction in Promoting Reconciliation." In *Forgiveness and Reconciliation: Religion, Public Policy, and Conflict Transformation*, edited by Raymond G. Helmick and Rodney L. Petersen, 129–50. Philadelphia: Templeton Foundation.

Hiebert, Paul G. 2008. *Transforming Worldviews: An Anthropological Understanding of How People Change*. Grand Rapids: Baker Academic.

———, R. Daniel Shaw, and Tite Tiénou. 1999. *Understanding Folk Religion: A Christian Response to Popular Beliefs and Practices*. Grand Rapids: Baker.

Hodgson, Marshall G. S. 1977. *The Classical Age of Islam*. Vol. 1 of *The Venture of Islam: Conscience and History in a World Civilization*. Chicago: University of Chicago.

Hofstede, Geert. 1991. *Cultures and Organizations: Software of the Mind*. London: McGraw-Hill.

———. 2001. *Culture's Consequences: Comparing Values, Behaviors, Institutions, and Organizations Across Nations*. 2nd ed. Thousand Oaks, CA: Sage.

References

https://www.hofstede-insights.com/country/iran/House, R. J., P. J. Hanges, M. Javidan, P. W. Dorfman, and V. Gupta. 2004. *Culture, Leadership, and Organizations: The GLOBE Study of 62 Societies*. Thousand Oaks, CA: Sage.

Houtsma, M. Th., A. J. Wensinck, T. W. Arnold, W. Heffening, and E. Lévi-Provençal, eds. 1913–36. *First Encyclopaedia of Islam*. Leiden, Netherlands: Brill.

Hughes, Thomas Patrick. 1995. *A Dictionary of Islam*. New Delhi: Asian Educational Services.

Ibrahim, Raymond. 2007. *The Al Qaeda Reader*. New York: Broadway.

Irani, George E. 1999. "Islamic Mediation Techniques for Middle East Conflicts." *Middle East Review of International Affairs* 3, no. 2. https://www.mediate.com/articles/mideast.cfm.

Kelman, Herbert. 1997. "Social Psychological Dimensions of International Conflict." In *Peace-Making in International Conflict*, edited by W. I. Zartman and L. J. Rasmussen. Washington, DC: U.S. Institute of Peace.

Khalidi, Tarif. 2009. *Images of Muhammad: Narratives of the Prophet in Islam Across the Centuries*. New York: Doubleday.

Khan, Muhammad Muhsin. 1979. *The Translation of the Meanings of Sahih al-Bukhari*, vol. 8. Chicago: Kazi.

King, Diane E. 2005. "Asylum Seekers / Patron Seekers: Interpreting Iraqi Kurdish Migration." *Human Organization* 64, no. 4: 316–26. http://uky.academia.edu/DianeEKing/Papers/90116/Asylum_Seekers_Patron_Seekers_Interpreting_Iraqi_Kurdish_Migration.

Kraft, Charles H. 1993. *Deep Wounds, Deep Healing: Discovering the Vital Link between Spiritual Warfare and Inner Healing*. Ann Arbor, MI: Servant.

Kraft, Kathryn Ann. 2007. "Community and Identity among Arabs of a Muslim Background Who Choose to Follow a Christian Faith." PhD diss., University of Bristol.

Laniak, Timothy S. 1998. *Shame and Honor in the Book of Esther*. Atlanta: Scholars Press.

Laroui, Abdallah. 1976. *The Crisis of the Arab Intellectual: Traditionalism or Historicism?* Translated by Diarmid Cammell. Berkeley: University of California.

Lewis, Bernard. 1995. *The Middle East: A Brief History of the Last 2,000 Years*. New York: Touchstone.

Little, Don. 2009. "Effective Insider Discipling: Helping Arab World Believers from Muslim Backgrounds Persevere and Thrive in Community." Unpublished thesis, Gordon-Conwell Theological Seminary.

———. 2015. *Effective Discipling in Muslim Communities: Scripture, History, and Seasoned Practices*. Downers Grove, IL: IVP Academic.

Love, Rick. 2000. *Muslims, Magic and the Kingdom of God*. Pasadena, CA: William Carey Library.

Mackey, Sandra. 1996. *The Iranians: Persia, Islam and the Soul of a Nation*. New York: Plume.

McIntosh, Phyllis. 2004. "Iranian-Americans Reported among Most Highly Educated in U.S." *FarsiNet*, January 26. http://www.farsinet.com/farsinet/iranian_americans.html.

Mercadante, Linda A. 2000. "Anguish: Unraveling Sin and Victimization." *Anglican Theological Review* 82, no. 2: 283–302.

Mernissi, Fatema. 1992. *Islam and Democracy: Fear of the Modern World*. Translated by Mary Jo Lakeland. Cambridge, MA: Perseus.

Miller, Darrow L., with Stan Guthrie. 1998. *Discipling Nations: The Power of Truth to Transform Cultures*. Seattle: YWAM.

Miller, Duane Alexander. 2012. "Iranian Diaspora Christians in the American Midwest and Scotland." *Global Missiology* 9, no. 2: 1–9. http://ojs.globalmissiology.org/index.php/english/article/view/720/1772.

Min, Pyong Gap, and Mehdi Bozorgmehr. 2000. "Immigrant Entrepreneurship and Business Patterns: A Comparison of Koreans and Iranians in Los Angeles." *International Migration Review* 34, no. 3: 707–38. http://www.jstor.org/stable/2675942.

Mischke, Werner. 2010. "Honor and Shame in Cross-Cultural Relationships." http://beautyofpartnership.org/about/free.

———. 2015. *The Global Gospel: Achieving Missional Impact in Our Multicultural World*. Scottsdale, AZ: Mission ONE.

Mobasher, Mohsen. 2006. "Cultural Trauma and Ethnic Identity Formation among Iranian Immigrants in the United States." *American Behavioral Scientist* 50: 100–117.

Muller, Roland. 2000. *Honor and Shame: Unlocking the Door*. Bloomington, IN: Xlibris.

———. 2013. *The Messenger, the Message and the Community: Three Critical Issues for the Cross-Cultural Church Planter*. Surrey, BC: CanBooks.

Musk, Bill. 1989. *The Unseen Face of Islam: Sharing the Gospel with Ordinary Muslims*. East Sussex, UK: Monarch.

Nasr, Seyyed Hossein. 1987. *Traditional Islam in the Modern World*. New York: Columbia University.

Nathanson, Donald. 1992. *Shame and Pride*. New York: W. W. Norton.

Neyrey, Jerome H. 1998. *Honor and Shame in the Gospel of Matthew*. Louisville: Westminster John Knox.

Nizami, Abu Yusaf Afzaluddin, and Mukhtar Chaudhry. 1993. *A Comprehensive Interpretation of Dreams*. Lahore, Pakistan: Mavra.

Noble, Lowell L. 1975. *Naked and Not Ashamed: An Anthropological, Biblical, and Psychological Study of Shame*. Jackson, MI.

Noor, Farish A. 2003. "What Is the Victory of Islam? Towards a Different Understanding of the Ummah and Political Success in the Contemporary World." In *Progressive Muslims*, edited by Omid Safi, 320–32. Oxford: Oneworld.

Patai, Raphael. 2007. *The Arab Mind*. Long Island City, NY: Hatherleigh.

Pattison, Stephen. 2000. *Shame: Theory, Therapy, Theology*. New York: Cambridge University.

———. 2011. "Shame and the Unwanted Self." In *The shame Factor: How Shame Shapes Society*, edited by Robert Jewett, 9–29. Eugene, OR: Cascade.

References

Pitt-Rivers, Julian. 1966. "Honour and social status." In *Honor and Shame: The Values of Mediterranean Society*, edited by J. B. Peristiany, 19–77. Chicago: University of Chicago.

Plueddemann, James E. 2009. *Leading Across Cultures: Effective Ministry and Mission in the Global Church*. Downers Grove, IL: IVP Academic.

Ramadan, Tariq. 2004. *Western Muslims and the Future of Islam*. New York: Oxford University.

Register, Ray, Jr. 2009. *Discipling Middle Eastern Believers*. Dayton, TN: Global Educational Advance.

Rosen, Lawrence. 2006. "Expecting the Unexpected: Cultural Components of Arab Governance." In *Law, Society, and Democracy: Comparative Perspectives*, edited by Richard E. D. Schwartz, 163–78. Vol. 603 of *Annals of the American Academy of Political and Social Science*. http://www.jstor.org/stable/25097763.

Saeed, Abdullah, and Hassan Saeed. 2004. *Freedom of Religion, Apostasy and Islam*. Burlington, VT: Ashgate.

Sahragard, R. 2003. "A Cultural Script Analysis of a Politeness Feature in Persian." Paper presented at the Pan-Pacific Association of Applied Linguistics. http://www.paaljapan.org/resources/proceedings/PAAL8/pdf/pdf034.pdf.

Said, Abdul Aziz, and Nathan C. Funk. 2001. "The Role of Faith in Cross-Cultural Conflict Resolution." Paper presented at the European Parliament for the European Centre for Common Ground, September. http://www.gmu.edu/programs/icar/pcs/ASNC83PCS.htm

Said, Edward W. 1979. *Orientalism*. New York: Vintage.

Sande, Ken. 1997. *The Peacemaker: A Biblical Guide to Resolving Personal Conflict*. Grand Rapids: Baker.

Scazzero, Peter. 2003. *The Emotionally Healthy Church: A Strategy for Discipleship that Actually Changes Lives*. Grand Rapids: Zondervan.

Sciolino, Elaine. 2000. *Persian Mirrors: The Elusive Face of Iran*. New York: The Free Press.

Sikand, Yoginder. 2006. "Madrasa Reforms: Pakistani Ulama Voices." *Muslim Public Affairs Journal* (April): 55–60.

Smith, Jane I. 1999. *Islam in America*. New York: Columbia University.

Smith, Steve. 2011. *T4T: A discipleship re-revolution*. Monument, CO: WIGTake Resources.

Spellman, Kathryn. 2004. *Religion and Nation: Iranian Local and Transnational Networks in Britain*. New York: Berghahn.

Stewart, Tat. 2005. "A Biblical Model for Shepherding MBBs." Paper presented at COMMA Consultation in Atlanta, October 20.

Stone, Matthew. 2015. "How Post-Traumatic Stress Disorder (PTSD) and Co-occurring Disorders Impact Ministries." Paper presented at COMMA consultation in Elmhurst, IL, October 15.

Taheri, Amir. 2008. *The Persian Night: Iran under the Khomeinist Revolution*. New York: Encounter.

Travis, John, and Anna Travis. 2008. "Deep-Level Healing Prayer in Cross-Cultural Ministry: Models, Examples, and Lessons." In *Paradigm Shifts in Christian Witness: Insights from Anthropology, Communication, and Spiritual Power*, edited by Charles E. Van Engen, Darrell Whiteman, and J. Dudley Woodberry, 106–15. New York: Orbis.

Trousdale, Jerry. 2012. *Miraculous Movements: How Hundreds of Thousands of Muslims are Falling in Love with Jesus*. Nashville: Thomas Nelson.

Tsakiridis, George. 2010. *Evagrius Ponticus and Cognitive Science: A Look at Moral Evil and the Thoughts*. Eugene, OR: Pickwick.

Van Donzel, E., B. Lewis, and Ch. Pellat, eds. 1978. *The Encyclopaedia of Islam*. Leiden, Netherlands: Brill.

Wansbrough, John. 1977. *Quranic Studies: Sources and Methods of Scriptural Interpretation*. New York: Oxford University.

Warner, Marcus. 2007. *Toward a Deeper Walk: Heart-Focused Training for the Journey of Life*. Highland Park, IL: Mall Publishing.

Weir, David. 2001. "Management in the Arab World: A Fourth Paradigm?" Paper presented at EURAM conference in Barcelona, Spain, December 2. http://www.leadersnet.co.il/go/leadh/ forums_files/4845731437.pdf.

Wilson, Sandra D. 2002. *Released from Shame: Moving Beyond the Pain of the Past*. Downers Grove, IL: IVP.

Wisley, Thomas, and Sandra Wisley. 2006. *Conflict Management and Resolution, Version 1.7*. Colorado Springs, CO: Development Associates International.

Ye'or, Bat. 1985. *The Dhimmi: Jews and Christians under Islam*. Teaneck, NJ: Fairleigh Dickinson University.

———. 1996. *The Decline of Eastern Christianity under Islam: From Jihad to Dhimmitude*. Teaneck, NJ: Fairleigh Dickinson University.

www.ingramcontent.com/pod-product-compliance
Lightning Source LLC
LaVergne TN
LVHW021205210325
806447LV00002B/451